Poverty, inequality and class structure

Edited by

DOROTHY WEDDERBURN

Reader in Industrial Sociology
Imperial College of Science and Technology

CAMBRIDGE UNIVERSITY PRESS

CAMBRIDGE
LONDON · NEW YORK · MELBOURNE

Published by the Syndics of the Cambridge University Press
The Pitt Building, Trumpington Street, Cambridge CB2 1RP
Bentley House, 200 Euston Road, London NW1 2DB
32 East 57th Street, New York, NY 10022, USA
296 Beaconsfield Parade, Middle Park, Melbourne 3206, Australia

Library of Congress catalogue card number: 73-80479

ISBNs: 0 521 20153 5 hard covers
       0 521 09823 8 paperback

First published 1974
Reprinted 1975 (twice)

First printed in Great Britain by
Cox & Wyman Ltd,
London, Fakenham and Reading
Reprinted in Great Britain at the
University Printing House, Cambridge
(Euan Phillips, University Printer)

CONTENTS

LIST OF CONTRIBUTORS

A. B. Atkinson Professor of Economics, University of Essex. Author of *Poverty in Britain and the Reform of Social Security* and *Unequal Shares. Wealth in Britain.* Editor of *Journal of Public Economics.*

Basil B. Bernstein Professor in the Sociology of Education, University of London. Author of *Class Codes and Control, Vol. 1. Theoretical Studies towards a Sociology of Language.* Editor of *Class Codes and Control, Vol. 2. Applied Studies towards a Sociology of Language.*

Christine Craig Research Officer, Department of Applied Economics, University of Cambridge.

J. H. Goldthorpe Official Fellow, Nuffield College, Oxford. Joint author of *The Affluent Worker, Volumes I–III.*

A. H. Halsey Professorial Fellow of Nuffield College, Oxford. Head of Department of Social and Administrative Studies. Author of *Education, Economy and Society*, joint author of *Power in Co-operatives.*

Margot Jefferys Professor of Medical Sociology and Director of the Social Research Unit, Bedford College, University of London. Author of *An Anatomy of Social Welfare Services* and *Mobility in the Labour Market.*

Mavis Maclean Research Fellow, Goldsmith's College, University of London. Author of *Housing.*

Ralph Miliband Professor of Politics, University of Leeds. Author of *Parliamentary Socialism* and *The State in Capitalist Society.* Co-editor of *The Socialist Register.*

J. L. Nicholson Chief Economic Adviser to the Department of Health and Social Security. Associate Professor of Quantitative Economics, Brunel University. Author of *Distribution and Redistribution of Income in the United Kingdom in 1959, 1957 and 1953. The Interim Index of Industrial Production* and *Variations in Working Class Family Expenditure.*

W. G. Runciman Fellow of Trinity College, Cambridge. Author of *Social Science and Political Theory. Relative Deprivation and Social Justice. Sociology in its Place and other Essays*, and *A Critique of Max Weber's Philosophy of Social Science.*

R. Scase Lecturer in Sociology, University of Kent.

Peter Townsend Professor of Sociology, University of Essex. Author of *The Family Life of Old People, The Last Refuge, The Social Minority* and *Sociology and Social Policy*, and co-author of *The Poor and the Poorest* (with Brian Abel-Smith), *Old People in Three Industrial Societies* (with Ethel Shanas and others), and *The Aged in the Welfare State* (with Dorothy Wedderburn).

Dorothy Wedderburn Reader in Industrial Sociology, Imperial College of Science and Technology. Author of *White-collar Redundancy, Redundancy and the Railwaymen* and joint author of *Workers Attitudes and Technology*.

NOTE ON THE CONTRIBUTIONS

The chapters by Nicholson, Maclean and Jefferys, Wedderburn and Craig, and Bernstein and Miliband were first read to Section N Meeting (Sociology) of the British Association Meeting at Exeter in September 1969 and I am grateful to Mr Donald Munro, Recorder for that section, for his assistance. They have been substantially revised. Goldthorpe's chapter was his Presidential Address delivered to Section N (Sociology) of the British Association in September 1969 at Exeter. It appeared in its original version in the Advancement of Science, December 1969. Bernstein's chapter is reprinted with the permission of the publisher from A. Harry Passow: *Opening Opportunities for Disadvantaged Learners* (New York: Teachers College Press) 1971. Townsend's chapter was originally prepared for a 1969 conference in Boston on *Stratification and Poverty* organised by the American Academy of Arts and Sciences under a grant from the Ford Foundation and revised in 1971 for a project of the Academy. A short version of this chapter was presented to the General Applications Section of the Royal Statistical Society on 6 March 1973. It will also appear in *Poverty*, Allen Lane, a division of Penguin Books Limited, by whose permission it is here reproduced.

ACKNOWLEDGEMENTS

I would like to thank Patricia Skinner and Christine Linehan of the Cambridge University Press who gave every help and encouragement to produce this volume. Christine Dawson, my secretary, has not only typed the manuscript but has also been a most valuable assistant in the actual organisation of the editorial chores.

All editors are indebted to those who contribute to the volumes which they edit, but I more than most. Many of these authors are my personal friends who over the years have generously shared their thinking with me and have enriched my understanding of the problems to which this volume addresses itself.

D. W.

Introduction

DOROTHY WEDDERBURN

'Poverty has always had several not entirely separable meanings and is always defined according to the conventions of the society in which it occurs.'[1] That poverty is a relative concept appears only to require an appeal to common sense. For it is apparent that the poverty of an Indian peasant who may today die from starvation is a qualitatively different state from that which afflicts those who may be called poor in European countries or in North America. Yet recently, in contrast to the immediate post-war period, poverty has once again emerged as an important social issue in many developed countries. This is not because of an objective change in economic conditions or as Miller and Roby have put it: 'because part of the population lived in worse circumstances than in previous generations'.[2]

For there can be no doubt the poor in Britain today are better off now in real terms than when Rowntree made his first poverty study in York at the end of the nineteenth century. At that time poverty meant complete destitution, the loss of home and furniture and relegation to the work-house. But the old standards of poverty no longer appear relevant to contemporary society. The need for poverty to be rediscovered as a contemporary problem arose because there was a lag between social consciousness and reality. In the thirties, the future of capitalism itself had seemed in question because of its inability to meet the elementary needs of millions of ordinary men and women. But after the Second World War, the worst aspects of poverty appeared to be eliminated by the achievement of relatively high levels of employment and by the extension of social welfare programmes.[3] For the rest it was widely assumed that economic growth would automatically prove to be a panacea. This optimism began to be questioned by both academics and politicians at about the same time in both the United States and Britain. From the fifties onwards, evidence appeared which shattered any complacency.[4] Today, in the United States, the richest country in the world, anti-poverty programmes are, or have been, an essential part of the political armoury of both major political parties, and since the early sixties the literature on poverty has multiplied rapidly.[5]

That poverty exists in developed countries is not now disputed, although its extent is questioned. Moreover, two major theoretical debates have emerged. Can poverty be discussed in isolation from the more general question of inequality? Some writers argue that attempts to do so reflect political preferences.

> The acceptable term 'poverty' has become the way of discussing the more disturbing issue of inequality.

and:

> The social welfare term 'poverty' does not incur the disturbance that does the political term 'inequality'. But the ambiguity of our use of 'poverty' is preventing the full-scale examination of the issues of inequality. Who gets what? Who does and should benefit from government subsidisation? What shape do we wish the income and social profiles of this country to have?[6]

The second debate turns upon the attempt to locate the causes of poverty and inequality. In the early period of industrialisation the dominant explanation for poverty was character deficiency, the moral lapses of the work-shy or feckless. As Professor Titmuss has reminded us, R. H. Tawney castigated such a view in no uncertain terms:

> The problem of poverty, he said, is not a problem of individual character but a problem of economic and industrial organisation. It has to be studied at its source and only secondly in its manifestations.[7]

The juxtaposition of character as against opportunity is echoed today in the exchanges between those who take a 'situational' view of the causes of poverty as compared with those who are preoccupied with the 'culture' of poverty.[8] But in addition attention has been redirected in a new way to the nature and causes of inequality. Social inequality both in its distributional and in its relational aspect has long occupied a central position in the discipline of sociology.[9] Poverty, on the other hand, has not. Discussing the work of the early empirical investigators of poverty, like Booth and Rowntree, John Rex says:

> But however valuable the collection of such information may be from a moral point of view it is still necessary to ask whether it is relevant to sociology, i.e. whether it tells us anything about the nature of 'society' or about the social relations which exist among men.[10]

Thus it may be asked is poverty different from inequality and if so in what respects? Moreover what are the significant relational aspects of inequality? It is to some of these issues that the present volume addresses itself.

Most of these papers were originally written for a meeting of Section N

(Sociology) of the British Association meeting at Exeter in 1969. The justification for publishing them four years later is twofold. First, the facts and the problems which they describe and discuss are still with us in very much the same form. Second, these papers, together with one or two others specially commissioned for this volume, represent an interdisciplinary approach to the problems of poverty, inequality and class. Economists, sociologists and political scientists are here contributing to an explanation of the *process* by which in an advanced industrial capitalist society, like Britain, conditions of poverty and inequality are generated and sustained. They may take as their starting point the distributional aspects of inequality – the way in which different factors such as income, wealth, education, and power are distributed among the population – but they also address themselves to the interconnection between these different institutional inequalities as well as to people's perceptions of them and to the political implication of such perceptions. In other words, there is a concern with what might be termed both the political economy of poverty and inequality, as well as with its ideological rationale, the set of values and beliefs which sustain or challenge the existing order.[11]

The authors do not share a common approach. Some are mainly pre-occupied with understanding poverty as a social problem for which appropriate social reforms may then be devised. Others are more concerned with the relationship between social inequality, political process and the possibility of wider structural change.

Section One discusses conceptual problems in the definition of poverty, the problems related to the measurement of poverty and inequality and reviews existing evidence about the extent of poverty and inequality in Britain today. It is indeed remarkable that since the so-called 'rediscovery' of poverty in the fifties there has been almost continuous criticism of the inadequacy of the basic data available in Britain for studying both problems of poverty and inequality, but still little has been done to remedy the defects. There has been a parallel discussion of the conceptual problems involved in defining poverty, but again, perhaps because of the magnitude of the resources required, few attempts have been made to operationalise new and more refined concepts.[12] In his chapter Townsend draws on the recent experience of poverty measurement in the United States to argue for a dynamic poverty standard not only because as society becomes wealthier the absolute level of old standards is outmoded, but because economic growth alters the availability of different types of commodities, radically changes life styles and the composition of the old standard becomes irrelevant.

'Poverty,' declares Townsend, 'can be defined objectively and applied consistently only in terms of the concept of relative deprivation.' Relative deprivation is used here, as it frequently is in other places in this volume, in an objective sense to describe situations where people possess less of some desired attribute, be it income, favourable employment conditions or power, than do others. The term can, however, also be used in a subjective sense, as for example in Scase's chapter, to describe a sense of deprivation not dependent upon an absolute level but relative to the perceived level of the attribute possessed by groups with which comparison is being made. As Runciman has argued elsewhere, the choice of reference groups may be crucial in determining social response to the objective condition of inequality.[13]

Many of the contributors stress the inadequacy of studies of poverty and inequality which are based only upon cash income. These are the data, however, which Atkinson is forced to use in his review of post-war attempts to measure poverty in Britain. All of these studies, in one way or another, have taken as their standard of poverty the national assistance or supplementary benefit scale rate. One of the major disadvantages of this standard is that there are no published data which enable public discussion of what implies in terms of contemporary patterns of expenditure and styles of living. Even the argument that since the scale rates are approved by parliament they represent in some sense or another a degree of social consensus about a minimum acceptable level of income is at least open to question, for some surveys have shown that the general public places a poverty level higher than this.[14] The main outcome of Atkinson's review is that, on the basis of the admittedly inadequate data available, in the sixties between 5 and 8 per cent of the population fell below the poverty level. There is little reason to suppose that the situation has improved much since then.

As for overall inequality in income distribution Atkinson argues that there is a considerable degree of concentration of income in Britain today. There was a trend to greater equality between the late forties and fifties, even into the early sixties. But the optimism that this was an automatic trend was unfounded, and even the meaning of greater equality in this context is not unambiguous. For while the share of the top 1 and 10 per cent of income receivers fell, so too did the share of the bottom 30 per cent. Clearly finer measures are required which enable us to examine disaggregated data, at least disaggregated to the extent that is to say, of enabling us to understand the social meaning of such relative shifts.

To some extent this is what Nicholson is doing in his chapter where he is exploring how families of different composition gain or lose as a result of *all* Government activities concerned with raising taxes, direct and indirect, and with the provision of benefits in cash and kind, i.e. with Government measures to redistribute income. His was a pioneering work with estimates which have been regularly prepared for some years now. In this chapter we have a ten-year series. The overall effect is a substantial reduction in inequality compared with the inequality in the distribution of initial income. The truly remarkable finding, however, is that although families of different compositions may have fared differently at different times the size of the overall reduction in inequality as a result of government activity is very little different now from that found in a roughly comparable study carried out in 1937, despite the greater pervasiveness of Government activities in the post-war period. Nicholson's discussion of the possible reasons for such stability reveals a complex picture of balances between the effects of economic demographic, technological and social change which appear to have had the net effect of cancelling each other out. Further analysis is clearly called for to increase our understanding of these processes not least because of the widespread belief in fiscal measures as a mechanism for social reform.

There is one notable omission from Section One, and that is a full discussion of the distribution of wealth. Runciman in his chapter discusses theoretically the importance of wealth in the generation and sustaining of inequality but he is primarily concerned with developing a model by means of which the processes by which accretions or diminutions of net economic power occur over a person's lifetime, might be studied. Like other data in this area the evidence which *is* available about the ownership of wealth can be criticised. But it suggests that wealth is more unequally distributed in Britain than in many other capitalist countries, even the USA, and whilst the share of the top 1 per cent of wealth holders in Britain may have fallen quite sharply in the last sixty years, the share of the top 10 per cent has only declined from 92 per cent in 1911–13 to 83 per cent in 1960, leaving a very high degree of concentration indeed.

> The evidence regarding change in the distribution of wealth may be summarised by saying that they suggest some decline in inequality but that there are reasons for believing that this reflects in part the rearrangement of wealth *within* families rather than the redistribution *between* rich and poor families.[15]

Wealth endows not only control over economic resources but greater choice and control over life-time activities and greater power. Runciman's chapter is the first one to relate economic resources to the concept of class. As a sociologist he is concerned to explore the possibilities that differences of attitudes and norms of behaviour between different classes may have a significant effect upon typical expectations of life chances. He hypothesises that there are powerful constraints not only of a structural but also of a cultural kind which serve to perpetuate marked class divisions and inequalities in society.

Runciman's chapter serves as a bridge to Section Two where we leave the political economy of poverty and inequality to examine deprivation as manifested through differential access to, or experience of, major social institutions. Major and continuing causes of poverty and deprivation are the many natural vicissitudes which prevent individuals from participating fully in the labour market, such as sickness, old age, and disability. There have been a number of studies of old age.[16] But Maclean and Jefferys' chapter reports on a study of a much neglected group, the disabled. It documents the economic effects of disablement and the inadequacy of the present benefit system. As important, however, is the light which their study throws upon the role of social attitudes in the process of deprivation, for example the low expectations which the disabled and their families have of what can or should be done to help them.

Social attitudes are also important in Bernstein's discussion of education. Many reformers have seen equal educational opportunity as a means of breaking through the generational poverty cycle. The concept of compensatory education which Bernstein attacks goes further, and attributes educational disadvantage not so much to the inequality of educational facilities as to the inability of working-class children to benefit from the facilities available because of what has been termed their linguistic deprivation, i.e. to something lacking in the family. Bernstein maintains first that such an argument could be diversionary because there is still a basic failure to provide an adequate initial physical educational environment for poor and working-class children. But second that the insistence upon the working-class child adapting to the middle-class environment of the school, rather than the other way round, disadvantages the child. It is an example of the way in which inequality in the power relationships created outside the school permeates what he calls the 'organisation, the distribution and evaluation of knowledge'.

Halsey, too, is concerned with education but from an action viewpoint. His chapter is a cool and critical analysis, by one directly involved, of the philosophy and theoretical assumptions underlying the British educational priority area and community development programmes which were based on the assertion that reform could be achieved through social science experiments. They concentrated upon a particular area of what might be called total deprivation – the urban poor deprived in terms both of economic and environmental resources. The theory of poverty upon which the programmes are based owes much to the transatlantic debate of the sixties where the cultural view – emphasising the importance of the different value orientations, family structure and interpersonal relations of the poor – was counterposed against the situational view – emphasising the importance of opportunity. Halsey believes that a constructive synthesis has emerged in Britain and that the British programmes seek to influence both economic and cultural factors. Whilst resources from central government are recognised as necessary, there is also a belief that local and private community resources must be tapped. But the projects are essentially reformist, for nowhere is there any consideration given to the possibility that poverty may be the result of society-wide structural characteristics. At the same time, however, Halsey does leave with us the question whether the CDP programmes themselves might be the means of awakening political pressures which would seek solutions beyond local institutions and frameworks.

The influence of United States thinking which emerges so strongly in this chapter serves to underline another important omission from this volume. For whilst there have been many people who have rightly objected to the identification of poverty in the United States as 'black poverty', problems of race do add another dimension to discussion of social inequality. The fact that in Britain, too, we have a racial problem serves to reinforce the argument for more study of the interconnection between situational and cultural factors in the causation and perpetuation of poverty. Should we share the confidence of one American sociologist who stated:

> ... I am confident that if men can be given a viable occupational role, if family income is sufficient to guarantee a decent living, if Negroes are freed from the material and emotional punishment of racial discrimination and are allowed to participate as first-class citizens in the political community, a healthy Negro family structure – which may or may not correlate with the middle-class ideal – will develop as a result.[17]

If we do, what policy measures are required?

With Wedderburn and Craig we turn back from the action orientation of Halsey to an overall examination of the link between the political economy of inequality and the power system which accompanies it in the work situation. Inequality of income is an accepted aspect of employment (which is not, of course, to say that it is always seen as morally justifiable). But we also find inequality in a wide range of other work conditions like the physcial working environment, the intrinsic interest of work, and the experience of power and authority. Such inequalities are here documented and shown to be very considerable, but there is also evidence which supports Runciman's contention that people select very narrow reference groups with which to compare themselves. As a result the inequalities are not in themselves a source of great discontent although there is a basic desire for improved conditions. This particular discussion of inequality leads us away from viewing inequality as a continuum to a consideration of certain crucial discontinuities of the kind which Runciman discussed in his chapter. It is possible to distinguish significant social groupings sharing similar work situations and life chances. There are sharp breaks between manual and non-manual workers, and within non-manual workers between routine clerical and technical workers and managers. Finally, the discussion in this chapter poses the question of whether there is any relationship between work constraints and cultural responses to them, and whether it would be possible to trace a connection between the worker's experience at work, including his experience of collective trade union action, and his attitudes and behaviour as a consumer and as a citizen.

Maclean and Jefferys discussed the efforts of the disabled to form a pressure group to deal with their economic difficulties, and Halsey, as we have seen, considered that one possible outcome of the attempt to mobilise community resources might be to mobilise community political pressure. But Miliband, in his discussion of political deprivation, does not offer a very comforting perspective on the political effectiveness of the poor. They have, as T. H. Marshall has so clearly documented, attained equality of citizenship but this does not imply equality of access to resources.[18] There is an acute dilemma here to which Miliband draws attention. The poor are *part* of the working class but they are largely excluded from the organisations which have developed to defend the interests of the working class, despite some recent growth in the concern shown by the trade unions for, say, the problems of the elderly. Miliband is presumably saying that the poor – by which he means the old, the disabled, the low paid – are part of the working class in the sense that they share the same relationship to the capitalist economic system as the skilled craftsman or car worker. But do the poor form a distinct grouping within the working class?

Political response to inequality is the subject of Scase's chapter. The subjective view of relative deprivation was concerned with the relationship between institutionalised inequalities and people's awareness of them.[19] Reference groups could be chosen to mitigate or to exacerbate perceptions of inequality and in Britain, Runciman's argument has been that the choice of reference groups was such as to minimise political grievance. There have been criticisms of Runciman's interpretation of his own data.

It has been suggested for example, that people might erroneously assume in interview situations that they are expected to draw upon their own limited experience and to make, what they feel are, realistic comparisons. Moreover, it is argued, Runciman's own data show a general sense of dissatisfaction with income levels among manual workers and a criticism of the established order.[20] But in his comparison between a sample of Swedish and British workers roughly comparable in objective conditions, Scase shows a much wider and more active awareness of inequalities among the Swedes, and a tendency to select much wider reference groups than among the British workers. The explanation he offers for this phenomenon lies in the role of the Swedish trade unions and of the Social Democratic Party as vehicles for translating the everyday experience of Swedish workers into a broader ideological context. In other words their personal experience is set in a context of beliefs and values which are such as to challenge the existing political economy of inequality whereas in Britain this is not the case. One of the continuing interests of the subjective view of relative deprivation and the role of reference groups is to explain how the choice of reference groups comes to be what it is. Parkin has argued that subordinate classes may have two levels of reference, one which arises from everyday experience in the work situation, and the other which is more abstract and which will be influenced by the interpretation offered by political parties and movements to their supporters.[21] The interest of Scase's Swedish and British comparison is in the apparent sharpness of contrast in the meaning systems offered by the institution of the labour movement. Although, as he himself points out, the heightened awareness of relative deprivation among the Swedish workers may lead to greater resentment because their 'influence' is not always perceived to produce social justice.

With John Goldthorpe's analysis we find a rather different approach to the significance of reference groups and relative deprivation. He argues that Runciman when discussing relative deprivation was over-occupied with the absence of *political* manifestation of grievances about inequality in Britain, whereas in fact, the major arena for the manifestation of grievances is that of economic life. Goldthorpe suggests the possibility that social inequalities do not pose threats to the stability of the political order but that they do militate against 'stable normative regulation in the economic sphere'. This analysis is particularly pertinent in the light of renewed attempts to establish a prices and incomes policy which are primarily concerned with the regulation of differentials within the area of earned incomes whilst ignoring the generalised context of overall inequality which exists in the wider society.

In the light of both the development of a new incomes policy and the attempts to legislate for 'good' industrial relations through the Industrial Relations Act 1971, Goldthorpe's appeal to Durkheim's observation appears particularly apposite,

> ce n'est pas assez qu'il y ait des règles: car parfois, ce sont des règles mêmes qui sont la cause du mal.

A collection of essays of this kind is perhaps bound to raise as many questions as are answered. But certain common themes emerge. First there is agreement about the inadequacy of existing data to study problems of poverty and inequality in the distribution of resources. Second, there is agreement that the really important issues are concerned with access to total economic resources including environmental resources, and to power. Third, there is agreement that the interaction between differential access to various kinds of resources with prevailing sets of values, beliefs and preferences produces cumulative and self-sustaining inequalities. The self-sustaining character of inequality constantly emerges as well as the part played by value systems in shaping the functioning even of institutions deliberately created to solve problems of poverty.

But the essays still leave unanswered the question whether poverty is a meaningful sociological concept as distinct from social inequality. We are still today, in Tawney's words, concerned with quantities. There is nothing very complicated or profound about the *mechanism* required to redistribute resources to the old, the sick and the disabled. But the amount of redistribution is a political issue which takes us back to the question of Miller and Roby 'what shape do we wish the income and social profiles of this country to have?' The self-sustaining nature of poverty appears more intractable. But is that only a transitional phase? When economic growth has produced a larger national cake and there has been some effective redistribution through measures of social reform, as Townsend suggests has occurred in Sweden, shall we be prepared to drop the word 'poverty' from our vocabulary? But will that then turn attention directly to the nature of inequality and to the characteristics of the class structure? The statistical representation of inequality appears as a continuum. Yet a number of these essays have suggested that there are significant social *groupings* sharing life situations and chances, and ordered in an unequal fashion. One conclusion which could be drawn is that awareness of inequalities will concentrate upon the differences *between* these groups, leading to more fragmentation and the development of conflicting interest groups. An alternative conclusion would be that there might emerge a recognition of communality of interest between some of them because the differences between them are insignificant compared with the differences between them and say the top 10 per cent of wealth holders. The intervention of ideology and meaning systems here become vital in determining which of these alternatives is likely to occur. Certainly the analysis of different responses to inequalities would support the view expressed by David Lockwood that the

> tension between ideology and reality is an additional reason why adherence to a status order is never unconditional even by those most indulged by its dispensation.[22]

NOTES

[1] E. J. Hobsbawm, 'Poverty', *International Encyclopaedia of the Social Sciences* (New York, 1968), p. 398.

[2] S. M. Miller and P. Roby, *The Future of Inequality* (New York, 1970).

[3] For a comparative discussion of the growth of social welfare programmes see Asa Briggs, 'The Welfare State in Historical Perspective', *European Journal of Sociology*, Vol. II (1961).

[4] Examples of some of the studies are: P. Townsend, *Poverty: Ten Years After Beveridge*, Planning No. 344, 1952. M. Harrington, *The Other America* (London, 1963). D. Cole Wedderburn, 'Poverty in Britain Today: The Evidence', *Sociological Review*, Vol. 10 (1962).

[5] See, for example, *Poverty Studies in the Sixties*, US Dept. of Health, Education and Welfare, Washington, 1970, a selected and annotated bibliography.

[6] S. M. Miller, Martin Rein, Pamela Roby and Bertram Cross, 'Poverty, Inequality and Conflict', *Annals of the American Academy of Political Science*, Vol. 373, September 1967.

[7] R. Titmuss, *Essays on the Welfare State* (London 1958), p. 18.

[8] H. J. Gans, 'Poverty and Culture: Some Basic Questions about Methods of Studying Life-Styles of the Poor', in ed. P. Townsend, *The Concept of Poverty* (London, 1970). See also for a specific example of this controversy in the United States Lee Rainwater and W. L. Yancey, *The Moynihan Report: The Politics of Controversy* (Cambridge, Mass., 1967). See also this Chapter p. 7.

[9] Ed. A. Beteille, *Social Inequality* (London, 1969), pp. 9–14.

[10] John Rex, *Key Problems of Sociological Theory* (London, 1961), p. 28.

[11] D. Lockwood editorial foreword to David Lane, *The End of Inequality* (London, 1971).

[12] Peter Townsend with Professor Abel-Smith has recently conducted a large scale study of household resources and standards of living in this country. This report is in preparation.

[13] W. G. Runciman, *Relative Deprivation and Social Justice: a study of attitudes to social inequality in twentieth century England* (London, 1966).

[14] D. Wedderburn, 'How Adequate Are Our Cash Benefits?', *New Society*, No. 263, 1967.

[15] A. B. Atkinson, *Unequal Shares. Wealth in Britain* (London, 1972), p. 24.

[16] For example, P. Townsend and D. Wedderburn, *The Aged in the Welfare State* (London, 1965); E. Shanas *et al., Old People in Three Industrial Societies* (New York and London, 1968).

[17] H. Gans, 'The Negro Family: Reflections on the Moynihan Report', in Rainwater and Yancey, *The Moynihan Report and the Politics of Controversy.*

[18] T. H. Marshall, 'Citizenship and Social Class' in *Sociology at the Crossroads* (London, 1963).

[19] Runciman, *Relative Deprivation and Social Justice.*

[20] J. H. Westergaard, 'The Rediscovery of the Cash Nexus' in ed. R. Miliband and J. Saville, *The Socialist Register* (London, 1970).

[21] F. Parkin, *Class, Inequality and Political Order* (London, 1971).

[22] D. Lockwood, editorial foreword to the *End of Inequality.*

Measuring inequality and poverty

1
Poverty as relative deprivation: resources and style of living

PETER TOWNSEND

Poverty can be defined objectively and applied consistently only in terms of the concept of relative deprivation. That is the theme of this chapter. The term is understood objectively rather than subjectively. Individuals, families and groups in the population can be said to be in poverty when they lack the resources to obtain the types of diets, participate in the activities and have the living conditions and amenities which are customary, or are at least widely encouraged or approved, in the societies to which they belong. Their resources are so seriously below those commanded by the average individual or family that they are, in effect, excluded from ordinary living patterns, customs and activities.

The consequences of adopting this definition will be illustrated to bring out its meaning. For example, research studies might find more poverty, according to this definition, in certain wealthy than in certain less wealthy societies, and although the poor in the former might be better off, according to some criteria, than the poor in the latter. Again, despite continued economic growth over a period of years, the proportion of the population of an advanced industrial society who are found to be in poverty might rise. Certainly some of the assumptions that are currently made in comparing and contrasting the more developed with the less developed societies and in judging progress in overcoming poverty in affluent societies would have to be revised. In the United States, for example, the assumption that the prevalence of poverty has been steadily reduced since 1959 may have to be abandoned, principally because the definition upon which prevalence is measured is rooted in the conceptions of a particular moment of history and not sufficiently related to the needs and demands of a changing society.[1]

The definition also has implications for policy, which should be recognised at the outset. Although all societies have ways of identifying and trying to deal with their problems, the social sciences are having an increasing influence upon decision-makers, both in providing information and implicitly or explicitly legitimating action. An important example in the history of the formulation of social policies to deal with poverty is the definition of the subsistence standard in the Beveridge Report of 1942. Beveridge adapted the definition used in measuring poverty by Seebohm Rowntree, A. L. Bowley and others in their studies of different communities in Britain and he argued that this was the right basis for paying benefits in a social security scheme designed to abolish want.[2] For over 20 years the rationale for the level of benefits paid in the British schemes of national insurance and supplementary benefit (formerly National Assistance) has rested upon the arguments put forward in the early years of the 1939 war. No attempt has yet been made to present an alternative rationale, although benefits have been increased from time to time in response to rises in prices and wages. A clear definition allows the scale and degree as well as the nature of the problem of poverty to be identified and therefore points to the scale as well as the kind of remedial action that might be taken. Such action may involve not just the general level of benefits, for example, but revision of relativities between benefits received by different types of family.

Previous definitions of poverty

Any attempt to justify a new approach towards the definition and measurement of poverty so that its causes and means of alleviation may be identified must begin with previous definitions and evidence.[3] The literature both about poverty and inequality are closely related and need to be considered in turn. Although poverty is more than inequality the poor undoubtedly receive an unequal share of resources and any explanation of this fact must be related to the larger explanation of social inequality in general.

Previous operational definitions of poverty have not been expressed in thoroughgoing relativist terms, nor founded comprehensively on the key concepts of resources and style of living. The concern has been with narrower concepts of income and the maintenance of physical efficiency. Among the early studies of poverty the work of Seebohm Rowntree is most important. In 1899 he collected detailed information about families in York. He defined families whose 'total earnings are insufficient to obtain the minimum necessaries for the maintenance of merely physical efficiency as being in primary poverty'.[4] Making shrewd use of the work of Atwater, a nutritionist who had experimented with the diets of prisoners to find how nutritional intakes were related to the maintenance of body weight, he estimated the average nutritional needs of adults and children, translated these needs into quantities of different foods and hence into the cash equivalent of these foods. To these costs for food he added minimum sums for clothing, fuel, and household sundries according to size of family. The poverty line for a family of man and wife and three children was 17s 8d per week, made up of 12s 9d for food, 2s 3d for clothing, 1s 10d for fuel and 10d for household sundries. Rent was treated as an unavoidable addition to this sum, and was counted in full. A family was therefore regarded as being in poverty if its income minus rent fell short of the poverty line.

Nearly all subsequent studies were influenced deeply by this application of the concept of subsistence. With minor adaptations a stream of area surveys of poverty based on Rowntree's methods were carried out in Britain between the wars.[5] Rowntree himself carried out further studies in York in 1936 and 1950.[6]

But the standards which were adopted proved difficult to defend. Rowntree's estimates of the costs of necessities other than food were based either on his own and others' opinions or, as in the case of clothing, on the actual expenditure of those among a small selection of poor families who spent the least. Does the actual expenditure of the poorest families represent what they *need* to spend on certain items? Neither in his studies nor in similar studies were any criteria of need independent of personal judgement or of the minimum amounts actually spent on certain goods put forward.

In the case of food it seemed at first sight that independent criteria of need had been produced. But there were three major faults in procedure. Estimates of the nutrients required were very broad averages and were not varied by age, and family composition, still less by occupation and activity outside of work. The foods that were selected to meet these estimates were selected arbitrarily, with a view to securing minimally adequate nutrition at lowest cost, rather than in correspondence with diets that are conventional among the poorer working classes. And finally, the cost of food in the total cost of subsistence formed a much higher percentage than in ordinary experience. In relation to the budgets and customs of life of ordinary people the make-up of the subsistence budget was unbalanced. For example, when Lord Beveridge argued in the war for a subsistence standard similar to the poverty standards of Rowntree and others, he recommended an allowance of 53s 3d a week at 1938 prices for a man, wife and three small children, including 31s for food (58 per cent of the total). But in 1938 families of the same size with roughly the same total income were spending less than 22s on food (41 per cent of the total).[7]

An adaptation of the Rowntree method is in use by the United States Government. The Social Security Administration Poverty Index is based on estimates prepared by the Department of Agriculture of the costs of food needed by families of different composition. A basic standard of nutritional adequacy has been put forward by the National Research

Council and this standard has been translated into quantities of types of food 'compatible with the preference of United States families, as revealed in food consumption studies'.[8] This is then in turn translated into the minimum costs of purchases on the market. Finally, by reference to the average sums *per capita* on food as a proportion of all income (derived from consumer expenditure surveys) it is assumed that food costs represent 33 per cent of the total income needed by families of three or more persons and 27 per cent of the total income needed by households consisting of two persons.

A number of points in the argument can be examined critically. First, the index is not re-defined periodically to take account of changing customs and needs. In one of her influential articles Mollie Orshansky writes, as if it were a virtue, 'Except to allow for rising prices, the poverty index has not been adjusted since 1959'. Between 1959 and 1966 'the average income of 4-person families had increased by 37 per cent but the poverty line by only 9 per cent'.[9] Yet the same writer had pointed out earlier, that 'social conscience and custom dictate that there be not only sufficient quantity of food but sufficient variety to meet recommended nutritional goals and conform to customary eating patterns'.[10] In a rapidly developing society like the United States dietary customs and needs are liable to change equally rapidly and estimates of need must be reviewed frequently. Otherwise the risk is run of reading the needs of the present generation as if they were those of the past. Foods are processed differently, and presented from time to time in new forms, whether in recipe or packaging. Real prices may rise without any corresponding improvement in nutritional content. In the United States as well as Britain household expenditure on food has increased faster than prices in the last 10 or 20 years but regular studies of nutrition have shown little change in nutritional intakes. This evidence provides the minimum case for raising the poverty line between two points in time by more than the rise in prices.[11] No price index can cope properly with changes in ingredients, quality and availability of and 'need for' goods and services.[12] Strangely Miss Orshansky fails to grasp the fact that the standard that she helped to work out for 1959 could only be justified in the stream of American domestic history in terms far more dynamic than the grudging movements in the price index. That the United States definition is static and historically barren is revealed in her honest admission that one of the things the Social Security Administration did not know was 'how to adjust a poverty line to conform to changes in productivity'.[13] That is a fundamental and very damaging admission.[14]

Second, the use of a nutritional basis is questionable, and failure to recognise this allows the full poverty standard to be fixed at a lower level than it otherwise would be fixed. Food costs were worked out which would obtain a minimally adequate diet, providing families restricted the kind and quality of their purchases and exercised skill in preparing as well as in buying food.[15] Nothing extra was allowed for eating meals out and the amounts were enough only for 'temporary or emergency use when funds are low'.[16] There are grounds for supposing that the standards pay insufficient heed to ordinary food customs and are inappropriate for more than a temporary period. The underlying definitions of dietary adequacy are insufficiently related to actual performance of occupational and social roles. Estimates of nutritional needs in fact include a larger element for activities which are socially and occupationally determined than for activities which are biologically and physically determined. Moreover, the former obviously vary widely among individuals and communities. While it may be very reasonable to average nutritional requirements, empirical studies of diets in relationship to incomes and activities have to be undertaken.

Finally, the question of finding criteria for needs other than food is dodged by estimating food costs and then taking these as a fixed percentage of the total budget stated to be necessary. The percentage varies for households of different size and is lower for farm families than for other families. How therefore, are the percentages chosen? Essentially they are a reflection of actual consumption, or more strictly, consumption in the mid-1950s.[17] But, again, although actual behaviour is more relevant than an arbitrarily defined category of 'poor' it cannot be regarded as a criterion of need. This remains the nagging problem about the entire procedure. All that can be conceded is that at least the United States method makes more allowance (although out of date) for conventional distribution of a poverty budget between food, fuel and clothing and other items, than the Rowntree method, which expected poor families to adopt a distributional pattern of spending quite unlike other families.

The circularity in the definition of poverty by the United States Social Security Administration is its weakest feature. In some respects budgetary practice is redefined as budgetary need. But arbitrary elements are also built into the definition from the start. Miss Orshansky is refreshingly candid about this. Beginning an expository article she writes: 'Poverty, like beauty, lies in the eye of the beholder. Poverty is a value judgement; it is not something one can verify or demonstrate, except by inference and suggestion, even with a measure of error. To say who is poor is to use all sorts of value judgements. The concept has to be limited by the purpose which is to be served by the definition . . . In the Social Security Adminis-tration, poverty was first defined in terms of the public or policy issue; to how many people, and to which ones, did we wish to direct policy concern.' Later she adds, 'A concept which can help influence public thinking must be socially and politically credible.'[18]

In these passages Miss Orshansky confuses different purposes. The point about a good definition is that it should be comprehensive, should depend as much as possible on independent or external criteria of evaluation, should involve the ordering of a mass of factual data in a rational, orderly and informative fashion, and should limit, though not conceal, the part played by the value judgements.

The limitations of the evidence of poverty

The evidence about poverty is voluminous but incomplete and inconsistent. Most of it is indirect, in the sense that particular aspects of poverty, such as bad housing, homelessness, overcrowding and malnourishment, the hardship of the unemployed, aged, sick and disabled and the severity of some working conditions rather than actual income in relation to com-munity living standards have been described and discussed. One tradition is the polemical, comprehensive account of working and living conditions, as for example, in some of the writing of Engels, Masterman and Orwell.[19] Another is the painstaking official commission of enquiry, ranging, for example, from the 1844 report of the Commission of Enquiry into the State of Large Towns to the 1965 report of the Milner Holland Committee on Housing in Greater London. A third is the punctiliously specific research study.

For example, there have been studies of the relationship between pre-natal nutritional deficiencies in mothers and organic and mental defects in their children,[20] more general studies of depression, apathy and lethargy resulting from inadequate diets and nutritional deficiency; books and papers containing evidence of the correlation between bad social conditions and restricted physical growth of children both in height and weight;[21] evidence too of the association between overcrowding and a number of different infectious diseases;[22] and evidence of the downward drift of income and occupational status in relation to schizophrenia.[23] This kind of evidence can certainly be used by the social scientist to build up a picture of the interrelationship of different problems and very rough estimates of the amount of, as well as the relative variations in, poverty. Different indicators can be used for this purpose, such as morbidity and mortality rates, percentage of households lacking certain amenities, unemployment rates, measures of the average height and weight of school-children and the percentage of families obtaining means-tested welfare benefits.[24] Perhaps insufficient work has yet been done on the correlations between indicators like these and variables such as population structure, employment structure and rateable value. Certainly elaborate work of this kind would be required to buttress any development of more general theories of poverty.

But the underlying work of developing a comprehensive definition of poverty in operational terms which can be applied in different countries and regions and which can permit measurement of a kind sensitive enough to show the short-term effect on the numbers in poverty of, say, an increase in unemployment, an unusually large increase in prices, or the stepping-up in value of social security benefits, is still in a very early stage. This remains true despite a longish history of empirical work in some countries.[25]

It is interesting to compare some recent quantitative analyses of the extent of poverty. In 1966 the British Ministry of Social Security found that 160,000 families with two or more children, or 4.1 per cent of such families, were living on incomes lower than the prevailing basic rates of national assistance.[26] In the same year, the United States Social Security Administration, using a more generous definition of adequacy, found that 13.6 per cent of all households with children (15.6 per cent with two or more children) and 17.7 per cent of all households were poor.[27] In 1966 in Melbourne 4.8 per cent of families with children (6.1 per cent of families with two or more children) and just over 7 per cent of all households were found to be in poverty.[28] But although the last of these three 1966 surveys copied methods used in the United States to estimate what incomes for families of different size were equivalent they each adopted a national or conventional and not independent standard. In Britain, the Ministry of Social Security simply adopted the basic scale rates paid by the National Assistance Board, plus rent, as the poverty line, and sought to find how many families had an income of less than the levels implied by those rates.[29] In Australia, the legal minimum wage plus child endowment payments was treated as equivalent to the poverty line for a man and wife and two children, and adjustments were made for families of different size. In each case standards which had already proved to be politically acceptable rather than other standards were invoked. The United States method has been described above and, though it is more complicated in that it consists of certain attempts to develop detached criteria and build rational procedures, rough and arbitrary judgements are made at the really critical stages of fixing the level of the poverty line.

In calling attention to the fact that much of the evidence about poverty depends on measures which are built, in the final analysis, on conventional judgement or experience rather than on independent criteria such evidence must not be discounted. If there are national standards of need, expressed through public assistance scales, a minimum wage or child endowment, knowing the number of people having incomes of less than these standards represents valuable information. Such information can also be collected for different countries. The moral is, however, to endeavour to distinguish between definitions of poverty which are in practice made by a society and those which depend on detached or scientific criteria.

Poverty and inequality

For various countries there is also a considerable amount of evidence about unequal distribution of incomes, and the proportion of aggregate incomes taken by the poorest 10 per cent or 20 per cent of income recipients. In one recent comprehensive review Harold Lydall found that the countries distributing employment income most equally were Czechoslovakia, Hungary, New Zealand and Australia. Those distributing them most unequally were Brazil, Chile, India, Ceylon and Mexico. Lydall attempted also to document trends in the distribution for different countries. He showed that in 10 of the 11 countries for which information was available inequality in the distribution of pre-tax incomes had not just remained stationary during the 1950s but had actually widened.[30] Most other attempts to compare distributions have been less carefully documented and have been reduced to rankings according to a single coefficient or the per cent of aggregate income taken by the upper 10 per cent of income units and by the lowest 50 per cent of income units.[31]

The methods that have been used to compare the distribution of income in different countries can be criticised on grounds that they are so crude as to be misleading. For example, the ranking of developed and developing countries according to a measure of inequality, such as the Gini coefficient, can change remarkably if alternative measures, such as the standard deviation of logarithms or coefficient of variation, are used.[32] The rankings are sufficiently diverse as to throw profound doubt on the accepted conclusion that inequality is greater in the developing countries. As Atkinson points out, nearly all the conventional measures are insensitive to whether or not inequality is more pronounced near the top rather than near the bottom of the distribution.[33] What is at stake is the concept of equality. An attempt is made in Figure 1.1 to bring out the ambiguities in present conceptions. In Country A the total range of the distribution of income is

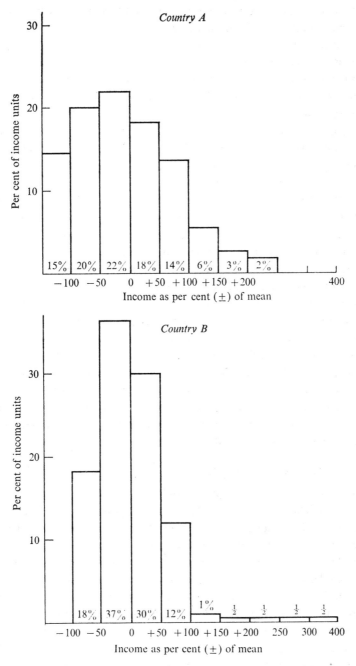

Figure 1.1 Illustration of the distribution of income in two countries

not as wide as in Country B, but 97 per cent of the population of the latter are concentrated over a narrower range of income. In which country is income distribution more unequal?

More fundamentally, the statistics themselves are suspect. For many countries the information for income units below taxable levels is either very sketchy or is ignored. While such factors may have small effects upon comparisons drawn between some developed countries they may be crucial for the developing countries. Moreover, income in kind is extremely important in those countries with large agricultural populations and yet the monetary equivalent is extremely difficult to estimate and take into account in the distribution of cash incomes. The problem is not much easier in the so-called developed countries, as is discussed in other chapters of this volume.[34] Inevitably we are driven to develop a more comprehensive definition of income and collect more comprehensive data on which to build theory. Better information about styles of living in different countries is also required. The same relative level of command over resources in each of two countries might permit minimal participation in such styles in one but not in the other.

Theories and data are, of course, interdependent. Bad theories may not just be the consequence of bad data, but also give rise to the collection of bad data, or at least the failure to collect good data. Economic theories of inequality tend to misrepresent the shape of the wood, and in endeavouring to account for it, fail to account for the trees. Sociological theories of inequality tend to avoid any specific examination of the correlation between economic resources and occupational status or styles of life and are as a consequence, unnecessarily diffuse.

Three forms of deprivation

A new approach to the definition and measurement of poverty, therefore, is needed. This depends on 'relative deprivation'. As already indicated a fundamental distinction is made between actual and perceived need, and therefore between actual and perceived poverty – or more strictly, between *objective* and *conventionally acknowledged* poverty. All too easily the social scientist can be the unwitting servant of contemporary social values and in the study of poverty this can have disastrous practical consequences. He may side with the dominant or majority view of the poor. If, by contrast, he feels obliged or is encouraged from the start to make a formal distinction between scientific and conventional perspectives he is more likely to enlarge knowledge by bringing to light information which has been neglected and create more elbow-room for alternative forms of action, even if, in the end, some colouring of scientific procedure by social attitudes and opinion or individual valuation is inescapable.[35] At least he is struggling to free himself from control and manipulation by the values which prevail within the constrictions of his own small society. Without pretending that the approach offered in these pages, or any alternative approach, can escape the exercise of judgement at key stages, it may open the way to cross national usage and limit the element of arbitrariness.

On the one hand we have to examine the structure and stability of living standards, and on the other the sectional and collective interpretations of, or feelings about, such living standards. Throughout a given period of history there may be no change whatever in the actual inequalities of wealth and of income and yet social perceptions of those inequalities and of any change in them may become keener. Alternatively, substantial changes in the structure of incomes in society may occur without the corresponding perception that such changes are taking place.

Examples can be uncomfortable. After the Second World War, for example, there was for over a decade very little critical discussion of social policy either in Britain or the United States and few studies by social scientists of the problems of minorities. Until the mid-1950s in Britain and until the late 1950s in the United States even the term 'poverty' had not been disinterred for the purposes either of popular or scientific discussion of contemporary society. But now, in the early 1970s, there has been over a decade of continuous debate, study and even action taking heed of the problem. There are, of course, processes going on by which grim facts are being made more palatable and theories of causation made less disturbing to established views of social management. There are also placebos which are being made to look like radical reforms. But no one can suppose that there was virtually no problem in the United States and Britain between the mid-1940s and the mid-1950s. Indeed, if the conclusions of the research undertaken by the United States Social Security Administration are to be believed, that 20 per cent of the population of the United States were in poverty in 1962, 18 per cent in 1964, 15 per cent in 1966 and only 12.6 per cent in 1970, then the proportion must have been very substantially larger than 20 per cent around 1950. If this evidence makes any kind of sense, it only dramatises the distinction between actuality and perception.

The distinction may also encourage the sociologist to pay a little more attention to actuality than he has done hitherto. The term 'relative deprivation' was coined originally by Stouffer and his colleagues,[36] and then elaborated valuably first by Merton, and then by Runciman,[37] to denote *feelings* of deprivation relative to others and not *conditions* of deprivation relative to others. Yet the latter would be a better usage. Little or no attempt has been made to specify and measure conditions of deprivation relative to others in recent work, perhaps because such conditions are recognised to be very complex phenomena requiring elaborate and patient fieldwork to precisely identify. The description and analysis of these conditions is important in many different ways. For example, skilled manual workers may feel deprived in relation to office staff, even though their take-home earnings may be as high, or higher, than the salaries of some of the office staff. However, they may have fewer resources of other kinds. We have to establish what are the inequalities in actual working conditions, security of employment, promotion prospects and fringe benefits and, in addition, the extent to which some workers may be excluded from sharing in the conditions available either to other groups of workers in the same industry, or workers comparable to themselves in other industries.[38] It is surely impossible to assess the importance of subjective deprivation as an explanatory variable independent of assessing actual deprivation.

A different example might be a group who are conscious of only small deprivation but who are, in fact, substantially deprived, by any objective criteria, such as some sections of the retired. By comparison with the earnings of older people who are still at work, or with the incomes of younger people without dependents, the incomes of retired persons in different countries are very low. The great majority have few assets.[39] Moreover, their deprivation is quite widely acknowledged by the rest of society (if not by Government) and public support is readily found for proposed increases in pensions. But although some pensioners' organisations campaign for large increases in pension rates most of the elderly themselves say they would be content with relatively small increases. Their expectations are modest.[40]

This example brings out very clearly how a distinction must be drawn not just between the actuality and perception of poverty but also between normative and subjective perceptions. So the social scientist has to collect evidence about (i) objective deprivation, (ii) conventionally acknowledged or normative deprivation, and (iii) subjective deprivation. The distinction between the second and third is in some ways a matter of degree. The former represents a dominant or majority valuation in society and the latter an individual valuation, but also a valuation of different kinds of minority group – or even a statistical representation of a large number of individual viewpoints. An individual may feel poor, especially by reference to past comfort, even when he is neither demonstrably poor nor acknowledged to be poor by society. Some retired persons, for example, have an income which is more than adequate according to either objective or conventional standards but which is inadequate according to their own customary or expected standards. Groups too may feel poor. A group of manual or professional workers who have earnings considerably higher than the mean may feel poor by reference to other groups. There are alternative ways of defining and measuring conventionally acknowledged or normative deprivation. In the course of history societies develop rules about the award of welfare payments and services to poor families. These rules can be said to reflect the standard of poverty conventionally acknowledged by these societies. The rates of payment under public assistance laws, for example, represent a contemporary social standard. The extent to which people in different societies in fact fall below national standards can be investigated.[41] Similarly, societies use minimum housing standards, whether of overcrowding or amenities. These standards tend to be changed from time to time in response to political pressures. They represent conventional or elitist values rather than standards the non-fulfilment of which represents objective deprivation.[42]

Each of the three types of deprivation deserves thorough documentation and measurement, as a basis for explaining social conditions, attitudes and behaviour. But by trying to separate subjective and collective views about poverty from the actual conditions which constitute the problem we are led to define them and their relationships rather more carefully.

Conceptions of relativity

The idea of 'the relativity' of poverty requires some explanation. The frame of reference in adopting this approach can be regional, national or international, although until formal ties between nation states are stronger or global corporations even more strongly entrenched the international perspective is unlikely to be given enough emphasis. The question is how far peoples are bound by the same economic, trading, institutional and cultural systems, how far they have similar activities and customs and therefore have similar needs. Needs arise by virtue of the kind of society to which individuals belong. Society imposes expectations, through its occupational, educational, economic and other systems and it also creates wants, through its organisation and customs.

This is easy enough to demonstrate for certain commodities. Tea is nutritionally worthless but in some countries is generally accepted, even by economists, as a 'necessity of life'. For many people in these countries drinking tea has been a life-long custom and is psychologically essential. And the fact that friends and neighbours expect to be offered a cup of tea (or the equivalent) when they visit helps to make it socially necessary as well: a small contribution is made towards maintaining the threads of social relationships. Other goods that are consumed are also psychologically and socially 'necessary' in the same sense, though to varying degrees. The degree of necessity is not uniform for all members of society, because certain goods and services are necessary for some communities or families and other goods and services for others. Repeated advertising and imitation by friends and neighbours can gradually establish a new product or a new version of an old product as essential in a community. Minority wants are converted into majority needs. People may buy first of all out of curiosity or a sense of display but later make purchases in a routine way. The customs which these purchases and their consumption develop become socially and psychologically ingrained.

Clothing is another good example. Climate may determine whether or not any soft forms of protection are placed over the body, and how thick they are, but social convention, itself partly dependent on resources available, determines the type and style. Who would dare to lay down a scale of necessities for the 1970s, for young women in Britain consisting of one pair of boots, two aprons, one second-hand dress, one skirt made from an old dress, a third of the cost of a new hat, a third of the cost of a shawl and a jacket, two pairs of stockings, a few unspecified underclothes, one pair of stays and one pair of old boots worn as slippers, as Rowntree did in 1899?[43]

But convention is much more than ephemeral fashion. It is a style of living also governed by industry and State laws and regulations. Industry conditions the population not only to want certain products and services but to put up with certain disservices. The Public Health and Housing Acts and regulations control sanitation, the structure, size and lay-out of housing, streets and shops. A population becomes conditioned to expect to live in certain broad types of homes, and to heat and furnish them accordingly. Their environment, and the expectations of society around them, create their needs in an objective as well as subjective sense. Similarly, society expects parents to provide certain things for their children, thereby creating needs. The goods and services provided for infants and at all stages of childhood are, through law, the school system, the mass media and so on, socially controlled. The needs which parents feel obliged to meet out of their incomes will depend, among other things, on formal rules about compulsory schooling, free schooling, free school meals and milk and free health services, as well as social norms about the wearing of shoes and school uniforms. Laws and norms are in delicate interdependence with need.

If poverty is relative cross-nationally or cross-culturally then it is also relative historically. It is relative to time as well as place. Needs which are a product of laws and social norms must change as new legislation is passed, social organisations grow and coalesce, automation develops and expectations change. Within a generation the possession of a television set in Britain has changed from being a doubtful privilege of a tiny minority to being an expected right of 95 per cent of the population. But this is only one example. The school-leaving age is being raised, and this will add to the family's needs – to support each dependent child for one year longer. The Parker Morris standards for housing, like earlier housing standards, have been accepted by the Government; new homes built to these standards will add items that each family will be expected to afford. In the 1880s and 1890s one room was the most that many working-class families could afford – or expect. Today, a two- or three-bedroomed house exacts larger real financial obligations. The attenuation of public transport services is brought about in some areas by the development of private transport and, if private transport becomes the norm, that can only be at greater real cost per family. Two or three weeks summer holiday away from home is another social revolution of the mid-twentieth century which, now that it has become a majority convention, adds to the needs which the average family is expected to meet.

With economic growth, though not necessarily in direct proportion to such growth, the needs which a family is expected to meet also increase. Standards rise subtly, sometimes imperceptibly, as society adapts to greater prosperity and responds to the changes demanded by industry, consumers, educationists and the professions. Certainly no standard of sufficiency could be revised only to take account of changes in prices, for that would be to ignore changes in the goods and services consumed as well as new obligations and expectations placed on members of the community. Lacking an alternative criterion, our best assumption would be to relate sufficiency to the average rise in real incomes.

There is one further important elaboration. If needs are relative to society, then they are also relative to the set of social sub-systems to which the individual belongs. This seems to suggest that a different definition of poverty is required for every society, or indeed every relatively autonomous community. But this tends to ignore the marked inter-relationship of many communities within regional and national economic, political, communication, welfare and other systems. Members of ethnic minorities can often be said to participate in commonly-shared rather than exclusive activities. They use the common system of transport, work in multi-racial occupations, go to multi-racial schools which broadly subscribe to national cultural values, and generally adapt in many ways to the conventions and styles of life of the national society. Many of their needs will therefore be the same as of persons who are not members of such minorities and the same as of persons who are members of other minorities. But to some extent their resources will be different and their activities and beliefs relatively autonomous. A national definition of need, and more particularly of poverty, will to that extent not apply to them. Little is yet known in any quantitative sense about the degrees of cultural self-containment of different ethnic minorities. Certainly in Britain it can be said that West Indian immigrant communities are far less self-contained than Pakistani communities. Again, while both Jews and Irish preserve a corporate identity and tend to play special, though different, functions in industrial cultural life it would be difficult to claim they live so differently and have needs which are so radically different from those of society at large that only an entirely different conception of poverty can meaningfully be applied to them. Still, in the absence of empirical evidence demonstrating degrees of integration of ethnic minorities in the wider society this difficulty about any 'relative' conception of poverty must remain.

It would be wrong, however, to call attention only to the possible divergence of racial or ethnic sub-systems from the social system as a whole. There are differences between rural and urban communities and even between different urban communities which would compel different overall definitions of their needs. The difficulty of allowing properly for the income in kind of the country-dweller (such as home-grown vegetables, free or cheap fuel, and tied accommodation) but also the lack of facilities available to the town or city dweller, especially if he is young (for example, entertainment, choice of shops and choice of indoor as compared with outdoor work) are reasonably well recognised. Inevitably both would have to be taken into account in any sophisticated investigation of poverty, not just in qualifying the results of any measure but also in applying that measure.

Style of living

A distinction must therefore be made between the resources which are made available by society to individuals and families and the style of life with which they are expected, or to which they feel prompted, to conform. This is the set of customs and activities which they are expected to share or in which they are expected to join. However, conformity is not rigidly prescribed. People engage in the same kind of activities rather than the same specific activities, just as they select from a fairly limited and familiar range of foodstuffs or other commodities. Different but overlapping sets of activities are expected of people of different age and sex and family membership. Communities differ according to geographical situation, composition and the kind of resources that are readily available to them. The style of living of a society consists more of elements which are heterogeneous but ordered and interrelated than they are rigidly homogeneous. Any attempt to define this style and represent it in some form of operational index, so that the conformity of a population can be measured statistically, is bound to be rough and ready. One kind of analogy could be drawn with the Retail Price Index. The Price Index does not show how much the cost of living may have changed between two dates for any particular family or section of the population but only in broad terms for society as a whole. There are difficulties in applying it to retirement pensioners or to the poor generally and to different regions. Techniques have to be developed so that applications to certain groups can be qualified; or a modified index, such as the index for retirement pensioners, is developed. But none the less it represents a useful point of departure and a means of accumulating, and generalising, knowledge.

Stratification and resources

What principles must therefore govern the attempt to obtain better information? We are concerned to identify the conditions and numbers of the poor relative to others in society. The population must be ranked in strata according to a criterion of inequality. But the criterion of cash income is inadequate. There are groups in the population with considerable income in kind, such as farmers and small-holders. There are people with small cash incomes but considerable assets, which elevate their standards of living. There are people with identical wages or salaries who differ greatly in the extent to which fringe benefits from employers add substantially to their living standards. There are people with identical cash incomes who differ greatly in the support they may obtain from free public social services, because they live in different areas, for example.

Living standards depend on the total contribution of not one but several systems distributing resources to individuals, families, work-groups and communities. To concentrate on cash incomes is to ignore the subtle ways developed in both modern and traditional societies for conferring and redistributing benefits. Moreover, to concentrate on income as the sole

Figure 1.2 Type of resource

1. *Cash income*	(*a*) earned	⎫
	(*b*) unearned	⎬
	(*c*) social security	
2. *Capital assets*	(*a*) house/flat occupied by family, and living facilities	
	(*b*) assets (other than occupied house) and savings	
3. *Value of employment benefits*	(*a*) employers fringe benefits: subsidies and value of occupational insurance	
	(*b*) occupational facilities	
4. *Value of public social services in kind*	including government subsidies and services, e.g. health, education and housing but excluding social security	
5. *Private income in kind*	(*a*) home production (e.g. of small-holding or garden)	
	(*b*) gifts	
	(*c*) value of personal supporting services	

criterion of poverty also implies that relatively simple adjustments, as might be made in a single scheme for negative income tax, will relieve it.

A plural approach is unavoidable. Thus, Figure 1.2 shows the types of resources arising from the principal systems of resource distribution. Even a fleeting reference to the different systems in society which distribute and redistribute resources, such as the wage-system, insurance and banking, social security and services like the National Health Service, may suggest that poverty is the creation of their complex interrelationship, or perhaps more fundamentally, of the values and norms upon which they rest or which they continuously reinforce. The practical implication is that the abolition of poverty may require comprehensive structural change in not one but several institutional systems. The problem is to establish the part that the different types of resource play in determining the overall standards of living of different strata in the population and, secondly, which of the systems underlying the distribution of that resource can be manipulated most efficiently to reduce poverty.

To obtain full information about all these types of resources for a representative cross-section of households is an ambitious but necessary task. Each of the types of resources can be defined in detail and converted (sometimes though with difficulty) into equivalent cash income values. The distribution of each in the population can be examined. Individual income units and households can be ranked according to each dimension and a measure of total rank achieved. The way can be opened for the measurement of the contribution made by different resource systems to both inequality and poverty. Following this approach we could also investigate the extent of rank agreement in society, that is, the extent to which the number of units which are ranked the same on all dimensions approaches the total number of units. The use in stratification theory by

Landecker, Lenski and Galtung and others of certain ideas about class and status crystallisation, rank disequilibrium, congruence and so on, can, of course, be adapted for poverty research. [44]

One of the purposes of combining the ranking of resources in different dimensions would be to allow us to distinguish between *total* and *partial* poverty. If resources are distributed by different institutional systems then it follows that although some people may lack a minimal share of any of these resources there will be others who lack a minimal share of one or two of these types of resources but have a substantial share of others. Thus in Britain there are, for example, fatherless families with identically low cash incomes but whose other resources differ sharply. There are those who live in the slum areas of cities in very bad, overcrowded housing, with schools and hospitals of poor quality near by. And there are those who live in new council housing estates on the fringe of cities or in new towns, in good housing with spacious, modern schools and hospitals near by with modern facilities and equipment. The standards of living of these two sets of families are not at all equivalent.[45] Whether instances such as these are common is unknown.

Another advantage is to trace more clearly the differences between *temporary* and *long-term* poverty. The distribution of resources changes over time. People are promoted within the wage-system; they change jobs, and become unemployed or sick; they obtain new dependants. It is impossible to conceive of social stratification as in fixed ranks, and clearly there may be major changes in the possession of resources both in the long-term, over the entire life-cycle, but also in the short-term, from month to month and even week to week. The life-cycle of poverty first described by Seebohm Rowntree requires contemporary documentation. A proportion of the population may always have been poor, but a much larger proportion have had occasional or periodic but not continuous experience of poverty. A large proportion still have lived or are living under the constant threat of poverty and regard some of the resources flowing to them, or available to them, as undependable. For the purposes of understanding the experience of poverty and the development of good policy it is most important to obtain the data to modify the over-confident division of the population into 'we the people' and 'they the poor'.

Inequality, however, is not poverty. Even if we succeed in identifying and measuring inequalities in the distribution of resources those in the lowest quintile or decile, say, are not necessarily poor. For example, the quintile with the lowest incomes in Sweden are not so badly placed as the corresponding quintile in the United States.[46]

Just as it is argued that a wider concept of 'resources' should replace 'income' in the study of inequality and poverty, so it is argued that 'style of living' should replace 'consumption' (or more narrowly still 'nutritional intakes') in determining what levels in the ranking of resources should be regarded as constituting deprivation. Some care is required in establishing the meaning of the concept, for it has been used in sociology in many different senses. For Weber, stratification by economic class and status could both be represented by style of living. 'Status honour is normally expressed by the fact that a special style of life can be expected from all who wish to belong to the circle.'[47] But Veblen and more recently sociologists such as Warner developed the concept into a system of what amounts to supercilious and derogatory distinctions in society. Everyone, or nearly everyone, was supposed to hold similar views about what was good and desirable. Modern studies have begun to break down this unrelieved picture of a uniformly acquisitive, materialistic, consumer society and a number of community studies in particular have shown that there are not just enclaves of traditional working-class culture but highly developed and pervasive styles of community living.[48] Tom Burns suggests that in contemporary urban society the principle of segregation is more and more strictly followed. In any large town or city there are social areas 'representing important expressive aspects not only of the income but of the occupations, social proclivities, educational background, and social pretensions of the people who live in them – or rather of the kind of people who are supposed to live in them'. In suburbs, neighbourhoods, and even blocks of flats there were, he continued, groupings of young married couples, middle-aged people, the retired or bachelor girls·and men. Consumption was the expressive aspect of style of life and 'style of life has developed a much greater significance as a mode of organising individual behaviour and leisure, careers and, therefore, as a form of social structure . . . Individuals do organise their lives in terms of a preferred style of life which is expressed concretely in terms of a pattern of consumption ranging from houses, and other consumer durables, to clothing, holidays, entertainment, food and drink.'[49]

Style of life is made up of very widely and very restrictedly shared elements. This must always have been so for reasons of cultural self-confidence and social control as well as individual and local community self-respect. But the mix for any particular section or group in society may be different and may change over time. There are types of behaviour which are nationally sanctioned and even upheld in law affecting working hours and conditions, child care, marital relations, spending and so on. There are public corporations and departments which endeavour to provide recognisably uniform services throughout the country. There are trade unions, which encourage their membership to adopt a nationally cohesive outlook and not diverse and perhaps contradictory branch opinions and activities. There are symbols of nationhood, like the Royal Family, the British policeman, a village green, a love of animals or of cricket, which are repeatedly invoked in family or local rituals. And through the mass communication industries – television, newspapers, popular magazines, the cinema and advertising – the cultural norms of society are both reflected and modified. The mass media help to standardise the kinds of leisure-time pursuits, child-rearing practices, manners and language which certain wide sections of the population will feel it is appropriate for them to adopt.

There are subtle gradations of styles of living ramifying through society as well as different mixes of national and local styles for different communities and ethnic groups. Different classes may engage in similar types of activity, such as going on a holiday or holding a birthday party for children, but do them differently. In developing an operational definition of style of living it is therefore necessary to distinguish (i) types of customs and social activities practised or approved by a majority of the national population; (ii) the types of customs and social activities practised or approved by a majority of people in a locality, community, class, racial group, religious sect or work group; and (iii) the specific content and manner of individual and group expression of both national and local customs or practices. It is hypothesised that with a diminishing level of resources people will engage less fully in the national 'style of living'. Below a certain level it is further hypothesised that participation will fall off more sharply. More exactly, as resources diminish at the lower levels of the distributional range participation will diminish disproportionately. In principle items for the index might be chosen at systematic intervals from an exhaustive list of customs practised by the majority or at least a substantial minority of a population, though obviously there would have to be controls for item 'inter-contamination', and the frequency and varying symbolic importance of the practice of different items. A summary list has to be the product of judgement and pilot experiment. The following index was developed for the purposes of analysing a national survey carried out in the United Kingdom in 1968–9.[50]

A deprivation index
> Per cent of sample population which:
> 1. Has not had a week's holiday away from home in last 12 months   53.6
> 2. *Adults only*. Has not had a relative or friend to the home for a meal or snack in the last four weeks   33.4

3. *Adults only.* Has not been out in the last four weeks to a relative or friend for a meal or snack   45.1
4. *Children only* (under 15). Has not had a friend to play or to tea in last four weeks   36.3
5. *Children only.* Did not have party on last birthday   56.6
6. Has not had an afternoon or evening out for entertainment in the last two weeks   47.0
7. Does not have fresh meat (including meals out) as many as four days a week   19.3
8. Has gone through one or more days in the past fortnight without a cooked meal   7.0
9. Has not had a cooked breakfast most days of the week   67.3
10. Household does not have a refrigerator   45.1
11. Household does not usually have a Sunday joint (3 in 4 times)   25.9
12. Household does not have sole use of four amenities indoors (flush W.C.; sink or washbasin and cold-water tap; fixed bath or shower; and gas or electric cooker)   21.4

Such indices provide the means of exploring whether or not there is a threshold of resources below which deprivation becomes marked. In principle they ·extend the selective use of more traditional indices of morbidity, nutritional deficiency, poor housing and mortality.

Conclusion

The social scientist is very frequently the victim of normative values and his perceptions and measures tend to be permeated by them. But if he feels obliged to make a distinction, as I have suggested, between subjective, collective and objective assessments of need then first he becomes much more aware of the forces which are controlling his own perceptions and second he becomes that much more prepared to break with the conventions which restrict and trivialise his theoretical work. I have suggested two steps that he can take towards the objectification of the measurement of poverty. One is to endeavour to measure all types of resources, public and private, which are distributed unequally in society and which contribute towards actual standards of living. This will tend to uncover sources of inequality which tend to be prescribed from public and even academic discourse. It will also help him more readily to compare different types of poverty. The other is to endeavour to define the style of living which is generally shared or approved in each society and find whether there is, as I have hypo-thesised, a point in the scale of the distribution of resources below which families find it increasingly difficult (proportionate to the diminishing level of resources) to share in the customs, activities and diets comprising that style of living.

But this does not leave measurement value-free. In the last resort the decisions which are taken to define the exact boundaries of the concept of resources and weigh the value of different types of resources have to be based on judgement, even if such judgement incorporates certain criteria of number and logical consistency. And decisions have to be taken about all the different ingredients of 'style of living', their relative importance and the extent to which they can be reliably represented by indicators used as criteria of deprivation by social scientists. Values will not have been eliminated from social research. But at least they will have been pushed one or two stages further back and an attempt made both to make measurement reproducible and more dependent on externally instead of subjectively assessed criteria.

It will be some time before theory and methodology can be put on to an agreed scientific footing. The problem of poverty had attracted a lot of concern and also justifiable anger. Many of the attempts to document and explain it have been grounded in limited national and even parochial, not to say individualistic, conceptions, which this paper has sought to demonstrate. Until social scientists can provide the rigorous conception within which the poverty of industrial societies and the third world can both be examined, and the relationship between inequality and poverty perceived, the accumulation of data and the debates about the scale and causal antecedents of the problem will in large measure be fruitless.

NOTES

[1] *The 1970 Manpower Report of the President*, by the US Department of Labor solemnly traces, like many other reports emanating from the US Government and also papers and books by social scientists, the fall in poverty between 1959 and 1968. But since a fixed and not an up-dated poverty line has been applied at regular intervals, this fall is scarcely surprising. The same trend could have been demonstrated for every industrial society in the years since the war, and indeed for nearly all periods of history since the Industrial Revolution.

[2] *Social Insurance and Allied Services* (The Beveridge Report) Cmd. 6404 (London, 1942).

[3] It is new only in the sense that the implications and applications do not appear to have been spelled out systematically and in detail. The line of thought has been put forward by many social scientists in the past. For example, Adam Smith wrote, 'By necessaries I understand, not only the commodities which are indispensably necessary for the support of life, but whatever the custom of the country renders it indecent for creditable people, even of the lowest order, to be without', *The Wealth of Nations*, Book 5, Chapter 2, Part I, 1776.

[4] B. Seebohm Rowntree, *Poverty: A Study of Town Life* (London, 1901).

Charles Booth's major work in London in the late 1880s was on a larger scale but employed a cruder measure of poverty. See his *Life and Labour of the People in London*.

5 See for example, A. L. Bowley and A. R. Burnett-Hurst, *Livelihood and Poverty, A Study in the Economic and Social Conditions of Working Class Households in Northampton, Warrington Stanley, and Reading [and Bolton]* (London, 1915), A. L. Bowley and M. H. Hogg. *Has Poverty Diminished?* (London, 1925). *New Survey of London Life and Labour* (London, 1930–35), M. S. Soutar, E. H. Wilkins and P. S. Florence. *Nutrition and Size of Family* (London, 1942).

6 *Poverty and Progress* (London, 1941) and, with G. R. Lavers, *Poverty and the Welfare State* (London, 1951).

7 Based on data in A. M. Henderson, 'The Cost of a Family', *The Review of Economic Studies*, Vol. xvii (2) (1949–50).

8 M. Orshansky, 'Counting the Poor: Another Look at the Poverty Profile', *Social Security Bulletin*, Vol. 28 (January, 1965), p. 5.

9 M. Orshansky, 'Who Was Poor in 1966?' *Research and Statistics Note*, US Dept. of Health and Education and Welfare, 6 December, 1967, p. 3. The *1970 Manpower Report of the President* puts the same point in a rather different way. 'Whereas in 1959 the poverty threshold represented about 48 per cent of the average income of all four-person families, in 1968 it represented only 36 per cent.'

10 Orshansky, 'Counting the Poor', p. 5.

11 Between 1960 and 1968 average expenditure per head in Britain on food increased by about 6 per cent more than prices but the energy value of nutritional intakes by only about 1 per cent and calcium by less than 3 per cent. However, there is no satisfactory comprehensive index for nutritional intakes. Ministry of Agriculture, *Household Food Consumption and Expenditure: 1968* (London, 1970), pp. 8, 57 and 64; *Household Food Consumption and Expenditure: 1966* (London, 1968), pp. 9 and 84.

12 This applies to most goods and services and not just foodstuffs. One instance might be given from recent US experience. Between 1958 and 1964 the price of refrigerators jumped from $217 to $261. But at the same time they became self-defrosting and incorporated more frozen food storage space. During the same period, 1958–64, the Consumer Price Index showed a decline of 11 per cent. Nevertheless a person with $217 could buy (a refrigerator) in 1958 but not in 1964. Department of Economic and Social Affairs, United Nations, *Social Policy and the Distribution of Income in the Nation* (New York, 1969), p. 53.

13 M. Orshansky, 'How Poverty is Measured', *Monthly Labour Review*, February 1969, p. 41.

14 There are few references to this conceptual problem in the American literature. Ornati does call attention to the problem but does not suggest how a fresh 'contemporary' standard for each period of time, which he recommends, can be worked out consistently. See O. Ornati, *Poverty Amid Affluence* (New York, 1966), pp. 28–31.

15 'All the plans, if strictly followed, can provide an acceptable and adequate diet but – generally speaking – the lower the level of cost, the more restricted the kinds and qualities of food must be and the more the skill in marketing and food preparation that is required.' M. Orshansky, 'Counting the Poor: Another Look at the Poverty Profile', *Social Security Bulletin*, Vol. 28 (January, 1965), p. 5.

16 This is a phrase used by the US Department of Agriculture in describing an 'economy food plan', costing only 75–80 per cent as much as the basic low-cost plan, quoted in M. Orshansky, *ibid.* p. 6. Later Miss Orshansky made the remarkable admission that 'The Agriculture Department estimates that only about 10 per cent of persons spending (up to the level in

the economy food plan) were able to get a nutritionally adequate diet.'
'How Poverty is Measured', *Monthly Labour Review* (February 1969), p. 38.

[17] Orshansky herself quotes a Bureau of Labour Statistics Survey for 1960–1, showing that food represented only 22 per cent of the expenditure of a household of three people, for example, compared with 31 per cent in the 1955 survey. Acknowledging that the percentage had decreased she stated that this 'undoubtedly reflect(ed) in part the general improvement in real income achieved by the Nation as a whole in the 6 years elapsed between the two studies'. Had the later percentages been adopted the poverty line would have been 14–1500 dollars higher for a family of three persons for example, and the total number of families in poverty would have been at least half as many again. Orshansky, *ibid.* p. 9. The percentage chosen is a further instance of the rigidity of the poverty line. In the last hundred years the proportion of the family budget spent on food has fallen steadily in the United States, Britain, Japan and other rich countries, and tends to be higher in countries which have a lower income *per capita* than the US. See, for example, Department of Economic and Social Affairs, *Social Policy and the Distribution of Income* (New York, 1969), pp. 53–6.

[18] M. Orshansky, 'How Poverty is Measured'.

[19] Compare, for example, F. Engels, *The Condition of the Working Class in England* (London, 1969) (first published in 1845); C. Masterman, *The Condition of England* (London, 1960) (first published in 1909) and G. Orwell, *The Road to Wigan Pier* (London, 1936).

[20] B. Pasamanick, A. Lilienfeld, and M. E. Rogers, *Prenatal and Paranatal Factors in the Development of Childhood Behaviour Disorders* (Baltimore, 1957).

[21] See, for example, B. Benjamin, 'Tuberculosis and Social Conditions in the Metropolitan Boroughs of London', *British Journal of Tuberculosis*, 47 (1953); F. J. W. Miller *et al., Growing up in Newcastle upon Tyne* (London, 1960).

[22] For example, L. Stein, 'Tuberculosis and the "social complex" in Glasgow', *British Journal of Social Medicine* (January, 1952); J. A. Scott, 'Gastro-enteritism in Infancy', *British Journal of Preventive and Social Medicine* (October, 1953).

[23] G. W. Brown *et al., Schizophrenia and Social Care* (London, 1966), E. M. Goldberg and S. L. Morrison, 'Schizophrenia and Social Class', *British Journal of Psychiatry* (1963).

[24] Methods of relating different indicators are discussed in C. A. Moser, and W. Scott, *British Towns: A Statistical Study of their Social and Economic Differences* (London, 1961). See also, B. Davies, *Social Needs and Resources in Local Services* (London, 1968); and for an illustration of the political uses of indicators of area deprivation, the Labour Party, *Labour's Social Strategy* (London, 1969).

[25] American work of a systematic kind could be said to date from W. E. B. Dubois, *The Philadelphia Negro,* first published in 1899 (New York, 1967). The early work in England of Booth and Rowntree in the 1880s and 1890s prompted a succession of studies in towns and cities. See, for example, Bowley, and Burnett-Hurst, *A Survey of Five Towns*; D. Caradog Jones, *Social Survey of Merseyside* (Liverpool, 1934); H. Tout, *The Standard of Living in Bristol* (Bristol, 1938), as well as Rowntree's own subsequent work.

For a review of English studies see, Political and Economic Planning, *Poverty: Ten Years after Beveridge*, Planning, No. 344 (1952). For a general review of surveys using the subsistence standard of measurement see A. Pagani, *La Linea Della Poverta,* Collana di Scienze Sociali (Milano, 1960).

[26] Ministry of Social Security, *Circumstances of Families* (London, 1967), p. 8.

[27] M. Orshansky, 'Who Was Poor in 1966', *Research and Statistics Note*, US

Department of Health, Education and Welfare, 6 December, 1967, Table 4. In Canada a similar kind of approach to that used in the United States produced an official estimate of 3.85 million people in poverty in 1967, or about a quarter of the population. The proportion was highest in the Atlantic Provinces. See a brief prepared by the Department of National Health and Welfare for presentation to the Special Committee of the Senate on Poverty, The Senate of Canada, *Proceedings of the Special Senate Committee on Poverty* (24 and 26 February, 1970), pp. 18–19 and 62.

28 Estimated from Table 7.5 in R. F. Henderson, A. Harcourt and R. J. A. Harper, *People in Poverty: A Melbourne Survey* (Melbourne, 1970), p. 117.

29 See also the discussion in Chapter 2.

30 H. Lydall, *The Structure of Earnings* (London, 1968), pp. 152–62, and 249–51. See the discussion for Britain in Chapter 2.

31 See K. R. Ranadive, 'The Equality of Incomes in India', *Bulletin of the Oxford Institute of Statistics* (May 1965), in his critical review of data used by S. Kuznets, 'Quantitative Aspects of Economic Growth of Nations: VIII, Distribution of Income by Size', *Economic Development and Cultural Change*, 11 (January 1963).

32 For example, see B. M. Russett *et al.*, *World Handbook of Political and Social Indicators* (New Haven and London, 1964), and Kuznets, 'Quantitative Aspects of Economic Growth of Nations'.

33 A. B. Atkinson, 'On the Measurement of Inequality', *Journal of Economic Theory* (September 1970), pp. 258–62.

34 'We have, at present, no means of estimating the effects of private fringe benefits on the degree of inequality of effective employment income . . . Private fringe benefits may offset a large part of the equalising effects of progressive income taxes.' Lydall, *The Structure of Earnings*, pp. 157–8.

35 Gunnar Myrdal is well aware of this problem and describes it in broad terms. 'The scientists in any particular institutional and political setting move as a flock, reserving their controversies and particular originalities for matters that do not call into question the fundamental system of biases they share . . . The common need for rationalisation will tend . . . to influence the concepts, models and theories applied; hence it will also affect the selection of relevant data, the recording of observations, the theoretical and practical inferences drawn explicitly or implicitly, and the manner of presentation of the results of research.' He argues that, 'objectivity' can be understood only in the sense that however elaborately a framework of fact is developed the underlying set of value premises must also be made explicit. 'This represents an advance towards the goals of honesty, clarity and effectiveness in research . . . It should overcome the inhibitions against drawing practical and political conclusions openly, systematically and logically. This method would consequently render social research a much more powerful instrument for guiding rational policy information.' G. Myrdal, *Objectivity in Social Research* (London, 1970), pp. 53 and 72.

36 S. A. Stouffer *et al.*, *The American Soldier* (Princeton, 1949).

37 R. K. Merton, *Social Theory and Social Structure*, revised edition (Illinois, 1957); W. G. Runciman, *Relative Deprivation and Social Justice* (London, 1966). Runciman's work is particularly valuable, not just because he expounds the practical relevance of the concept to contemporary problems, such as wage bargaining, but because he shows its relevance to the analysis of political behaviour generally.

38 See Chapter 7.

39 D. Wedderburn, 'The Financial Resources of Older People: A General Review', and 'The Characteristics of Low Income Receivers and the Role of Government' in E. Shanas *et al.*, *Old People in Three Industrial Societies* (New York and London, 1968).

40 See, for example, D. Wedderburn, 'A Cross-National Study of Standards

of Living of the Aged in Three Countries', in P. Townsend (ed.), *The Concept of Poverty* (London, 1970), p. 204.

[41] In a secondary analysis of income and expenditure data the social or normative standard of poverty was discussed and applied and the number and characteristics of people living below that standard identified. The authors did not, of course, claim that this was an objective or an ideal definition of poverty – though their work was sometimes subsequently misinterpreted as such. B. Abel-Smith and P. Townsend, *The Poor and the Poorest* (London, 1965). For a similar approach see Ministry of Social Security, *Circumstances of Families* (London, 1967).

[42] The present definition of overcrowding adopted by the Registrar General is one and a half persons per room. A 'bedroom standard' of overcrowding has been devised, which makes greater provision for family norms about the age and sex of children who share rooms. A 'minimum fitness' standard for housing has also been worked out recently by the Denington Committee. Ministry of Housing, Central Housing Advisory Committee, *Our Older Homes: A Call for Action* (London, 1966).

[43] Rowntree, *Poverty, a Study of Town Life*, pp. 108–9 and 382–84.

[44] The possibilities are discussed in Townsend, *The Concept of Poverty*. There are two special difficulties in deriving total rank in stratification theory from individual rank dimensions. Total rank is very difficult to express if the form of distribution varies in each individual dimension. It is also difficult to express if there is no criterion according to which the different dimensions can be weighted. The conversion of values in the different dimensions into equivalent cash incomes offers a means of overcoming the second problem. However, such a conversion may overlook subtleties in the different meanings placed on the value of assets, goods and services in everyday social life.

[45] The tendency for families of widows and children to have higher living standards than other fatherless families is traced in D. Marsden, *Mothers Alone* (London, 1969). There appear to be inequalities in the ownership of assets, particularly housing and household durables, as well as in treatment under social security.

[46] They have about 6 per cent of pre-tax income, compared with about 4 per cent in the United States. The top quintile have about 43 per cent compared with 46 per cent. H. Lydall, and J. B. Lansing, 'A Comparison of the Distribution of Personal Income and Wealth in the United States and Great Britain', *American Economic Review* (March 1959); United Nations, *Economic Survey of Europe in 1956* (Geneva, 1957). Chapter IX, p. 6.

[47] H. Gerth and C. W. Mills, *From Max Weber: Essays in Sociology* (London, 1946), p. 187.

[48] See, for example, P. Willmott and M. Young, *Family and Class in a London Suburb* (London, 1960); M. Stacey, *Tradition and Change: A Study of Banbury* (London, 1960).

[49] T. Burns, 'The Study of Consumer Behaviour: A Sociological View', *Archives of European Sociology*, VII (1966), pp. 321–2.

[50] An elaborate survey of household resources and standards of living was carried out in that year by Professor Brian Abel-Smith and the author, with a research team working at the University of Essex and the London School of Economics and Political Science. The report is in preparation. Pilot work was completed during 1964–8. See, for example Marsden, *Mothers Alone*; Land, *Large Families in London* (London, 1969); Townsend (ed.), *The Concept of Poverty*.

2

Poverty and income inequality in Britain[1]

A. B. ATKINSON

This chapter surveys the work that has been done on measuring poverty and income inequality in Britain. Three main questions will be discussed. First, how unequal are incomes in Britain? Here the chapter will concern itself both with the number of people living below a certain poverty line and with the distribution of income in more general terms. Second, is inequality increasing or decreasing? Are the differences in the living standards of the rich and the poor widening or narrowing? The chapter will examine how far it is possible to answer such questions with available information. Third, what are the main sources of inequality in incomes? This question is not one which can be discussed here at any depth, but there are some important and straightforward questions which can be answered. Who are the poor? Are they chiefly old people, or families with low wages? How far can the observed inequality of income be explained by people being at different stages of the life cycle?

Many conceptual problems arise in measuring poverty and inequality. The chapter therefore deals first with the theoretical issues involved in measuring inequality. It then turns to a review of some of the empirical work undertaken in Britain. Such a survey is necessarily selective. In particular the present discussion does not deal with the effect of Government policy on the distribution of income. J. L. Nicholson gives an account in another chapter of this volume of his pioneering work on measuring the overall redistributive effect of the Government budget, and elsewhere I have discussed the contribution of the present social security system to dealing with the problem of poverty.[2] Nor does the paper discuss other important aspects of economic inequality such as the concentration of wealth-holding. It is confined to the studies that have been made in the fields of poverty and of inequality in the distribution of income.

Conceptual issues in measuring inequality

Since concern with inequality stems ultimately from some concept of social welfare, many of the problems discussed in this part of the paper involve social values. The aim of this discussion is to clarify the issues involved and to bring to light situations where values are being introduced implicitly rather than explicitly into the measurement of inequality.

What is being measured

The first area where conceptual problems arise concerns the definition of the basic unit for which information should be analysed. Should it be the individual, the nuclear family or the household? This question may best be understood in terms of the degree to which a group of persons share their income. Suppose, for example, that we were to take the individual as the basic unit. We should then find a large number of married women with very low money incomes. Since by convention in our society most married couples do share their income and since this applies also to dependent children, the natural unit may appear to be the nuclear family. Should one, however, go further and adopt the household as the basic unit?[3] In answering this, we have to decide first how far incomes are in fact shared within the household; if there is no income-sharing, there would be no obstacle to treating families separately in respect of their incomes. If income-sharing takes place, we have then to consider how far we should want to take this into account. This is a difficult question to resolve. In the case of old people, it can be argued that their incomes should be adequate in their own right and that they should not need to depend on help from relatives and our assessment of the adequacy of their incomes should be independent of whether or not they live with their children. But this argument may appear less attractive at the other end of the age scale when the question is whether a young adult living at home, supported by his parents, should be regarded as being in poverty if his own personal income is low.

The choice between the family and the household unit depends on the purpose for which the measure is required. If, for example, we are concerned to measure poverty, the adoption of a household basis assumes that income-sharing in fact takes place, and should be taken into account. To the extent that these conditions are not satisfied, we shall underestimate the magnitude of the problem. It has been shown by Morgan in the United States that the extent of this under-statement may be considerable,[4] and the sensitivity of the income distribution to the definition of the unit was brought out very clearly by the study of Cole and Utting.[5] Moreover, in so far as there are changes over time in the pattern of household formation, the use of the household base will bias estimates of changes in the extent of poverty over time. It will be biassed upward, for example, if the dominant changes are for young people to leave home sooner and for old people to continue living on their own longer.

The second conceptual problem concerns the period over which resources should be measured. The shortest period that could practically be taken is a week. It can be argued, however, that weekly income is very sensitive to chance fluctuations, a person may have been working a short shift in that particular week or have received a special bonus. The importance of short-run variations was first stressed by Friedman,[6] who pointed out that the distribution of income measured over a short period would show greater inequality than 'normal' income. Whether the alternative approach of measuring resources over a longer period (such as a month or a year) should be adopted depends again on both empirical and normative judgements. The empirical question concerns the extent to which people are able to average their incomes over time by borrowing or lending. In fact it seems reasonable to assume that at the lower end of the income scale the scope for averaging is very limited, certainly so far as borrowing is concerned, but that at the upper end the situation is different. This clearly leads to difficulties when considering the distribution as a whole. The normative question concerns the extent to which we think that people *ought* to be assumed to average their incomes.[7] As in the case of income-sharing within the household, we may want to adopt a different approach for different questions. If we are measuring poverty, we may want to know how many people have current weekly incomes below a certain standard, ignoring the fact that a month later they may be better off. On the other hand, when measuring inequality, it may be more reasonable to try and approximate 'normal' income by taking income measured over a longer period.

An extension of this argument is to consider aggregating a person's income over the whole of his life and to concern ourselves not with *current* income but with *lifetime* income. This will clearly give quite different results for at any moment there are people who currently have low incomes, but will have higher incomes later in their life (for example students or apprentices) while others will have had higher incomes in the past (for example pensioners). If our concern is with measuring poverty, then the lifetime income approach is not very relevant: for example, the fact that an old person had a high income thirty years ago does not make up for the pension being below his needs today. On the other hand, when measuring the degree of inequality, there are many attractions in treating a person's lifetime as a whole rather than considering different periods in isolation.

There are obvious difficulties in obtaining the data required to measure income inequality on a lifetime basis. Even if we were to start collecting information now about individual cohorts, we should not have any answers for fifty years. On the other hand, obtaining figures retrospectively involves serious problems. Information obtained from memory would be unreliable and piecing together figures from the Inland Revenue returns, even if access were granted, would be an immense undertaking. One study has, however, been made by Soltow of lifetime income inequality in the Norwegian city of Sarpsborg.[8] He obtained information from the tax returns, which are available for inspection by the general public, on the annual income of a group of men over the period 1928–60 and showed that inequality in total income over this period was significantly less than the inequality in single years. Given that this kind of information is not likely to be available in Britain, we may none the less be able to make some deductions about lifetime inequality from the degree of inequality within age groups. If, for example, incomes were the same for everyone in an age group but increased with age, the distribution over all age groups would show inequality, but there would be no lifetime inequality and this would be revealed by looking at individual age groups. This is an artificial example and in practice the life-cycle pattern of incomes would differ between social groups; however, examination of the extent to which inequality is attributable to differences between age groups would allow us to eliminate those life-cycle differences which are common to all individuals.

We have, so far, referred to income and resources as synonymous, but there are a number of problems concerning the measure of resources. First, there is the definition of income. Although there are still disagreements among economists, most are broadly agreed that income should be regarded as 'the value of rights which a person might exercise in consumption without altering the value of his assets'.[9] In other words, income is equal to the market value of all goods consumed plus the increase in the value of a person's wealth between the beginning and the end of the period (where this includes the increase in the value of existing assets as well as the acquisition of new assets). The important feature of this 'ideal' definition is its comprehensiveness. To quote the Minority Report of the Royal Commission on the Taxation of Profits and Income:[10]

> No concept of income can be really equitable that stops short of the comprehensive definition which embraces all receipts which increase an individual's command over the use of society's scarce resources – in other words, his 'net accretion of economic power between two points in time'.

Moreover, it is this comprehensiveness which distinguishes the definition from the present tax practice and, as we shall see later, there are a number of important items which would be considered income according to our 'ideal' definition, but which do not appear in the Inland Revenue statistics: for example, capital gains and imputed rent on owner-occupied houses.

Second, we might ask whether expenditure or wealth might not be a more appropriate measure of resources than income. The argument for expenditure may take two forms, both of which are discussed fully by Kaldor in his book on the expenditure tax.[11] There is the Hobbesian argument that consumption represents what people take *out* of the common pool, whereas income is more a reflection of what they put *in*. There is also the quite different standpoint which accepts income as the correct measure, but argues that expenditure may represent a better indicator of 'true' income than the income recorded by the Inland Revenue figures. Capital gains, for example, do not appear in the Inland Revenue figures, but people take them into account when deciding how much to consume. This argument has particular force if we are concerned with lifetime inequality, since current expenditure may be superior to current income as an indicator of lifetime income. Suppose, for example, that there are two pensioners, one of whom had a high income while working and was able to accumulate savings, the other did not. They may now have the same income, but the first is able to maintain a higher level of consumption because he is able to draw on his capital. The existence of lifetime inequality will be suggested by the differences in expenditure but not by current incomes. This difficulty might, of course, be circumvented by considering not only current income but also wealth; but there is then the problem of combining income and wealth into a single measure of welfare.[12]

Methods of analysis

In considering the method of analysis to be applied once the basic form of the data has been determined, we can distinguish two approaches. The first is concerned with establishing what proportion of the population falls below some specified poverty standard, and the second is concerned with measuring the degree of inequality in the distribution as a whole. In the measurement of poverty, the crucial problem is that of determining the poverty standard to be applied. In the pioneering work of Seebohm Rowntree in Britain in 1899, the method followed was to calculate for each family 'the minimum necessaries for the maintenance of merely physical efficiency'.[13] This was done by estimating the nutritional requirements of families of different sizes, translating these into quantities of different foods and hence into money terms, and adding the rent paid and certain minimum amounts for clothing, fuel and sundries. However, this approach involves a number of serious conceptual problems, which were recognised by Rowntree and have been discussed at length by Townsend.[14] Even in the case of food, it is extremely difficult to determine 'requirements' with any precision, and rather than any one absolute level of subsistence needs, there is a broad range where physical efficiency declines with falling food intake. Where precisely the line is drawn depends on the judgement of the investigator and the idea of a purely physiological basis to the poverty standard is lost. For this reason, recent studies have adopted rather different approaches to the definition of poverty. In Britain, the definition has conventionally been based on the standards of eligibility for National Assistance/Supplementary Benefits – or the minimum standard of living that the Government considers necessary at a particular time. This approach was used by Abel-Smith and Townsend in their study *The Poor and the Poorest*, who justified it on the grounds that:[15]

> Whatever may be said about the adequacy of the National Assistance Board level of living as a just or publicly approved measure of 'poverty', it has at least the advantage of being in a sense the 'official' operational definition of the minimum standard of living at any particular time.

A very important feature of the poverty standard is the way in which it changes over time (see p. 62). If an absolute subsistence approach is adopted then logically it should only rise to allow for increased prices – the real poverty standard should be unchanged. In practice, however, almost all studies of poverty have adopted a relative standard. In his study of 1936, Rowntree's real poverty standard was considerably higher than in 1899. In view of this, it seems best to recognise explicitly that any poverty line will be influenced by current living standards and that poverty can only be defined in relation to the living standards of a particular society at a particular date. Our concern is then with people whose incomes fall below an acceptable minimum relative to the general level of incomes, and the poverty line will rise with rising standards of living. In the United States, it has been argued by Fuchs that the poverty standard should in fact be linked to the median level of income.[16]

The poverty standard has a number of other important dimensions. Allowance has to be made for the needs of families of different sizes. The relative scales under Supplementary Benefits for adults and children of different ages are shown in Table 2.1.[17] These relativities have their origin in the Beveridge Report of 1942, when he calculated a set of subsistence scales for adults and children of different ages following a rather similar approach to that of Rowntree. When National Assistance was introduced in 1948, the scale rates were based broadly on the Beveridge proposals and since then even with the introduction of Supplementary Benefits, they have remained virtually unchanged. The continuing rationale of these differentials

Table 2.1: *Supplementary Benefit rates for families of various sizes 1970*

	Percentage of single person's rate[a]
Married couple	164
Child aged:	
Less than 5	29
5–10	34
11–12	43
13–15	46
16–17	58

[a] No allowance is made for the long-term addition.
Source: Department of Health and Social Security Annual Report 1970 (London, 1971), p. 124.

must be subject to question: and although the difficulties involved are considerable, this issue should receive more attention.[18] Wynn has shown that the differential rates are different in other European countries and that in particular the rates for adolescent children are more generous.[19]

In measuring poverty, the aim must be to apply a uniform standard in real terms. Thus allowance should be made for geographical differences in the cost of living. This problem arises most acutely in the case of rents, and this is recognised in the Supplementary Benefit scale in Britain in that a separate allowance is paid to cover housing expenditure provided that it is considered 'reasonable'. No other adjustment is made under the Supplementary Benefit scale for differences in the cost of living between areas. In view of the paucity of information about regional price differentials, it is not possible to assess the inequity which this involves, and this is clearly an area in which more information is necessary.[20]

If we turn to the measurement of inequality in the distribution as a whole, the question arises whether there is any convenient measure by which the overall degree of inequality may be summarised. Such a measure would be of use both as an indicator of the extent of concentration at a point in time, and as a means for comparing distributions at different dates or in different countries.

One convenient way of summarising the information collected about the distribution of income is in terms of a Lorenz curve (see Figure 2.1), which shows the proportion of total income received by the bottom x per cent of income-receivers. If the distribution were perfectly equal, the bottom 10 per cent, for example, would receive 10 per cent of the total income, and the Lorenz curve would follow the diagonal ('line of complete equality' in Figure 2.1). If there is inequality, the bottom 10 per cent

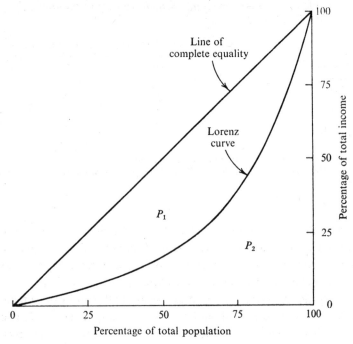

Line of
complete equality

Lorenz
curve

P_1

P_2

Figure 2.1

receive less than 10 per cent of total income, and the Lorenz curve lies below the diagonal. The Lorenz curve provides a means of comparing the degree of inequality in two distributions: for if the Lorenz curve for one distribution, *A*, lies everywhere above that for another distribution, *B*, then distribution *A* can be said to be unambiguously more equal (see Figure 2.2*a*).[21] The difficulties arise where the Lorenz curves intersect (see Figure 2.2*b*) – which frequently happens. What can be said about the degree of inequality in such a case? The usual approach is to use one of the conventional summary statistical measures, such as the Gini coefficient, the relative mean deviation or the coefficient of variation. Of these the Gini coefficient is perhaps the most popular, and it has a simple geometric interpretation as the ratio of the area between the diagonal and the Lorenz curve to the total area of the triangle.[22] On this basis, one can see by eye that the distribution *A* in Figure 2.2*b* would be considered more equal than distribution *B* according to the Gini measure.

The Gini coefficient is often presented as a purely 'scientific' measure of inequality. But it must implicitly embody values about the distribution of income, since without introducing such values one cannot (in the example

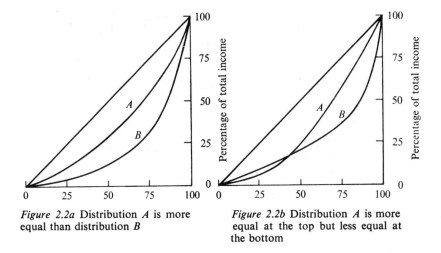

Figure 2.2a Distribution *A* is more equal than distribution *B*

Figure 2.2b Distribution *A* is more equal at the top but less equal at the bottom

given) weigh the lesser inequality of distribution *A* at the top against the greater inequality at the bottom. Moreover, when one examines the values implicit in the Gini coefficient, there is no reason to believe that they correspond to any values that we should like to hold regarding equity – indeed there is little reason to expect that they should, since the coefficient was put forward as a purely statistical measure rather than as representing any considerations of social welfare. In view of this, I have recently argued that we should adopt the alternative approach of considering directly the values regarding the distribution of income that we should like to incorporate.[23] Suppose that we assume that there is some consensus about the acceptability of varying degrees of inequality, so that with each distribution of income is associated a certain level of social welfare. Then on certain assumptions this gives rise to a new measure of inequality which I have referred to as the *equally distributed equivalent* measure.[24] This measure involves a parameter ϵ which reflects the weight attached by society to the inequality in the distribution of income. If ϵ is high, then society is particularly averse to inequality, if $\epsilon = 0$ then it is indifferent. Once ϵ has been agreed, the measure has an intuitive interpretation as the proportion of the present total income that would be required to achieve the same level of social welfare as we have now, *if all incomes were equally distributed*. A value of 70 per cent means that if incomes were equally distributed we should need only 70 per cent of the present national income to reach the same level of social welfare – or alternatively that the gain from redistribution to bring about equality is equivalent to raising national income by 30 per cent. (A *low* value denotes a *high* degree of inequality.) The precise

Table 2.2: *Characteristics of income surveys in Britain*

	Inland Revenue survey	Central Statistical Office estimate (based on Inland Revenue survey)	Family Expenditure survey
Income unit	Based on nuclear family. May diverge because: (i) income of children not necessarily aggregated with that of parents (ii) wife's earnings may not be aggregated where below deduction limit (iii) dependent relatives with incomes below the exemption limit are included	As Inland Revenue	Household (although basic questionnaire contains information about income units)
Time period	Annual income	As Inland Revenue (although on a calendar year basis)	'Normal' income where: Earnings = 'normal' earnings Social Security benefits = current week (except where off work for less than 13 weeks where normal earnings recorded) Other income = average of past 12 months
Definition of income – divergences from 'ideal'	Excludes capital gains, imputed rent on owner-occupied houses, certain social security benefits such as sickness and unemployment benefits and Supplementary Benefits, and certain income in kind	Includes social security benefits and income in kind of domestic servants and farm workers, otherwise as Inland Revenue	Excludes capital gains, and income in kind. Under-statement of income is quite likely (particularly income from self-employment and investments)

Information about needs	Number of members of income unit. Difficulties where: (i) allowances for children not claimed (where not paying tax), (ii) where units change status in the course of the year (births, deaths, marriages, etc.)	No information about number of members of income unit	Basic questionnaires contain: (i) number and ages of children, (ii) expenditure on different items (inc. housing), (iii) composition of income. This information is summarised in published tables
Coverage of survey	All income units with incomes over £275 reviewed for tax purposes. Double-counting may occur because of marriages and divorces, and there may be spurious units where incomes belonging to the same family are not aggregated	All income units with incomes over £50 year. Double-counting may occur as with Inland Revenue and (i) where income not aggregated (covenants and scholarships) and (ii) where dependent relatives appear also in own right	All private households (people living in hotels, boarding houses, hostels or institutions being excluded) No possibility of double-counting
Sample size	110,000 in 1967–8	As Inland Revenue	11,000 since 1967 (5,000 in earlier years). Problem of 'blowing-up' in view of absence of adequate control totals
Response rate	100 per cent	As Inland Revenue	Response rate averages around 70 per cent. Possible bias due to (i) underrepresentation of old and sick, (ii) over-representation of families with children

meaning of ϵ and the application of this equally distributed equivalent measure is illustrated below.

Studies of income inequality in Britain

Before surveying some of the recent work in Britain on the measurement of income inequality, it is necessary first to discuss the principal sources of information about the distribution of income in Britain. There are two of these, the Family Expenditure Survey (FES) and the Inland Revenue (IR) survey of personal incomes which also forms the basis of the estimate of income distribution prepared by the Central Statistical Office (CSO) and published in the National Income Blue Book.[25] The chief characteristics of these surveys are summarised in Table 2.2. One major difference between them is that the IR survey is based upon family incomes (with the exceptions noted in Table 2.2) whereas the information published in the FES is based on the household and therefore includes the income of all household members.[26] The 1968 FES shows that about 20 per cent of households were not of the nuclear family type,[27] so that the difference is an important one.

These surveys are not designed with the aim of deriving information about the distribution of income, and for this purpose they both suffer from serious drawbacks. The definition of income used in the IR survey diverges in a number of important respects affecting both the top of the distribution (capital gains) and the lower end (certain social security benefits), from the ideal definition discussed earlier. The estimates of the total number of income units is distorted by the exclusion of a substantial number of income units at the lower end of the distribution with incomes below the exemption level and by some double-counting. Moreover the only information which the IR survey provides about needs is the number of people per income unit. The CSO estimates are better in that they include social security benefits in total income and make adjustments for units below the exemption level. On the other hand, they do not provide any information at all about the composition of income units.

The FES does not suffer from a number of the deficiencies of the IR survey; its definition of income includes social security benefits and there are no problems about the exclusion of units or double-counting. It also provides more information about needs, and would provide even more if access were available to the raw returns. It is, however, based on an extremely small sample (covering about 1 person in 7,000); there are problems due to non-response and possible under-reporting of income; and there are difficulties in 'blowing up' the results to cover the whole population.[28]

It should be clear from this brief discussion of the various sources that there are no clear grounds for preferring one to another. Rather the choice between them depends on the purpose for which the distribution is required.

The measurement of poverty in Britain

The first systematic attempts to measure poverty in Britain were those of Seebohm Rowntree and Charles Booth at the end of the last century. In 1899 Rowntree carried out a survey of the city of York in which he estimated that 9.9 per cent of the population were living in poverty. As we have seen, his poverty line was based on the concept of an absolute subsistence standard, and more recent work has followed a rather different approach. The poverty line commonly adopted has been the standard of eligibility for Supplementary Benefits so that a person is considered to be living in poverty if his income is not sufficient to bring him to the level of someone receiving this basic benefit.

To give some indication of the relationship of this poverty standard to the general level of incomes, the Supplementary Benefit scale (including an allowance for rent) for different types of family is shown in Table 2.3 (column 1) as a percentage of the take-home pay of a man with earnings equal to the average for manual workers. Thus, in 1969 a pensioner couple on Supplementary Benefits would have received about half the amount they would have got if the man had been working and receiving the average earnings for a manual worker; and even for a family with six children the corresponding proportion was only three-quarters. An alternative indication of the level of the poverty line is given by expressing the Supplementary Benefit scale as a proportion of the average expenditure by families of different sizes (column 2 of Table 2.3) which again suggests that the poverty line falls a long way short of the general standard of living.

We turn now to a review of recent studies of poverty in Britain.[29] The pioneering study from which most of the recent interest in poverty stems is that carried out by Abel-Smith and Townsend.[30] They had access to the basic returns from the Family Expenditure Surveys of 1953–4 and 1960, and used these to estimate the proportion of households that were below the National Assistance scale (in 1953–4 this was assessed in terms of expenditure and in 1960 in terms of income). In order to allow for the fact that in many cases allowances are paid for special needs, they examined not only those with incomes below the National Assistance scale but also those who were less than 40 per cent above. The households falling below these poverty standards were classified according to their sources of

Table 2.3: *Supplementary Benefit scale in relation to income and expenditure*

| Family type | Supplementary Benefit scale[a] plus rent allowance as a percentage of | |
	Take home pay for male manual worker with average earnings (1969)[b]	Average expenditure of family that size (1968)[c]
Single pensioner	38	57
Pensioner couple	52	44
Unemployed man with:		
Wife + 1 child (aged 7)	56	44
Wife + 2 children (aged 4, 7)	60	46
Wife + 4 children (aged 4, 7, 10, 12)	67	*
Wife + 6 children (aged 2, 4, 7, 10, 12 and 14)	72	*

[a] The Supplementary Benefit scale is that introduced in October 1968. It includes an allowance for average rent and (in the case of the pensioner households) the long-term addition.

[b] Based on average earnings of adult male manual workers in manufacturing and certain other industries (average April and October 1969) after deducting income tax and National Insurance contributions but including Family Allowances.

[c] From *Family Expenditure Survey* 1968 (*denotes expenditure figures not available).

income, household size, age and whether or not they were in receipt of National Assistance. In 1968, Gough and Stark published a study of low incomes in 1954, 1959 and 1963 based on the Inland Revenue survey of personal incomes adjusted in a number of important respects.[31] The basic unit of analysis was the nuclear family, and in this respect their measure is closer to that employed by the Supplementary Benefits Commission in determining eligibility than the household-based data used by Abel-Smith and Townsend. On the other hand as we noted above, the Inland Revenue survey provides little information about needs and a number of major assumptions had to be made: for example, that all households had an average level of housing expenditure and that all children were of an average age. Moreover, the IR figures are grouped by broad income ranges and this involves the use of interpolation techniques, which may introduce considerable error into the estimates of the numbers with low incomes. A more recent estimate is that based on the 1969 Family Expenditure Survey and given in Atkinson.[32] Since access was not available to the raw returns, but only to the grouped data, a number of assumptions similar to those of Gough and Stark had to be made regarding average rent and the ages of children. For this reason the figures are considerably less reliable than those of Abel-Smith and Townsend, although they have the advantage of being based on a larger sample. A 'minimum' estimate of the number in poverty was also made for 1966 using the surveys of the incomes of retirement pensioners and families receiving Family Allowances carried out by the Government in 1965 and 1966 respectively.[33] Since the information collected in these surveys was precisely of the form required (applying the standard of eligibility for Supplementary Benefits), this provides a reliable figure for reference purposes; and since there are undoubtedly people in poverty outside these two groups it also provides a minimum estimate.

The results of these studies are summarised in Table 2.4 which shows the proportion of the population having incomes below the Supplementary Benefit scale (or the scale rate plus 40 per cent). There are clearly wide disparities between the studies – both in the absolute numbers in poverty and in the trends over time – that call for comment.

There are two reasons why we would expect estimates based on the FES to under-state the number of people with incomes below the Supplementary Benefit scale. Firstly, the household unit assumes a degree of income-sharing which is not allowed for in the provisions for Supplementary Benefits.[34] By adopting a household base, the estimates of Abel-Smith and Townsend for 1953–4 and 1960, and that of Atkinson for 1969 overlook cases where, for example, an old person living with children may have an income below the scale rate although the sum total of the household income is above. The enquiry into the circumstances of retirement pensioners showed that about one in five of the retirement pensioners with incomes below the scale were non-householders and a further substantial number were heads of households which included other non-dependent adults. Unless the other members of these households also had incomes below or close to the poverty line, they would not have appeared to have been poor on the basis of the FES. The second reason why use of the FES is likely to lead to an under-statement is that it is based on 'normal' rather than 'current' income. People who have been out of work for less than three months are recorded as continuing to receive normal earnings, although they may well fall below the Supplementary Benefit standard in the period of unemployment. The evidence of the 1966 enquiry into families with two or more children showed that in the case of low income families where the father was sick or unemployed, about a third had been off work for less than three months. If we make an approximate allowance for the omission of these families and of pensioners living with other adults, the proportion of the population below the poverty line in 1967 rises to around $4\frac{1}{2}$ to 5 per cent.

a

Table 2.4: *Summary of results of recent poverty studies in Britain*

| | | | | Percentage of population with total income[c] below: | |
| | | | | Supplementary Benefit scale | Supplementary Benefit scale plus 40 per cent |
Year	Study	Source	Base		
1953–4	Abel-Smith and Townsend	FES	Household/Expenditure	1.2	7.8
1960	Abel-Smith and Townsend	FES	Household/Income (Expenditure)[a]	3.8 (4.3)	14.2 (12.4)
1969	Atkinson	FES	Household/Income/Assumptions about average rent, age of children	3.4	—
1966	'Minimum' (Atkinson)	[b]	Family/Income/Pensioners and families receiving Family Allowances only	3.7	—
1954	Gough and Stark	IR	Family/Income/Assumptions about average rent and ages of children	12.3	21.0
1959	Gough and Stark	IR	Family/Income/Assumptions about average rent and ages of children	8.8	18.1
1963	Gough and Stark	IR	Family/Income/Assumptions about average rent and ages of children	9.4	20.7

[a] Based on a special analysis of the expenditure of a sub-sample of households.
[b] Based on Government enquiries into families receiving Family Allowances and pensioner households
[c] Income is the total from all sources including Social Security benefits and Supplementary Benefit where this is received.

In the estimates of Gough and Stark based on the Inland Revenue survey, the use of annual income leads to an under-statement of the number with incomes below the Supplementary Benefit scale in a given week. Moreover, no allowance is made for any income tax or National Insurance contributions paid, so that take-home pay may well be lower than suggested by their figures. On the other hand, they may over-estimate the amount of poverty because of the assumptions they are forced to make. The 'needs' of an income unit may be over-stated (where children are born in the course of the year or married persons die); there will be some over-statement as a result of the assumptions about family composition; spurious extra income units may appear (children or students with earnings, adults with small covenants, etc.); and although the effect of these individual items is small, together they may account for 1 to 2 per cent over-statement.

The FES-based estimates therefore suggest that in the 1960s around 5 per cent, and the IR-based estimates around 8 per cent (allowing for some net over-statement) of the population had incomes below the SB scale. Where exactly between these two estimates the true figure lies cannot be determined on the basis of the information now available.

The figures in Table 2.4 reveal differences not only about the extent of poverty, but also about the trends over time. In particular, the estimates of Abel-Smith and Townsend suggest an upward trend in the 1950s and those of Gough and Stark a downward trend.

In trying to reconcile those results it should be remembered that neither is a perfect measure of the extent of poverty at a particular date, and both may involve biasses in the estimates of change over time. In the case of Abel-Smith and Townsend, their 1953–4 estimates were based on expenditure and those for 1960 on income, and it is known that expenditure tends to be over-stated in the FES and income understated.[35] They were well aware of this difficulty and were guarded about the conclusions that could be drawn. They did in fact make an estimate of the figures for 1960 in terms of expenditure (the figure shown in brackets in Table 2.4). In view of the fact that these estimates had to be based on a very small sub-sample, there are grounds for doubting their accuracy. A second source of bias in the Abel-Smith and Townsend estimates stems from the use of a household base; and as suggested earlier, a tendency for old people to live on their own longer or for young people to leave home sooner would cause an upward bias in the increase in the number of people below the poverty line. As for the Gough and Stark estimates the downward trend could possibly be explained by the inclusion of more 'spurious' low income units in the earlier year. It is interesting to note that the number of one person low income units falls from 2.6 million in 1954 to 1.7 million in 1959, when there are reasons to expect it to increase (such as an increase in the number of old people). The difficulties regarding interpolation referred to earlier are also very important here, and the change in the number of low income units may be very sensitive to the precise method used.[36] There are, therefore, a number of factors which may explain the discrepancy between the findings of the two studies, but in the absence of further information it is not possible to say which are the most important.

In interpreting the evidence about trends there are a number of factors which have to be borne in mind. First, in using the Supplementary Benefit scale as a poverty standard, it is clearly important to examine the way in which it has changed over time in relation to the general level of incomes. Lynes[37] has compared the increase in the National Assistance scale, as it then was, over the period 1948–61 with the rise in personal disposable income and allowed for the fact that the prices of goods bought by low income households had risen faster than the general cost of living index. If we take the period considered by Abel-Smith and Townsend, the real value of the scale rate for a single pensioner rose by 12 per cent whereas the average real disposable income per person increased by 24 per cent. This means that the poverty standard applied by Abel-Smith and Townsend had increased less rapidly than the incomes of the general population – so that if all incomes had risen proportionately, we should have expected the extent of poverty to decline. It is important to bear this in mind when interpreting their results.

Similarly, there is the question of demographic changes. These were discussed by Abel-Smith and Townsend who pointed to the increase between 1953 and 1960 in the proportion of the population over 65, and the fact that the number of families with six or more children rose by 45 per cent. To this extent the increase in poverty shown by their figures can be attributed to an increase in the population at risk rather than to a worsening of the position of old people and large families. However, these developments cannot explain all the observed increase in poverty, and the proportion with low levels of living increased for households of every size.

This discussion has been limited to the changes over the 1950s and does not throw any light on the recent debate as to whether poverty increased under the Labour Government of 1964–70. However, it does bring out the difficulties involved in answering this question – and the need for information on the same basis for different years, the need for agreement about the change in the poverty standard relative to the general level of incomes, and for interpreting the evidence in the light of demographic and other developments.

Finally, in order to draw conclusions for policy purposes, more is needed than simply aggregate figures for the number in poverty. We need to know which groups of the population are most severely affected. Of the studies referred to above, only *The Poor and the Poorest* provides any detailed information about the composition of low incomes households and this is summarised in Table 2.5. It is interesting to note first the large proportion

Table 2.5: *Characteristics of households with low incomes–1960*

Age	Percentage of total persons with incomes below National Assistance scale (Per cent)
Under 5	12
5–15	21
16 and over	67
Household size (Persons)	Percentage of total households with incomes below National Assistance scale plus 40 per cent (Per cent)
1	41
2	29
3	9
4	7
5	5
6 or more	9
All	100
Primary source of income	Percentage of total persons with incomes below National Assistance scale (Per cent)
Pensions	37
Other state benefits	44
Earnings	18

Source: Abel-Smith and Townsend, *The Poor and the Poorest*, Tables 16, 17, and 18.

of low income households consisting of only one or two persons; on the other hand, families with children are clearly important, since a third of the people below the Supplementary Benefit scale were aged under 16. Abel-Smith and Townsend also classified households according to their primary source of income and this revealed the surprising result that around 18 per cent depended chiefly on earnings. In other words, there were many people in poverty even though they were in full-time work, a finding which was later confirmed by the 1966 enquiry into families receiving Family Allowances. It is interesting to look at the picture presented by Rowntree's original 1899 survey. In this he found that 'The life of a labourer is marked by five alternating periods of want and comparative plenty'. The periods of want were first those of childhood, second when he himself had children, and third when he was too old to work. The evidence from *The Poor and the Poorest* suggests that the picture is not very different today. Although the relative importance of old age as a cause of poverty has increased since 1899, it still seems to be true that poverty is associated with these three stages in a person's life-cycle. As was pointed out by Rowntree, this means that the proportion of the population who are in poverty at some time in their lives is very much higher than the proportion found to be in poverty at a particular moment of time.

Income inequality in Britain

The study of inequality in the distribution of income in Britain has a long history, dating back to the estimates of Gregory King for 1688, which gave the number and average incomes of 26 classes of persons in England and Wales ranging from temporal lords with average yearly incomes of £3,200 through 'freeholders of the better sort' with an annual income of £91 to 'vagrants, gipsies, thieves and prostitutes' with an annual income of £2 a year. This section surveys the estimates that have been made covering the post-Second World War period, and in particular the work of Paish, [38] Lydall,[39] R. J. Nicholson,[40] Prest and Stark[41] and the critical study of Titmuss.[42] These studies have all been based primarily on the Inland Revenue survey of incomes. In what follows the principal conclusions of these studies are discussed, with particular attention being given to the deficiencies of the data and the problems of interpretation.

Table 2.6 shows the estimates derived from the National Income Blue

Table 2.6: *Distribution of Income (before tax)*

| | Percentage share of total income received by: | | | | |
Year	Top 1 per cent	Top 5 per cent	Top 10 per cent	Top 40 per cent	Bottom 30 per cent
1949	11.2	23.8	33.2	68.1	12.7
1957	8.2	19.1	28.1	65.7	11.3
1959	8.4	19.9	29.4	67.8	9.7
1960	8.5	19.9	29.7	68.2	9.8
1961	8.1	19.2	28.9	67.5	10.0
1962	8.1	19.2	28.9	67.5	9.8
1963	7.9	19.1	28.7	67.7	9.7
1966	7.8	18.9	28.6	67.1	10.5
1967	7.4	18.4	28.0	66.9	10.4

Source: R. J. Nicholson, 'The Distribution of Personal Income', *Lloyds Bank Review,* No. 83 (1967) Table 3 (extended to 1967).

Book (the CSO estimates) which form the basis of the work of R. J. Nicholson. If we concentrate on the most recent year (1967) these show that the top 1 per cent of income units received 7 per cent of total income before tax, the top 10 per cent received 28 per cent and the bottom 30 per cent received 10 per cent. These figures suggest considerable concentration in the distribution of income in Britain. Is it possible, however, to give more precise expression to this by some summary measure of the degree of inequality? The conventional approach is to use the Gini coefficient, but as argued earlier it may in some ways be more useful to adopt the 'equally distributed equivalent' measure outlined above. This measure depends on a parameter ϵ representing the degree of acceptability of inequality (according to the social consensus). This parameter has the following interpretation. Suppose that there are two people, one with twice the income of the other, and that we are considering taking £1.00 from the richer man and giving £X to the poorer (the remaining £1 − £X being lost in the process – e.g. in administering the transfer), how far can £X fall below £1.00 before we cease to regard the redistribution as desirable? (Clearly, if we are at all concerned with inequality £X = £1.00 is considered desirable.) The answer to this question determines the value of ϵ. For example, $\epsilon = 1$ corresponds to our regarding it as 'fair' to take £1.00 from the richer man and give £0.50 to the poorer; and $\epsilon = 2$ to it being regarded as fair to take £1.00 and give £0.25 to the poorer man.

If we apply the equally distributed equivalent measure to the before tax distribution of income in Britain in 1967 and take $\epsilon = 1$, we obtain a measure of inequality of 77 per cent. This means that the gain from bringing about complete equality in the distribution of income would be equivalent in social welfare terms to the gain resulting from a 23 per cent increase in national income. It is interesting to compare this figure with the kind of gain that has been talked about in connection with other economic policies. For example, the immediate gain from joining the Common Market has been estimated at less than 1 per cent of national income, and the loss due to the possible disincentive effects of income tax at 1 per cent. The measure of gain from bringing about equality of incomes is greater than 15 per cent for ϵ larger than 0.6 which corresponds to regarding it as fair to take £1.00 from a rich man and give £0.66 to a man with half his income.

There are, however, a number of ways in which the CSO figures are deficient as a basis for assessing inequality. Firstly, no allowance is made for the differing needs of income units and families with six children are treated in the same way as a single person. One of the chief aims of the study by Prest and Stark was to correct for this, and they adjusted the CSO data to a family size basis using the family circumstances information in the IR survey. Secondly, we have seen earlier that there are a number of errors in the IR/CSO estimates which may lead to the introduction of spurious low income units. In their study, Prest and Stark made allowances for some but not all of these deficiencies. The resulting adjusted distribution among equivalent adults (i.e. allowing for family size) are shown in Table 2.7. Comparing the results for 1963 with those derived

Table 2.7: *Adjusted distribution allowing for family size*

	Percentage share of total income received by:				
Year	Top 1 per cent	Top 5 per cent	Top 10 per cent	Top 40 per cent	Bottom 30 per cent
1954	8.9	19.8	28.8	64.5	12.1
1959	8.0	18.7	27.6	63.3	13.3
1963	7.3	17.7	26.9	63.2	13.5

Source: I am grateful to Dr T. Stark for making available to me the basic figures from which this table has been calculated. The method of estimation is described in Prest and Stark, 'Some Aspects of Income Distribution in the U.K.', *Manchester School*, Vol. 35 (1967).

from the straightforward CSO estimates in Table 2.6, the degree of concentration is rather less. In each case the share of the top percentiles is lower, and the share of the bottom 30 per cent rises from 10 per cent to over 13 per cent. One of the most serious omissions from the definition of income in the basic CSO data is undoubtedly capital gains. Prest and Stark estimated the capital gains accruing in 1959 from information on asset-holding and allocated these to different ranges of income. The effect on the shares of different income groups is shown in Table 2.8. There is a marked in-

Table 2.8: *Distribution of income allowing for capital gains–1959*

	Distribution allowing for capital gains	Corresponding distribution with no allowance for capital gains
Percentage share of:		
Top 1 per cent	14.1	8.3
Top 5 per cent	26.6	19.7
Top 10 per cent	35.6	29.2
Top 40 per cent	68.5	65.6
Bottom 30 per cent	11.7	11.6

Source: See Table 2.7. These figures differ from those shown in Table 2.7 because they are based on partially adjusted data rather than fully adjusted.

crease in inequality – as one would expect in view of the fact that capital gains accrue largely to people in the upper income ranges. The share of the top 1 per cent rises from 8 per cent to 14 per cent and the share of the top 5 per cent from 20 per cent to 27 per cent. As the authors point out, however, capital gains accruing in 1959 were exceptionally high, so that the effect in other years would probably have been smaller.[43]

So far we have concentrated on the distribution among the whole adult population and have taken no account of the life-cycle factors discussed earlier in the chapter. It is possible that at least part of the observed inequality may be attributed to life-cycle differences in income, and as suggested earlier it may be possible to explore this by considering inequality within age groups. The FES data are the only ones which give a distribution of households by income and the age of the head of the household. This was used by Prest and Stark to estimate the degree of concentration of income within age groups. The estimates are necessarily approximate, since no information is given in the FES about the mean income of each cell and it has to be assumed that the mean income for a certain income range is the same for all age groups. In Table 2.9 I have set out correspond-

Table 2.9: *Distribution of income by age groups–1968*

	Percentage share of total income in each age group				
Age of head of household	Top 1 per cent	Top 5 per cent	Top 10 per cent	Top 50 per cent	Top 75 per cent
Under 25	3.0	10.8	18.5	65.4	86.6
25–9	2.8	11.7	19.3	64.6	85.3
30–9	2.6	11.8	20.0	65.3	85.8
40–9	2.3	11.2	21.6	68.2	87.8
50–9	2.5	12.0	23.1	70.9	89.5
60–4	3.2	14.6	23.9	73.1	91.3
65–9	4.7	18.3	29.3	75.6	90.6
70–4	5.1	20.9	32.3	75.8	90.7
75 and over	5.7	19.3	31.5	76.3	90.2
All households	2.9	13.9	23.0	72.5	91.2

Source: Basic data taken from FES, 1968, Table 28. Percentiles estimated by logarithmic interpolation.

ing results from the 1968 FES.[44] There is a marked tendency for inequality to rise with age. For those aged 39 or less the share of the top 10 per cent of income-receivers is around 20 per cent of total income for that age group, but for those over 65 the corresponding figure is about 30 per cent. If life-cycle factors were an important explanation of the observed inequality in the distribution as a whole, we should expect the inequality within age groups to be very much less than that in the overall distribution. However, this is not the case.

One of the prominent issues in the literature and in public debate is whether income inequality has decreased over time. The original finding of Paish using the CSO figures was that the share of the top income groups fell between 1938 and 1949 and again between 1949 and 1955. Similarly, Lydall concluded that 'there had been a continuous trend towards greater equality' and that this remained when adjustments were made for excluded income. R. J. Nicholson, however, argued that the trend had ceased in the later 1950s, and this is certainly suggested by the figures shown in Table 2.6. On the other hand, the estimates adjusted to an equivalent adult basis made by Prest and Stark show a continuing trend towards greater equality up to 1963.

Before we can accept the conclusions of these studies, there are a number of questions that should be considered. Suppose that we take the figure for the years 1949 and 1959 given in Table 2.6. These show the shares of the top 1 per cent and 10 per cent as falling considerably. On the other hand, the bottom 30 per cent also lost ground and their share fell from 12.7 per cent to 9.7 per cent. As R. J. Nicholson (and earlier Paish) pointed out, the redistribution had been from the extreme ends to the middle ranges. The Lorenz curves corresponding to the two distributions in fact intersect. We cannot therefore say unambiguously that one is more unequal than the other. The rich have lost ground but so have the poor, and we have to weigh one against the other. The method of doing this suggested above was to calculate the equally distributed equivalent measure. It then turns out that the distribution in 1959 would be regarded as more unequal than that in 1949 if ϵ is greater than 0.6. In other words, in terms of the interpretation suggested earlier, if we think that taking £1 from a rich man and giving £0.66 to a man with half his income would be fair, then we would not in fact consider that inequality had declined. Even accepting the basic CSO figures, therefore, it is not clear that the degree of concentration has fallen and the conclusion must be that it depends on what one means by inequality.[45]

Even if one accepts the view that inequality has declined, this could have been brought about by changes in the structure of society rather than by a genuine movement towards greater equality. These factors include changes in the age structure of the population, the fall in the age of marriage, the growth of occupational pensions and other provisions for retirement. The fall in the age of marriage is important because single women tend to

appear in the lower part of the income distribution and part of the reduction in inequality may be attributable to low income units joining together
in holy matrimony. The age factor may be expected to work in the opposite
direction. Since old people tend to have low incomes, and income is
distributed more unequally in the older age groups, the growing proportion
of old people will tend to raise the observed degree of inequality.[46]

The relationship between changes in the current distribution of income
and the lifetime distribution may be illustrated by reference to the growth
of occupational pension schemes. The effect of occupational pension
schemes as far as the IR statistics are concerned is to raise incomes when
retired at the expense of income when working (since, for example, the
interest on pension funds is not included in current income received by an
individual when at work). Under the schemes income is effectively spread
more evenly over a person's life. This leads to a reduction in inequality in
the instantaneous distribution of income, although there has not necessarily
been any reduction in lifetime inequality.

Finally, there are the deficiencies of the basic data. Here the question is
not the deficiencies as such, but whether their importance has changed
over time, thus biassing a *comparison* of the degree of inequality in different
years. In fact, there are good reasons for expecting this to be the case. The
relative importance of capital gains undoubtedly increased over the 1950s.
The abolition of the tax on Schedule A means that since 1964 the whole,
rather than simply part, of the imputed rent on owner-occupied houses
is missing; and over the period as a whole owner-occupation has been
increasing. Various 'fringe' benefits not included in income have also
undoubtedly increased in importance. Lastly, we must bear in mind the
important question of the change in *real* incomes as opposed to the change
in *money* incomes. If the cost of living has risen more for the poor than for
the rich, because 'necessities' have gone up more than 'luxuries', then the
inequality of real incomes may have increased even though money incomes
show a reduction in inequality. This has been explored by Lydall, Brittain[47]
and others and the broad conclusion seems to be that prices in fact rose
more slowly for those with high incomes in the 1950s.[48] All these factors
lead one to expect, therefore, that the published estimates of the distribution of income over-state the trend towards greater equality – at least
during the 1950s.

In the introduction to *Income Distribution and Social Change*, Titmuss
draws attention to the reliance that has been placed on the trends in the
degree of inequality shown by the Inland Revenue statistics. It was on
the basis of these figures, for example, that Sir Edward Boyle stated in the

House of Commons in 1961 that 'we have a better and fairer distribution of incomes today than we had ten or eleven years ago'. This view is shared by many others, although Professor Titmuss' study has undoubtedly given pause to its advocates. From the present discussion, it will, I hope, be clear that in our existing state of knowledge it is impossible to draw any such firm conclusions.

Concluding comments

Throughout this survey, I have tried to emphasise the importance of the gaps in our existing knowledge about inequality in Britain. At a conceptual level, there is a range of issues which have not attracted the attention which they warrant – the measurement of inequality, the distinction between current and lifetime income, the allowance to be made for children of different ages in defining a poverty standard. When we turn to consider the data available in Britain, we have seen that there is a pressing need for more information. To acquire such information would require resources; however, it is impossible to devise policies to deal with poverty and inequality without adequate information about its extent and causes.

NOTES

[1] I am very grateful to Dorothy Wedderburn and Peter Townsend for their critical comments on an earlier draft of this chapter. I should also like to thank M. J. H. Mogridge, J. L. Nicholson, R. J. Nicholson and T. Stark for their suggestions and help.
The final version of this chapter was essentially completed in September 1970, and no account is taken of work appearing after that date.

[2] A. B. Atkinson, *Poverty in Britain and the Reform of Social Security* (Cambridge, 1969).

[3] A 'household' is defined by the Family Expenditure Survey as those persons 'living at the same address having meals together and with common housekeeping'.

[4] J. N. Morgan, 'Measuring the Economic Status of the Aged', *International Economic Review*, Vol. 6 (1965), pp. 1–17.

[5] D. Cole and J. E. G. Utting, 'The Distribution of Household and Individual Income', *Income and Wealth*, Series VI (Cambridge, 1957).

[6] M. Friedman, *A Theory of the Consumption Function* (Princeton, 1957).

[7] It should be borne in mind that the *security* of a regular income is an important factor: a person might prefer a steady income to a fluctuating one with a higher average.

[8] L. Soltow, *Toward Income Equality in Norway* (Wisconsin, 1965).

9 This definition is associated particularly with the name of Henry Simons –
   see his *Personal Income Taxation* (Chicago, 1938), pp. 49–50.

10 Royal Commission on the Taxation of Profits and Income, *Final Report,*
   Cmnd. 9474 (London, 1955). Memorandum of Dissent, para. 5.

11 N. Kaldor, *The Expenditure Tax* (London, 1955).

12 For a discussion of this problem, see B. Weisbrod and W. L. Hansen, 'An
   Income-Net Worth Approach to Economic Welfare', *American Economic
   Review*, Vol. 58 (1968). The treatment that they propose is based on the
   arbitrary assumption that people liquidate their assets over the rest of their
   life. A further important problem of measuring income is that of valuing
   such items as fringe benefits, income in kind and the use of public social
   services.

13 S. Rowntree, *Poverty – A Study of Town Life* (London, 1901).

14 P. Townsend, 'Measuring Poverty', *British Journal of Sociology*, Vol. V
   (1954); 'The Meaning of Poverty', *British Journal of Sociology*, Vol. XIII
   (1962), and Chapter 1.

15 B. Abel-Smith and P. Townsend, *The Poor and the Poorest* (London, 1965),
   p. 17.

16 V. Fuchs, 'Comment' in L. Soltow (ed.), *Six Papers on the Size Distribution
   of Income and Wealth* (New York, 1969).

17 National Assistance became Supplementary Benefits in 1966.

18 For discussion of this point, see J. L. Nicholson, *Redistribution of Income
   in the United Kingdom in 1959, 1957 and 1953* (Cambridge, 1965). See also
   C. Bagley, *The Cost of a Child* (London, 1969) and J. L. Nicholson, *New
   Society*, 3 April 1969.

19 M. Wynn, *Family Policy* (London, 1970).

20 For a recent discussion of the dependence of food prices on the level of
   neighbourhood income, see the study by R. E. Alcaly and A. K. Klevorick,
   'Food Prices in Relation to Income Levels in New York City', *Journal of
   Business*, Vol. 44 (1971), pp. 380–97.

21 This is true where we are concerned with the shape of the distribution independently of the general level of incomes (as is usually assumed to be the
   case). For a precise statement and proof, see A. B. Atkinson, 'On the
   Measurement of Inequality', *Journal of Economic Theory*, Vol. 2 (1970),
   pp. 244–63.

22 In terms of Figure 2.1, it is the ratio of the area P_1 to the area $P_1 + P_2$.
   Its popularity is illustrated by the following remark: 'It has generally been
   agreed that the best single measure of inequality is the ... Gini Index of
   concentration.' J. N. Morgan, 'The Anatomy of Income Distribution',
   Review of Economics and Statistics, Vol. 44 (1963), pp. 270–83.

23 Atkinson, 'On the Measurement of Inequality'.

24 *ibid.*

25 I have used the term 'Britain' rather loosely. The IR survey covers the
   United Kingdom, as has the FES since 1958.

26 The information collected on the basic forms allows income to be calculated
   on an income unit (family) basis, but this is not published – see W. F. F.
   Kemsley, *Family Expenditure Survey – Handbook on the Sample, Fieldwork
   and Coding Procedures* (London, 1969), p. 63.

27 Defined as a single person (with or without children) or a married couple
   (with or without children).

28 Kemsley, *Family Expenditure Survey*.

29 This survey only covers studies published at the time of writing (September, 1970). No reference is made to the sample survey carried out in 1969
   by Abel-Smith and Townsend, and the discussion of this section will no
   doubt need to be modified when the results of this important study become
   available. Similarly no reference has been made to the special analyses of
   the FES data carried out by the Government.

[30] Abel-Smith and Townsend, *The Poor and the Poorest.*

[31] I. Gough and T. Stark, 'Low Incomes in the United Kingdom', *Manchester School*, Vol. 36 (1968).

[32] A. B. Atkinson, 'Policies for Poverty', *Lloyds Bank Review*, No. 100 (1971), pp. 17–28.

[33] Ministry of Pensions and National Insurance, *Financial and other circumstances of retirement pensioners* (London, 1966). Ministry of Social Security, *Circumstances of Families* (London, 1967).

[34] The only amounts taken into account are an 'assumed contribution' towards rent and any regular help of a significant kind on which a cash value can be placed.

[35] For a discussion of this point see Kemsley, *Family Expenditure Survey* and D. Cole and J. E. G. Utting 'Estimating Expenditure Saving and Income from Household Budgets', *Journal of the Royal Statistical Society*, Series A, Vol. 119 (1956).

[36] The equation used for interpolation was fitted to each year separately. If the distribution of income units within the lowest income range for single persons had been the same in 1959 as in 1954, the number of low income units would have been very much higher in 1959 (letter from Dr Stark).

[37] T. Lynes, *National Assistance and National Prosperity* (London, 1962).

[38] F. W. Paish, *Studies in an Inflationary Economy* (London, 1962).

[39] H. F. Lydall, 'The Long-Term Trend in the Size Distribution of Income', *Journal of the Royal Statistical Society*, Series A, Vol. 122 (1959), pp. 1–37.

[40] R. J. Nicholson, 'The Distribution of Personal Income', *Lloyds Bank Review*, No. 83 (1967), pp. 11–21.

[41] A. R. Prest and T. Stark, 'Some Aspects of Income Distribution in the UK since World War II', *Manchester School*, Vol. 35 (1967), pp. 217–43.

[42] R. M. Titmuss, *Income Distribution and Social Change* (London, 1962).

[43] Lydall, 'The Long-Term Trend in the Size Distribution of Income', made adjustments for other kinds of income excluded from the CSO figures: contributions to superannuation schemes, the excess of imputed rent over the Schedule A assessment for owner-occupied houses, etc. The effect of these adjustments on his estimate of the top 1 per cent share of *after-tax* income in 1957 was to raise it from 4·9 per cent to 6·7 per cent.

[44] As is to be expected, the estimates of the overall distribution are very different from those obtained from the IR survey, see Tables 2.6 and 2.7. The lower share of top income-receivers undoubtedly reflects the under-reporting of investment and self-employment income.

[45] If one takes the adjusted Prest and Stark distribution it is not clear whether the Lorenz curves intersect – this depends on the method of interpolation adopted.

[46] Prest and Stark's estimates based on the inequality within age groups suggest that this would in fact have had a noticeable effect.

[47] J. A. Brittain, 'Some Neglected Features of Britain's Income Levelling', *American Economic Review*, Vol. 50 (1960), pp. 593–603.

[48] R. G. D. Allen, 'Changes in the Distribution of Higher Incomes', *Economica*, Vol. 24 (1957), pp. 138–53, shows that the price index for the 'high income' group rose at the same rate as the general index; however, the index for a single pensioner rose very much faster.

3

The distribution and redistribution of income in the United Kingdom[1]

J. L. NICHOLSON

Introduction

All of us pay taxes of one kind or another. Most working people also pay National Insurance and National Health Service contributions, which cover a substantial part of the cost of National Insurance benefits and a small part of the cost of the National Health Service. Much of the revenue from general taxation is used to pay for the various social services – which include State education and the National Health Service as well as payments in cash and in subsidies – from which practically all of us benefit at some stage in our lives. A large part of the revenue from taxation goes, of course, on military defence, the maintenance of law and order, and central and local government (including the costs of collecting taxes and contributions and of distributing benefits). While few would doubt the need for maintaining the whole apparatus of a modern state, most people would probably be unable to attribute money values to the benefits which they personally derive from each of these services. Some of the revenue from taxation also goes on museums, libraries, parks and so on which are undoubtedly a source of personal enjoyment to individuals and families, and on services like roads which benefit private individuals as well as industry and other users. There is, however, no satisfactory way of measuring or estimating the value of any of these services to particular households. Similarly, some forms of tax cannot, in the present state of knowledge, be regarded as paid by or deductible from the incomes of families or individuals (corporation tax – the incidence of which is a matter of debate – is one example). There is nevertheless considerable interest in adding up and comparing the amounts which people in different circumstances pay or receive in all those taxes and social service benefits which it is reasonable and possible to allocate to individuals and families, and seeing how much on this basis different families gain or lose on balance, even if the resulting picture may seem incomplete.

There is, indeed, room for debate about the combined long-run effects, including their interactions on each other, of some of the taxes and benefits included in this analysis; and original income (defined as income before taxes or benefits) may itself be influenced by the whole system of taxes and benefits. But, for purposes of the present discussion these questions are set aside.

The net result of all taxes and benefits is to redistribute income – between families with relatively high and those with relatively low incomes, between large and small families, between those who spend money on drink, tobacco, petrol, and those who live in local authority dwellings the rents of which are subsidised. The nature and the extent of redistribution of income and the various factors which influence it are subjects which merit careful study. We can estimate the degree of inequality of original income and the effects on inequality of all allocable taxes and benefits combined, and of each of the main forms of tax or benefit separately.

Estimates have been regularly prepared for some years now, based on the detailed information obtained from the Family Expenditure Survey which has been carried out by the Department of Employment every year since 1957. This is a sample survey in which some 3,200 households co-operated each year up to 1966. Since 1967, when the size of the sample was increased, some 7,000 households have co-operated each year. Each household provides detailed information about all forms of income, including cash benefits received from the State, payments of income tax and surtax, the kind of education which any member of the household is receiving; and so on. Each adult in the household is asked to keep a full record of all expenditure incurred during fourteen consecutive days and over longer periods for some items.[2] This is still, admittedly, a relatively small sample to support an elaborate analysis for each main size and type of family. The collection of so much information on a voluntary basis and the preparation of these estimates present numerous difficulties and problems, and a number of assumptions and approximations have to be made. It is therefore necessary to exercise caution and to remember the explanations and qualifications and the sampling errors when looking at the results.[3] It may be useful to begin with a short account of the main problems of estimation and how they are dealt with.[4]

Brief explanation of the estimates

Direct taxes on personal income include income tax and surtax and employees' contributions to National Insurance and National Health Services.[5] Death duties, being a tax on capital rather than income, are excluded. Capital gains, in accordance with national income conventions, are excluded from income, and taxes on capital gains are likewise omitted. It is perhaps arguable that capital gains should be included in personal income, and in that case capital gains tax would be regarded as a direct tax on income.[6]

Direct benefits include both benefits paid in cash and benefits in kind. Cash benefits include Family Allowances, pensions and National Insurance benefits (but not scholarships and education grants). Benefits in kind include the National Health Services, State education (including scholarships and education grants), school health services, school meals, milk and welfare foods. In estimating the benefits from State education, it is assumed *faute de mieux* that all children at each of eight main types of educational establishment derive the same benefit, equal to the average expenditure per child by the State on that type of education.[7] The benefits derived from the National Health Services, in the absence of detailed information about the extent to which different people make use of the various services, can only be roughly allocated to individual families; it is assumed that the total value of all the services is the same for all persons in each of six age and sex categories of the population, and is equal to the estimated average expenditure by the State per person (net of charges) in each category.

No attempt is made to estimate the benefits derived from Government expenditure on administration, defence, police, museums, libraries, parks, roads, and so on. Most of these items are not generally regarded as bringing tangible benefits that can be expressed in terms of additions to the incomes of individual families. Defence, which is much the largest item, as well as police, prisons and such like, have been aptly termed 'regrettable necessities' rather than benefits and it is quite appropriate to exclude items which fall in this category. A further group of items – tax collection, the administration of National Insurance and Supplementary Benefits, the upkeep of local offices – are the unavoidable costs of providing social services and are not themselves regarded as benefits, even though the costs of comparable benefits under private insurance policies would inevitably include the costs of administration. Only a relatively small share of Government expenditure goes on environmental services which directly benefit private families;[8] the extent to which different people make use of these amenities, some of which are also used by industry and the Government, varies considerably and it would be difficult to determine the value of any of these services to each individual family.

The only indirect benefits included in the estimates are housing subsidies, defined as the excess of the estimated economic rent over the actual rent paid by tenants of local authority dwellings. Agricultural subsidies are regarded as part of the original, earned income of farmers who could otherwise earn comparable incomes in other employment; they are not treated as benefits to consumers since they merely have the effect of keeping the prices of domestic produce down to the same level as the prices of imported foods which, since war-time controls were lifted, have mostly been unrestricted. It is arguable that means-tested remissions of taxes and charges ought to be treated as indirect benefits. The method of calculating housing subsidies means that they include rent rebates, while rate rebates are reflected in reductions in the amounts paid in local rates. Income tax allowances for, e.g. dependants are similarly reflected to the extent that they reduce income tax payments.

Indirect taxes, or taxes on expenditure, are either paid directly by consumers, e.g. local rates and motor vehicle duties, or are assumed to be fully reflected in the prices paid by consumers when buying commodities which are subject to tax, e.g. purchase tax and customs and excise duties. Although it is sometimes criticised, good theoretical arguments can be adduced for this assumption which is borne out by the changes in prices on the many occasions when such taxes have been increased. It is the simplest assumption to make and is invariably used in estimates of this kind.

The following general qualifications which affect the accuracy of the estimates should be borne in mind. First, since the basic information is obtained from a small sample of families, the results are subject to the normal errors expected in probability samples.

Secondly, the average amounts recorded as being spent on alcoholic drink and tobacco are much lower than would be expected from the known tax yields – a common feature of expenditure surveys. After allowing for expenditure by people not living in households, something like half the taxes on drink and a quarter of the taxes on tobacco are not accounted for. All the recorded figures of expenditure on these items have therefore been increased in the same proportion, so as to bring average expenditure into line with the known tax yield in each year.

Thirdly, if the sample is grossed up to provide estimates for the whole population, comparison with national accounts data indicates a deficiency in some forms of income, particularly investment income; but precise checks are not possible because the national income figures include unknown amounts relating to residents in institutions.

Fourthly, in recent years between 70 and 75 per cent of the households included in the sample have co-operated by providing all the information requested; there is the possibility that families which do not co-operate differ in certain respects from those which do.[9]

Summary of results

The general results set out in Table 3.1 show, as might be expected, that families in the lowest income ranges gain much more from benefits than they pay in taxes, while families with the highest incomes pay rather more in taxes than they receive in benefits. Within a given income range, the largest families gain most (or lose least) and the smallest families gain least (or lose most) on balance, from all taxes and benefits combined. In general, the smaller the income of the family and the larger the size of the family, the greater is the net gain (or the smaller is the net loss) from benefits and taxes as a proportion of income, while the larger the income of the family and the smaller the size of the family, the larger generally is the net loss (or the smaller is the net gain) from taxes and benefits as a proportion of income.

It is usual to compare the incidence of taxes and benefits on different groups of households in terms of the proportion which they bear to the income of the households. It is conventional to describe a tax as progressive if, in general, it absorbs a larger proportion of high than of low incomes, and regressive if it generally absorbs a smaller proportion of high than of low incomes. Similarly, a benefit is termed progressive if, in general, it forms a larger proportion of low than of high incomes; this is true of all the benefits included in these estimates. It is worth noting here that, while a flat rate tax, examples of which are rare,[10] must be at least mildly regressive, a flat rate benefit is very progressive.

It is possible to estimate the progressiveness or regressiveness of each tax or benefit for a particular size and type of family (e.g. a couple with two children), but to do the same for different types of family combined involves a further problem – that of estimating equivalent household scales, which measure the relative needs of households of different size and type.[11] This problem is most acute when one is trying to show the effects of taxes and benefits for pensioner and non-pensioner families combined. Hence the main estimates so far produced are confined to showing the average effects on 'vertical' inequality – between income ranges – for the six main types of family combined (those consisting of single persons, or of two adults with 0, 1, 2, 3 or 4 children) and do not include 'horizontal' redistribution – between different sizes and types of family. Further work is needed before such estimates can be compiled.

The combined effect of all taxes and benefits is progressive in the sense

Table 3.1: *Net total benefits received (+) less total taxes paid (−)Averages^a 1971*

£ per year

	Range of original income: £ per year														
	Under 381	381–	461–	557–	674–	816–	987–	1194–	1446–	1749–	2116–	2561–	3099–	3750 and above	Average over all income ranges
All households in the sample	+494	+399	+303	+250	+193	+62	− 5	−136	−242	−359	−472	−672	−885	−1594	−259
Retired households^b															
1 adult	+358	+174	+115	+39	+24	−46	−136	−293							+273
2 adults	+546	+373	+329	+288	+180	+218	+45	+42	−251	−411					+383
Non-retired households															
1 adult	+339	+115	+15	− 20	− 91	−250	−286	−393	−590	−713	−836		−1428		−250
2 adults	+511	+465	+254	+367^c	+204	− 18	−139	−292	−432	−573	−762	−927	−1134	−2075	−569
2 adults, 1 child	+992			+224		+45	−122	−216	−310	−486	−546	−754	−914	−1505	−423
2 adults, 2 children	+840				+203	+99	+78	− 66	−186	−288	−409	−591	−808	−1312	−328
2 adults, 3 children						+456	+213	+141	− 65	− 95	−260	−264	−512	−1227	−100
2 adults, 4 children						+453	+365	+164	+124	+129		−154			+ 41

^a Averages are not shown for income ranges where there are fewer than 10 households.

^b Households where the income of members who are at least 60 and retired or unoccupied amounts to at least half the gross income of the household.

^c Total benefits include £170 from State education (including scholarships and grants from public funds).

just defined, and also in the sense of favouring large as against small families. For each type of family, direct and indirect taxes combined form a remarkably stable proportion of income over a wide range of incomes; and they generally form a smaller proportion of the income of large than of small families, but the differences in this case are not very marked. While income tax (including surtax) is progressive, National Insurance and National Health Service contributions (particularly the flat rate contributions) are regressive and most indirect taxes are also regressive, so that the net redistributive effect of all taxes combined, measured in proportion to income, is very slight considering their magnitude. While this broad generalisation applies to groups of households in different income ranges, the proportions of income paid in taxes by households within each income range show substantial variations, depending in particular on how much they spend on drink and tobacco. And while indirect taxes as a whole are regressive, the incidence of different indirect taxes varies.

All social service benefits are progressive. Family Allowances and State education appear to have only mildly progressive effects on 'vertical' inequality; but they must, in addition, have very progressive effects on 'horizontal' inequality, because they favour large families. It is largely because flat rate benefits form a much larger proportion of low than of high incomes that benefits as a whole are much more progressive than taxes as a whole.

Housing subsidies are small in comparison with other benefits; in proportion to income, they are largest for households in the lowest income ranges and are thus progressive.

The results are conveniently condensed in terms of the Gini coefficient of inequality which is generally regarded as the best single measure of inequality and is the one which is most widely used. Expressed in percentage form, the Gini coefficient can vary between the extreme limits of 0 (if all incomes were equal) and 100 (if all income went to one individual); in practice, the Gini coefficient rarely lies outside the narrower range 20–45. Thus the higher the value of the Gini coefficient, the greater the degree of inequality; and a given reduction in the value of the Gini coefficient measures the extent to which inequality has been reduced.[12]

The Gini coefficient naturally has the limitations of any measure which summarises a particular aspect of a distribution in a single figure. Changes in different parts of the distribution may offset each other – the relative positions of different social groups, for instance, may be interchanged – leaving an overall measure of this kind unchanged. Several studies have however shown that, in numerous countries which are at very different stages of development and in a single country at widely different periods, the shape and form of the distributions of income have been remarkably similar. Radical changes in economic and social structure which have large effects on particular groups have had very little effect on the shape and form of the distribution as a whole. Because of this, the Gini coefficient has a degree of general validity which makes it possible to use it for comparative analysis. A change in the Gini coefficient resulting from a particular tax or benefit does not, in itself, indicate whether it affects people at all levels of income, or mainly those with high or low incomes. But the nature of the tax or benefit usually makes it obvious which income levels are mainly affected.

Some of the more interesting results, expressed in terms of this coefficient, are set out in Tables 3.2 and 3.3. These tables exclude pensioner households (so defined if at least three-quarters of the household income is derived from old age pensions, National Insurance pensions and supplementary pensions and allowances) because the net benefit which most of them receive consists in the transfer of income from non-pensioner households; the estimates do, however, include a good many retired persons falling outside this definition, most of whom are in the lowest income ranges. Estimates which were prepared for 1957 and 1959 are not shown here since the work was then in an early, experimental stage and, because of subsequent improvements in the procedures and methods used, they are not fully comparable with the estimates for 1961 onwards. In order to reduce the influence of sampling errors, Table 3.2 shows the estimated average effects of taxes and benefits for pairs of adjacent years in the period 1961–6, when each year's sample of households was about half the size of the samples from 1967 onwards, and for single years thereafter. The most important change in method, introduced in 1969, was in the treatment of employers' contributions to National Insurance, as a result of work on the economics of social security. This change will itself have caused slight increases in the estimates shown in Table 3.2 (except in line 3). The broad conclusions may be summarised as follows.

1. The degree of inequality of original income, allowing for sampling errors, was practically stable throughout the years 1961–8, the Gini coefficient averaging 31.6 in this period. There is evidence of a slight increase in the inequality of original income from 1969 onwards, but part of the increase in the Gini coefficient (about 0.4) is the result of the change in the treatment of employers' contributions to National Insurance. The degree of inequality of final income remained remarkably constant throughout the whole period 1961–71, the Gini coefficient averaging a little under 25.

Table 3.2: *Gini coefficients of 'vertical inequality'*

Percentages

	1961–2[a]	1962–3[a]	1963–4[a]	1964–5[a]	1965–6[a]	1967	1968	1969[b]	1970[b]	1971[b]
Weighted average of Gini coefficient for six main types of family[c]										
1 Original income[d]	31.3	32.4	32.9	31.3	30.6	31.2	32.1	33.3	33.4	34.0
2 Income after direct benefits[e]	25.2	26.0	26.5	24.8	23.8	24.3	24.5	25.4	25.7	25.9
3 Income after direct taxes and benefits	23.0	23.5	24.1	22.7	21.6	22.0	22.4	22.7	22.9	23.4
4 Income after all taxes and benefits	24.3	24.9	25.9	24.7	23.5	23.8	24.7	24.8	24.7	25.0
Percentage reduction in Gini coefficient from										
5 Direct benefits[e]	19.4	19.8	19.6	21.0	22.0	22.2	23.8	23.7	23.1	23.8
6 Direct taxes and benefits	26.6	27.6	26.8	27.5	29.2	29.7	30.1	31.8	31.5	31.2
7 All taxes and benefits	22.3	23.2	21.4	21.3	23.1	23.6	22.8	25.4	26.1	26.4

[a] Averages for two years.
[b] The estimates for 1969 onwards (except for line 3) are not strictly comparable with those for earlier years – see text, page 81 and footnote 5, page 94.
[c] The Gini coefficients for each type of family are here combined with fixed weights, the average relative numbers in 1963–7. The six main types of family which account for roughly three-quarters of non-pensioner households co-operating in the surveys are: one adult; two adults; two adults, one child; two adults, two children; two adults, three children; two adults, four children.
[d] The estimated standard error of the Gini coefficient of original income shown here is of the order of 0.5.
[e] The method described in footnote [b] to Table 3.3 was used from 1969 onwards. Figures shown here for the years 1964–8 having been derived by a similar method; those for 1961–3 are not on a fully comparable basis.

Table 3.3: *Progressive/regressive effects of different taxes and benefits in 1970[a] [b] (ranked in order of progressiveness)*

	Effect on 'vertical' inequality measured by change in Gini coefficient[c] (percentage points)	Effect on Gini coefficient[c] per £100 of tax/benefit per household (percentage points)
Benefits (all progressive)		
Supplementary Benefit	−0.55	−5.45
Taxable pensions	−3.58	−5.12
Unemployment Benefit	−0.20	−4.08
Sickness Benefit	−0.58	−3.95
Disability pensions	−0·15	−3.00
Industrial Injury Benefit	−0.04	−2.25
National Health Service	−1.57	−1.95
Housing subsidies	−0.22	−1.74
Maternity Benefit	−0.05	−1.50
Family Allowances	−0.26	−1.36
Welfare foods	−0.09	−1.15
Education (incl. scholarships)	−0.63	−0.83
Progressive taxes		
Surtax	−0.27	−4.79
Income tax	−2.66	−1.16
Duties on wines	−0.03	−0.63
Purchase tax on motor vehicles	−0.03	−0.30
Regressive taxes		
Indirect taxation on intermediate products (rates)	+0.05	+0.21
Employees' National Insurance contributions	+0.13	+0.22
Purchase tax on clothing and footwear	+0.03	+0.39
Employers' National Insurance contributions	+0.12	+0.42
Duties on oil	+0.16	+0.48
Local rates (net)	+0.23	+0.53
Betting taxes	+0.02	+0.56
Indirect taxation on intermediate products (oil)	+0.15	+0.75
Indirect taxation on intermediate products (other)	+0.09	+0.76
Duties on beer	+0.26	+1.27
Purchase tax on foods	+0.08	+1.32
Duties on tobacco	+0.83	+1.50
Miscellaneous indirect taxes[d]	+0.11	+1.73

[a] Certain taxes have been excluded, either because they are relatively neutral (e.g. S.E.T.) or because they show wide fluctuations from year to year in the effect per £100 of tax/benefit (e.g. duties on spirits).

[b] In producing these estimates, individual taxes and benefits are assumed to be deducted or added in sequence, so that the separate effects of each form of tax and benefit (there are some 40, not all included in this table) necessarily add up to the total effect of all taxes and benefits. The particular sequence used, though inevitably somewhat arbitrary, is considered reasonable and, for instance, places taxable benefits in front of, and non-taxable benefits after, direct taxes.

[c] Weighted averages for the six main types of family (see footnote to Table 2.2).

[d] Mainly excise duties on matches and radio/TV and other (excluding driving) licences; also certain stamp duties, and fees paid to public authorities.

2. All taxes and benefits combined cause a substantial reduction in inequality, reducing the Gini coefficient by about 22/23 per cent in the early 1960s, and by about 26 per cent in the beginning of the 1970s. Thus the increase in the inequality of original incomes in the last few years of the period was accompanied and largely offset by an increase in the extent of redistribution through all taxes and benefits. The increased redistribution in recent years is mainly attributable to the improvements which were made in direct benefits, particularly National Insurance and Supplementary Benefits (see Table 3.2, lines 5 and 7); but to some extent the increase in redistribution, and also the increase in inequality of original income, in 1969–71 is due to the rise in the level of unemployment.

3. Professor Barna's estimates for 1937, though using different sources of data and somewhat different methods and so not strictly comparable with ours, showed a surprisingly similar degree of inequality of income before and after redistribution, and a similar reduction in inequality from all taxes and benefits, to those shown in recent years.[13] The Gini coefficients he obtained for 1937 (adjusted as far as possible for the main differences in method) were 33 before and 25 after redistribution, a reduction of about 24 per cent. One point concerning this comparison needs to be noted. The high level of unemployment in 1937 compared with post-war years would have increased both the degree of inequality in original income and the extent of redistribution, which includes the effect of unemployment benefit; it would also have contributed to the degree of inequality after redistribution.

4. Total payments in all taxes combined have formed a remarkably constant proportion of original income among families of any given type at different levels of income; in 1971 taxes absorbed on average about 38 per cent of original income, or 35 per cent of original income plus cash benefits, for all types of families combined. Among the families of one type in a given income range, the proportion paid in all taxes must of course vary according to their expenditure habits. The progressive effect of some taxes is largely offset by the regressive effect of others and all taxes combined have very little net effect on the Gini coefficient of inequality. This conclusion applies only to 'vertical' inequality, i.e. between families of a given size and type at different income levels, and excludes 'horizontal' redistribution between families of different size or type. Total taxes as a proportion of income show a moderate tendency to decline as the size of family increases. Thus, if 'horizontal' redistribution were included, the net effect of all taxes might be mildly progressive. Among progressive taxes, income tax (including surtax) has much the largest redistributive effect.

Among regressive taxes, duties on tobacco are the most regressive; others which have marked regressive effects are duties on beer, local rates and both employees' and employers' flat-rate National Insurance contributions. Purchase tax as a whole is mildly regressive and SET (assumed to be included in prices) is roughly neutral.

5. As the overall effects of progressive and regressive taxes largely offset each other, it follows that the net effect on ('vertical') inequality of all taxes and benefits combined is roughly equal to the net effect of all benefits combined. All benefits are progressive in the sense that they form a larger proportion of the income of families with relatively low incomes than of families with relatively high incomes; and most benefits are more progressive than any taxes. Benefits at flat rates, unrelated to the level of income, naturally form a much higher proportion of low than high incomes and for this reason have a greater redistributive effect than benefits that are positively correlated with income, such as earnings-related supplements to sickness and unemployment benefits, or than practically any form of tax. The only tax of comparable progressiveness is surtax but, as the total amount of surtax is small compared with other taxes and benefits, it has only a small redistributive effect. The most progressive benefit for a given total cost is Supplementary Benefit, or what used to be called National Assistance – not surprisingly since it is available only to families with incomes below given levels, and is *inversely* related to the level of income. (See Table 2.3.)

6. Benefits as a whole and each of the main benefits are also progressive in the sense of forming a higher proportion of the original income of larger families than of smaller families at a given level of income. But, as the needs of larger families are greater than those of smaller families, the additional progressive effect of benefits on the 'horizontal' distribution of income cannot, in the absence of acceptable and up-to-date equivalence scales, at present be measured (cf. p. 80 above).

Some possible explanations of the results

Until a great deal of further work has been done, we can only speculate on the possible reasons for these results. It is nevertheless instructive to discuss the different kinds of factors which may have had some influence, even if we cannot at present quantify their effects.

That the extent of redistribution – that is, the proportionate reduction in the degree of inequality of income resulting from all taxes and benefits – should have remained fairly stable is not altogether surprising. Consider taxes first. As money incomes rise over the years, income tax and surtax –

so long as personal and other allowances are unchanged – gradually bite off an increasing share of the higher incomes, while also extending to lower levels of real income. Thus, even when rates of income tax and surtax remain constant, their progressive effect will increase slowly over time. On the other hand, the recurring need for additional revenue has also caused indirect taxes to be increased from time to time and, as their total yield has generally risen faster than total disposable income, their regressive effect has tended to rise over the years. If the total amount paid by every family in a given form of tax increased in exactly the same proportion as their total personal income, and if the distribution of original income remained constant, the effect of the tax on the Gini coefficient of inequality would be unchanged. The total yield of indirect taxes (including SET) has risen faster in recent years than the total yield of direct taxes; but, since the progressive effect of direct taxes is generally greater than the regressive effect of indirect taxes (for a given yield), it is not too surprising that the effects of increases in the two kinds of tax have more or less offset each other.

Now consider benefits. In recent years, successive Governments have followed the practice of regularly increasing National Insurance and Supplementary Benefit rates and, in doing so, they have ensured that benefit rates have risen at least as much as prices so as to maintain their value in real terms; in fact the improvements have generally resulted in benefit rates following movements in money wages more closely than movements in prices. If rates of benefit and total personal income kept exactly in step with each other, and if the distributions of original income and of benefits remained constant, the effect of direct benefits on the Gini coefficient of inequality would remain unchanged. It is also fair to say that, given a broad degree of continuity in Government policy, social security cash benefits, Government expenditure on other social services (health, education, housing subsidies) and the general upward trend of money incomes are all, to a considerable extent, subject to common influences. In these circumstances, it is not really surprising to find that the progressive effect on the distribution of income of all social service benefits combined appears to have changed rather little over the years. The increase in the redistributive effect of direct benefits in 1968–71 (though partly attributable to the rise in unemployment) is doubtless in line with the intentions of Government policy at the time.

Thus the extent of redistribution, being not entirely but in large measure the outcome of Government policy, would not in the present circumstances of this country be expected to change much, at any rate in short periods. It is more difficult to explain why the degree of inequality in original income should have remained fairly stable, even apparently over quite a long period which included the war. Before considering this problem, some general qualifications need to be mentioned.

First, capital gains are not included in the figures of original income. If they had been included, the degree of inequality in original income would be greater than our figures indicate. The inclusion of capital gains and capital gains tax would, in addition, slightly reduce the progressiveness of all taxes combined, at any rate in the years before 1965, since capital gains tax was first introduced in April 1962 when it applied mainly to gains realised on securities bought and sold within six months and these form only a small proportion of all capital gains. Thus before 1962 incomes would be increased without total tax payments being increased, and in 1962–4 with only a small increase in tax payments. From April 1965, the tax was extended to capital gains realised on all sales of securities, but the average rate of tax has been somewhat less than 30 per cent which is the maximum rate of tax except on the relatively small amounts of short-term gains; whereas at present all taxes absorb on average roughly 35 per cent of original income (including cash benefits). In addition, capital gains which are not realised, and most gains on the sales of owner-occupied houses, are free of tax.

Secondly, any income which people who co-operate in the surveys fail to report is naturally omitted; this applies to all income which succeeds in evading or avoiding direct taxes on income. If the unreported income of different groups of families was proportional to their reported income, it would not affect our estimates of the degree of inequality of original income, although the estimates of the redistributive effects of all taxes and benefits, which depend on the proportions which they bear to original income, would be slightly reduced. But if, as seems more likely, the amount of unrecorded income bears some relation to taxable income, our estimates would also understate the degree of inequality in original income.

Thirdly, our estimates exclude the incomes of any families in the sample which contained an adult who did not co-operate in providing full details of his (or her) income and expenditure. If such families, which form about 30 per cent of the total sample, had approximately the same income distribution and other characteristics as the families which co-operated, our estimates of inequality and of the effects of taxes and benefits would be unaffected. But, to mention one possibility of which there are some indications, if the proportion of co-operating families in the original sample is generally lowest among those with the highest and/or lowest incomes, our estimates would understate the degree of inequality of original income and, at the same time, would somewhat understate the progressiveness of both taxes and benefits.

These three qualifications all work in the same direction in suggesting both that the degree of inequality of original income may be slightly greater than our estimates indicate, and that it may possibly have risen slightly in recent years.[14] Since the first two qualifications suggest that our estimates may slightly overstate while the third suggests that they slightly understate the extent of redistribution, it seems likely on balance that our estimates overstate the extent of redistribution.

In sum, between 1957 and 1968 there may have been a slight change in the degree of inequality of original income which our estimates, because of omissions or incomplete co-operation of families in the sample, may not have detected. The evidence nevertheless points to a remarkable stability in the degree of inequality. There are, of course, many factors which can influence the distribution of personal income. Those to be mentioned here fall into four distinct categories which have different origins and therefore different policy implications.

A. *Demographic changes*

Because the earnings of men and women usually differ and because incomes also vary with age, changes in the sex and age composition of the working population as well as changes in the proportions of households of different size and type may affect our estimates of the degree of inequality of family income, even when the incomes of men and women of any given age are unchanged.[15] For instance, since the excess of the number of women over the number of men in the population has gradually declined, there are now smaller proportions of single women and of widows under retirement age than formerly. The temporary increase in the number of births in the two or three years immediately after the war caused an increase in the relative numbers of young people aged 9–11 in 1957, and 19–21 in 1967 when their earnings, at an early stage in their working lives, would be relatively low. Again, the proportion of the working population aged 50–65 has been rising, and at these ages the incomes of most wage-earners are declining, while those of many salary-earners are still rising. Since the effects of these various demographic changes partly offset each other, they may on balance have had little effect on the degree of inequality of incomes; but this is only a guess.

B. *Changes in household structure*

The general rise in real incomes, the building and increased availability of new houses, and improvements in benefits themselves have, doubtless in conjunction with other factors, caused some households to split up, since some of the people who previously lived with relatives can now afford to live separately. And more marriages now occur among the younger age groups than previously. These changes affect the relative numbers of households of different size and at different income levels and, in themselves, are likely to have caused an increase in the degree of inequality, as measured by our estimates. But, since they are the deliberate expressions of preference by the people concerned, it is unlikely that social policy would want to discourage such changes.

C. *Changes in working habits*

The proportion of women, particularly married women, in the working population has been rising and the majority of working wives belong to families, usually with few or no children, in the middle rather than high or low income ranges. On the other hand, increasing numbers of people are retiring as soon as they reach the qualifying age for receiving National Insurance retirement pension, partly perhaps because of the improved rates of pension; so the increase in the proportion of people joining the ranks of pensioner households at or near pensionable age has probably reduced the number of occupied people with low earnings. Both these changes would tend to cause a slight reduction in the inequality of original income of families belonging to the working population, while the second will have increased inequality among the whole population. But, again, such changes result from free and deliberate choices made by the individuals concerned.

D. *Economic factors*

Changes that are mainly attributable to economic and technological developments include the following.

(i) The number of salary earners relative to the number of wage earners has risen. While many of the newer salaried posts are probably those with relatively low or medium levels of pay, salary levels are generally maintained in middle age, so that this change is unlikely to have had much influence on the degree of inequality of income either way.

(ii) Income tax and surtax have been biting not only on a steadily increasing number of incomes each year but also, with the declining value of money, on successively lower bands of real incomes (except for the reductions in the starting point of surtax in 1961–2 and 1969–70). Some self-employed people and employees may have tried to offset these high and increasing rates of tax by demanding higher pre-tax earnings; to the extent that they succeed in obtaining higher pre-tax incomes, the degree of inequality in original incomes will have increased, but so will the extent of redistribution from income tax and surtax.

(iii) It is difficult to gauge the success of prices and incomes policies or, because of the labyrinth of causes and effects, how much influence they are likely to have had on the distribution of income. If the policy in 1966–9 was more effective on incomes than on prices (which are difficult to control when changes in quality occur, or new models are introduced), real wages and salaries would have been restrained more than real profits and inequality would tend to be increased. But if, as some informed people believe, the policy was more effective on prices than on incomes (because of trade union pressures), it will have had the opposite effect and, since people living on fixed incomes – mainly pensioners and widows – would also have benefited, inequality would tend to be reduced. If the policy was equally effective (or ineffective) on both fronts, its influence would have been neutral.

(iv) The policy of dividend restraint – aimed at restraining increases in dividends above the amounts paid in 1965 – needs to be considered in conjunction with prices and incomes policy. To the extent that prices policy was effective in preventing profits from rising, the possibilities for increasing dividends would anyway be somewhat limited. But in the many cases where the policy would not prevent profits from rising dividend restraint can be effective. The temporary and subsequent effects of dividend restraint need to be considered separately. While it is in force, dividend restraint will tend to reinforce the effects of prices and incomes policies, both by making those policies more acceptable and by preventing shareholders from benefiting, at a time when other people are unable to benefit, from increases in productivity (which can allow profits to rise while prices are stable). Without enforced dividend restraint, prices and incomes policy would have a productivity loophole favouring shareholders and, to that extent, its influence on the distribution of income would be less effectively neutral. The after-effects of these policies, once prices, incomes and dividend restraint is lifted, are more complex, depending very much how long and how willingly the policies were in force and how effective they were. It is not the intention of these policies that losses of income should be made good later. But any feelings of pent-up demand being released might have effects that are difficult to anticipate. In the absence of any additional taxation (e.g. a special surcharge), it is arguable that any undistributed company profits which had meanwhile accumulated might lead to temporary additions to dividends, or to increases sooner or later in capital values, thus making up for the dividends withheld in the period of restraint. It is also reasonable to assume that some of the undistributed profits would lead to increased investment. Wages and salaries, if they simply resumed their trend prior to incomes policy, and if productivity had continued to rise throughout, might therefore be expected to receive a smaller share of income for a limited period after restraint has ended. Much depends, however, on the changes that have meanwhile taken place in productivity. Since the outcome of wage and salary settlements depends to a large extent on recent movements in productivity, as well as on recent and prospective company profits, the shares going to different groups will depend on the outcome of fresh negotiations as well as on industry's prospects. If the aftermath of a period of income restraint may temporarily favour one group, it seems likely that, as the information becomes generally available, other groups will not be long in restoring the balance.

(v) Any effects of devaluation of the pound in November 1967 would only begin to be visible in the estimates for 1968. To the extent that it was successful in achieving its aims, devaluation should, by increasing the prices of imports, have caused the general level of real wages to be less than it would otherwise have been. At the same time the reduction in the prices of exports to foreigners allowed room for prices of exports to rise sufficiently to cover increases in costs, including the costs of imported materials, without reducing profit margins. Devaluation could thus be expected to cause the share of profits in the national income to be slightly higher than it would otherwise be, and would tend to cause a slight increase in the degree of inequality of incomes.

(vi) Fluctuations in the general level of activity (the trade cycle) may be expected to have two opposing effects on inequality. Those forms of income which respond most easily and quickly to changes in the general level of activity, particularly profits and incomes of the self-employed, are distributed more unequally than other forms of income; and they form a higher proportion of total income in years of greater prosperity. This by itself would lead one to expect a higher degree of inequality of original income in the more prosperous years. On the other hand, a rise in unemployment and the resulting increase in the number of people with very low incomes would lead one to expect a higher degree of inequality of original income in the less prosperous years. Since the estimates suggest that the degree of inequality was higher in the years 1962–4 and 1969–71, which were years of relatively high unemployment, than in 1965–8 (see Table 3.2), it appears from the evidence of the relatively short period 1961–71 that the second influence is more important than the former. It is understandable that the effect on the inequality of incomes of a proportion of the working population being without jobs should be substantial and proportionately greater than the effect of changes in profits on the incomes of the people concerned.

(vii) As a result of increases from year to year in the level of prices, people with fixed incomes, e.g. widows with private pensions, or people whose incomes are reviewed infrequently, e.g. certain groups of low-paid workers,[16] are likely to experience, if not a reduction, a slower increase in real income than other people. Thus inflation, or rapid increases in costs and prices, may produce an increase in the degree of inequality – although the largest group of people affected are retired persons, the majority of whom are excluded from the estimates quoted in Table 3.2.

Concluding remarks

In the years since 1957, the effects of the majority of the changes discussed above are likely to have been fairly small; and to some extent they must have offset each other. Indeed, our estimates (Table 3.2) seem to indicate either that most of the effects have been too small to cause any marked change in the degree of inequality of original income, or that the changes which have caused it to increase and those which have caused it to decline (allowing for the influence of sampling errors) have to a large extent balanced each other. Since a change in original income is generally accompanied by a change in total tax payments in the same direction, the effect of each of the factors mentioned on the extent of redistribution – as measured by the Gini coefficient which is a measure of proportional inequality – is likely to be much reduced.

The important point emerging from this analysis is that the four types of influence distinguished above – demographic movements, changes in household structure, working habits and economic developments – arc of very different significance, Demographic changes are largely the result of long-term influences which take a generation or more to work through; they are not immediately influenced by the actions of individuals or by Government policy. Changes in household structure are in a different category because, though also reflecting long-term trends, they result from personal and voluntary decisions made by families and individuals and do not directly concern other people. Changes in the extent of participation

D

in work are also largely the result of personal and voluntary decisions; and, since the additional income of an extra bread-winner in the family is the reward for additional work which increases total national output, the distribution of income amongst the rest of the population is not directly affected. Thus the first three types of influence are different in kind from changes which are either economic in character or result from economic or technological developments, which can be influenced directly, whereas the others can only be influenced indirectly, by the Government's social and economic policies.

To arrive at a proper understanding of what has been happening, it would be necessary to estimate, separately and in combination, the effects on inequality of incomes of each of these four types of influence. Much further work needs to be done – and this is perhaps our main conclusion – before we can hope to reach this position.

NOTES

[1] A great deal of the work involved in producing these statistics, which are derived from the Department of Employment continuous Family Expenditure Survey, has been undertaken, from the very beginning, by Miss Phyllis Nye (Central Statistical Office). I am grateful to Mr Matt Semple for helping to assemble the results quoted in this paper, and to Mr Eric Dawe for helping to improve the draft in the light of valuable comments from other colleagues. The author alone is responsible for the views here expressed, however imperfectly.

[2] See also Table 2.2, Chapter 2 of this volume for a further description of The Family Expenditure Survey.

[3] The detailed results have been regularly published in *Economic Trends*. The latest results, for 1971, and comparisons with the results for earlier years, appeared in the November 1972 issue. Further details for low income households appeared in July 1968.

[4] For a fuller discussion of conceptual and estimation problems, see the present writer's *Redistribution of Income in the United Kingdom in 1959, 1957 and 1953* (London, 1965); and *Redistribution of Income – Notes on some Problems and Puzzles*, Review of Income and Wealth, Series 16, Number 3, September 1970 (International Association for Research in Income and Wealth, New Haven, Conn., USA).

[5] Prior to 1969, employers' contributions to National Insurance and the National Health Services, in accordance with the conventions used in national income estimates, were regarded as part of original income and as a direct tax on income. Recent work on the economic aspects of pension schemes suggests that, since employers' contributions form an integral part of labour costs, it is reasonable to assume that they contribute to prices.

From 1969 onwards, employers' contributions have therefore been treated as an indirect tax on all domestically produced goods and services.

6   Cf. Memorandum of Dissent by G. Woodcock, H. L. Bullock and N. Kaldor, *Final Report of Royal Commission on the Taxation of Profits and Income* (Cmd. 9474, June 1955) and see also the discussion of an ideal definition of income in Chapter 2 of this volume, p. 46.

7   Up to 1968, similar benefits were attributed to children attending private schools (not separately mentioned) on the grounds that the right to free State education was itself a benefit; but since 1969 such children have not been allocated any benefit from State education.

8   Namely, roads and public lighting; water, sewerage and refuse disposal; public health services; parks and pleasure grounds; libraries, museums and the arts; police (certain functions such as controlling traffic); fire service; local welfare services.

9   Cf. W. F. F. Kemsley, *Family Expenditure Survey: Handbook on the Sample, Fieldwork and Coding Procedures* (HMSO, 1969), pp. 28–30 and 88–90.

10   In the UK, only the flat rate employees' National Insurance contributions can be so described; though specific excise duties on mass-consumed goods come near to qualifying.

11   Very briefly, the problem is: how should we relate to each other the incomes of families of different composition, or in quite different circumstances? At what relative levels are the incomes of families of different size (e.g. couples with no children and those with several children), or the incomes of pensioners and of families of occupied persons, equivalent in the sense that there would then be no inequality after allowing for the different needs arising from differences in family composition?

12   The alternative measure proposed by Professor A. B. Atkinson (Chapter 2, page 51) is based on a particular form of social welfare function which includes an additional parameter (ϵ) for which it is difficult to choose a generally acceptable value. The Gini coefficient, while it may involve an implicit value judgement, avoids this difficulty and also has a simple statistical interpretation. At least for some values of the parameter ϵ, the use of Professor Atkinson's measure is anyway unlikely to affect the present broad comparisons.

13   Tibor Barna, *Redistribution of Incomes through Public Finance in 1937* (London, 1945). The main differences between his estimates and ours are discussed in J. L. Nicholson, *Redistribution of Income in the United Kingdom in 1959, 1957, and 1953* (London, 1965), pp. 60–1.

14   Pareto coefficients calculated from Inland Revenue data on the distribution of taxable income of people with relatively high incomes show a slight reduction in inequality in recent years, from 2.32 in 1959–60 to 2.55 in 1969–70 (*Inland Revenue Survey of Personal Incomes 1969–70*, p. 2). But these data are not comparable with our estimates since, firstly, they cover less than half of the total number of incomes; secondly, they relate to income tax units rather than families which may contain more than one income tax unit; thirdly, taxable income differs from the concept of original income by including taxable benefits and excluding income in kind. Hence it is not surprising if the distribution among less than half of all tax units, at the higher levels of income, shows different results from estimates of family income derived from a sample of the whole population at all income levels.

15   Estimates embracing both pensioner and non-pensioner families would also be affected, probably quite substantially, by the steadily growing proportion of old people in the population.

16   Cf. National Board for Prices and Incomes: Report No. 169, *General Problems of Low Pay* (HMSO, 1971), Table H, p. 16.

4

Occupational class and the assessment of economic inequality in Britain

W. G. RUNCIMAN

The inadequacy of the existing data for a thorough assessment of the degree of economic inequality in Britain has been discussed in chapter 2. It is not merely that the standard sources, whether official returns or sample surveys, are of questionable accuracy, but that they omit a wide range of sources of both income and wealth altogether: tips, expense accounts, charitable donations, pilferage, bribery, moonlighting, faredodging, shoplifting, evasion of tax and debt, and gifts *inter vivos* contribute significantly (in the sense that many hundreds of millions of pounds are involved) to the distribution of income and wealth. Yet they are barely touched on in academic studies of it.[1] Worse still, from the standpoint of the sociologist concerned with the assessment of economic inequality in its fullest sense and not simply with the distribution of net tangible assets and cash earnings, there is no unanimity on how it is appropriate to take account of outgoings which can be treated as mandatory,[2] disutilities (of which time spent is the most obvious) attaching to the nature and source of income, shares in communal assets, facilities or resources which cannot be assigned even a notional market value, or anticipated future benefits directly consequential upon the person's present situation. To assess economic inequality calls for some measure in terms of which the position of the representative members of different classes can be compared, but despite all that continues to be written on the topic we do not yet have one.

Yet the situation may not after all be quite so bad as this introduction suggests. In the first place, it may be doubted how far either the shape or the span of the distribution of either income or wealth as we now estimate it would be altered. Neither the undocumented sources of income nor the unresolved difficulties of measurement are confined to one part of the distribution alone. We cannot of course be certain, but it is at least plausible to suppose that we should still be left with the already familiar frequency distribution.[3] Second, a good deal is already known about the extremes of the distribution, even if more is known about the poor than the rich.

The literature on poverty includes a number of detailed empirical studies,[4] and although the rich are not very well documented[5] we do know that the Inland Revenue's estimates based on estate duty assessments standardised for age significantly underestimate the wealth of the very rich; and we also know that without progressive taxation of capital gains, effective estate duty and a levy on personal capital[6] the concentration of wealth will continue to be a very great deal higher than that even of pre-tax incomes, let alone of incomes after income tax and all other redistribution effected through the fiscal system.[7] Thus although more detailed and systematic investigation would be needed before we could claim to know at all accurately just how rich the rich are by comparison with everyone else, there is no reason to suppose that conclusions would have to be drawn from the results which would seriously upset any now accepted opinions of either sociologists or economists about them.

Third, the difficulty in assigning a cash value to assets, revenues and benefits which are not already in a marketable form may not be so formidable as it appears. Of course, such valuation will be 'subjective'. But from the sociologist's viewpoint, as opposed perhaps to the economist's, the important question is not what the asset would fetch if marketed but what its possessor would accept as compensation for its loss. Take the example of expense accounts. Many receipts under this heading are equivalent to an increment in post-tax income and should be treated as such. But by no means all are. A company director spending a fortnight in an expensive hotel at his firm's expense may seem to be enjoying a benefit which should be assessed at the cash cost of his fare, room, meals, drinks and whatever else he puts on his bill. But is he giving himself a holiday under the bogus guise of a commercial purpose, or is he spending all day and half the night trying to sell a product in which he has no interest to people he dislikes in a place from which he is longing to get away? To assess the benefit accruing to him, we should take not the cash total of the expenditure which his job entitles him to recover, but the sum which *he* would accept in lieu as a post-tax increment to salary.[8] In the first case, there could well be no difference at all; in the second, he might even accept a diminution. Fringe benefits, whether the managing director's chauffeured car or the Mersey docker's 'welt', are worth what the recipient thinks they are worth, and to assign them a cash value on this basis, discounted as necessary, is both meaningful and valid.

The more serious difficulty which stands in the way of an adequate assessment of economic inequality is that of making appropriate allowance for the future pattern of accretion in net economic power[9] of the members of different classes. The impossibility of forecasting that pattern, to say nothing of selecting the appropriate discount rate to be applied, is obvious enough. Yet this is in a sense the most important single aspect of economic inequality. Calculation of the distribution of income and assets at only a single point in time can be grossly misleading even when all sources have been included in the calculation. What matters is how far this can be extrapolated both forwards and backwards to cover the lifetimes of the representative members of the classes into which the population is to be divided; and even this requires comparisons standardised for age.[10] If an assessment of economic inequality is based simply on the contrast between the rich and the poor, it will turn out in Britain as elsewhere that the old are significantly over-represented among the latter. But an analysis of just how relatively poor they are will not yield the answer to questions about the nature and degree of inequality between classes in contemporary Britain so much as to questions about the history of the national economy and the 'Welfare State' over the last half-century. What is needed is a comparison between members of classes (or 'socio-economic groups'), whether the Registrar-General's or some other, standardised both for age and for household composition.

Yet this too is not impossible in principle. Any projection of future earnings, let alone of other benefits or allowances, capital appreciation, changes in the incidence of tax, and so forth is bound to turn out in the event to have been mistaken, and perhaps badly so. But then any description of the system of stratification in any country may be outdated by economic or political changes even before the researcher has had time to write up his results. A person's position in the hierarchy of economic class at any one point in time is a function of typical expectations of *Lebenschancen* extrapolated as best they may be from the existing data available. In a relatively stable advanced industrial society such as Britain, there is sufficient information available about potential earnings within broad occupational categories for the expectations attaching to each category under existing conditions to be approximately calculable.[11] Chances of promotion, opportunities for saving and investment, provisions for retirement through pension schemes, annuities or endowment policies, expectations of inheritance, appreciation of household or other property, and access to credit or mortgage facilities can all be estimated at least up to a certain point for a person in a normal full-time occupation whose family and household circumstances are known to the researcher, and who is willing to discuss them frankly and in detail. In theory, given sufficient information, it would be possible to express all these in a composite figure for net present value, as is done for example in calculating the relative values of apprenticeship to a skilled trade and a labouring job with higher immediate earnings but lower future prospects.[12] In practice, the margins are bound to be too wide to make the employment of so precise a calculation appropriate. But there is nothing fundamentally inaccessible about these features of economic position, however uncertain the eventual outcome of any one chosen person's life and career.

This applies also to such 'subjective' differences in attitudes and norms as can be shown both to have a material effect on accretion or diminution of net economic power over a person's career or lifetime and also to be typically associated with occupational or socio-economic class. The suggestion that these differences should be incorporated into an assessment of economic inequality between one class and another may seem to be an invitation to stray beyond the testable (or at least eventually testable) reportage of facts into the speculative explanation of them. But once again, from the standpoint of the sociologist rather than the economist these are differences no less relevant than differences in access to credit or provision for retirement. If economic class is taken to signify systematic, collective differences in typical expectation of life chances, then these things are not merely symptomatic but actually constitutive of it. It does not matter for this purpose whether 'subjective' attitudes or comparative and/or normative reference groups are taken as themselves influencing patterns of saving and consumption or whether both are seen as the common effects of deeper institutional and psychological causes.[13] The fact remains that members of different classes do tend to contrast their positions with, and take their standards from, persons or groups whom they see as fairly similar to themselves; and to the extent that this is so, attitudes to the acquisition and disposal of income and wealth tend to be self-perpetuating within classes and to determine differences in the typical expectations of the members of the classes between which economic inequality is to be assessed. Nowhere in the literature on wealth and poverty is there an attempt to calculate the long-term effects which these attitudes may have. But although they are of course difficult to estimate at all precisely, they are by no means wholly inaccessible to the thoroughgoing participant-observer or even to the doorstep interviewer.

So far the question has been left open whether persons, income units or households should be used as the basis of comparison.[14] But I think it follows from what I have been saying that the most appropriate would be household heads with resident spouses and the modal number of dependent children.[15] Given what is known about the costs less allowances and tax remissions of the children's upbringing, the prospective cycle of net contributions to the household budget by the children and both their parents, and the likely pattern of savings and consumption of the household as such, a comparison between household heads of the same age would be the most meaningful single measure of economic inequality as generated (or if you will, imposed) by the structure and workings of the social system. To work from comparisons between individuals, even if standardised for age, means ignoring differences at the level of the household which often override individual habits and patterns of both receipts and expenses; to use households raises the difficulty of variations of household composition over time; and to use income units has no other recommendation in its favour than that they are used by the Revenue – whose figures are almost valueless for the purposes of the sort of assessment of inequality which on the argument of this paper, is called for.

Suppose, accordingly, that all this data were available for a representative sample of household heads. Into how many classes would we wish to divide them? The view of economic inequality and its assessment being put forward here leads to a classification (whatever the distribution among classes might turn out to be) in terms neither of income nor of wealth as these are customarily defined and estimated, but rather in terms of the potential for formation of a net surplus of assets after normal household expenses – 'normal' being defined precisely by reference to the 'subjective' attitudes of the households concerned. By this standard, the natural division is not into two (proletariat and bourgeoisie), or three (upper, middle and lower class), or five (the 'social classes' used since 1911 by the Registrar General to break down the occupational classification), or six (the market researchers' A, B, C1, C2, D and E), but four. Crudely put, the four are: those for whom the net accumulation of assets is easy; those for whom it's not easy, but they manage it; those for whom it's not easy, and they don't manage it; and those for whom only a windfall will make it possible.

At the extremes, this classification neither raises any problems nor solves any. It is obvious that those at the top end of the distribution are able to generate and deploy a large excess of resources even after meeting a level of routine household expenditure many times higher than the mean, and the cumulative spiral of savings and investments at this level is what keeps the Gini coefficient for inequality of wealth where it is. Similarly, the virtual impossibility of breaking out of the 'poverty trap' for a household head with dependents who is in an unskilled job in a region where living costs are high and housing is scarce can be readily documented. But the middle of the distribution is altogether more problematical, and raises questions not merely about the meaning and validity of the traditional line between manual and non-manual occupations but also about the possibility of a definable take-off point above which net accumulation becomes increasingly more feasible and below which only atypical habits and attitudes will make it possible at all.[16]

Where differences in attitude are involved, the most familiar and best-documented contrast is that between the reference groups of manual and non-manual workers and their families. There are, of course, wide variations within both categories. But modal stereotypes can be constructed from the evidence of community studies, attitude surveys and a variety of impressionistic but none the less first-hand evidence. Whatever their nature may be – whether structural, cultural or historical – there are evidently strong influences on manual as contrasted with non-manual workers which incline them to collective rather than individual norms,[17] short-term rather than long-term gratifications,[18] and a sense of relative deprivation which on matters of economic class is likely to be of a fraternalistic rather than an egoistic kind.[19] Much of this is evidently bound up with a quite explicit recognition of the very limited opportunities which a stable advanced industrial society provides for intra-generational mobility and the contrast between the ascent of a career ladder characteristic of non-manual occupations and the improvement in common conditions of remuneration and employment characteristic of manual work. Thus, for example, even the 'vanguard' of skilled workers in Luton studied by the authors of the *Affluent Worker*, many of whom were optimistic about their future and ambitions for their families and themselves, were found to have 'not so much a belief in their own individual capacities to "make good" as, rather, a belief in the probability or inevitability of uninterrupted economic advance along a broad front'.[20] But rational though this outlook may be, the actual difference in the amount, as opposed to the pattern, of earnings between many manual and many non-manual household heads is sufficiently small for the strategy and tactics of domestic economy characteristic of the second to be not at all impracticable for the first. Given that, for whatever reasons, vehicle-builders,[21] printers, dockworkers or metal spinners don't take out mortgages, invest in unit trusts, make use of the tax advantages of life insurance or budget their household expenditure to the extent that clerks, salesmen, technicians and managers do, how does this affect their relative class position? If, by a wave of the wand, they were suddenly implanted with middle-class reference groups, how much better off could they turn out to be?

This question has a particular interest in what has been called the 'social and cultural "buffer zone" between the middle class and working class proper'.[22] But if there is indeed a sort of self-sustaining spiral in which the objective and subjective aspects of economic class reciprocally influence each other, then it would be important to calculate these effects both higher and lower on the scale than in the area where the classification into 'manual' or 'non-manual' is itself ambiguous. It is likely that in at least some cases the combination of social attitudes and family circumstances (which can, of course, themselves be mutually reinforcing) will outweigh the actual pattern of earnings as a determinant of long-term economic position even for heads of households quite widely apart in the classification of occupations. Whatever the lack of facts and figures based on detailed empirical research, there are a number of general considerations which can be adduced to suggest where and how these influences may be most important.

Consider first of all the situation of heads of households among the skilled working class. Here the argument for the possibility, at any rate, of net accumulation rests on the conjunction of a number of influences each of which can be separately documented (whether or not they would in fact be found to combine among significant numbers of actual families). There is first of all the increase in real incomes extending back for a generation and more,[23] which if combined with a retention of traditional norms and standards[24] would at the peak points in the cycle of household earnings generate an investible surplus.[25] Second, there is the success of the trade unions concerned in diminishing the risks of periodic unemployment for their members: even if it is true, as is sometimes alleged, that the success of the best-organised unions secures wage increases for their members sufficient to outpace inflation only at the cost of a diminution of future membership and increased unemployment among other less well-paid and less well-organised workers, there are undoubtedly some sections of the skilled working class for whom this important aspect of economic *Lebenschancen* is no more unfavourable than many workers in non-manual occupations.[26] Third, there is the recent expansion in job opportunities for both women and adolescents which has favoured working-class more than middle-class households both because more working-class wives have engaged in full-time work and because more working-class adolescents contribute earnings in their teens than their middle-class counterparts who are more likely to continue their education. And fourth, there are the circumstantial restrictions which quite apart from differences of attitude and taste reduce both the motive and the opportunity for certain categories of expenditure, such as housing. If, on this view, real incomes continue to rise and the incidence of tax is so adjusted by successive governments as to prevent the net rise being checked by punitive marginal tax rates, then net accumulation among the skilled working class is a possibility which will fail to be realised only if economically 'irrational' attitudes to savings and consumption are retained.

The most obvious counter-argument, however, is that the continuing difference between manual and non-manual households lies less in the distinctive standards and attitudes of the traditional working class than in the traditional standards and attitudes of the middle class. Once again, adequate documentation is simply not possible in the present state of our knowledge: there is nowhere any representative, detailed quantitative evidence for the pattern of savings and investments in non-manual households over the career of the household head.[27] But the general argument for the importance of the continuing difference rests on two grounds: first, the attitudes which naturally result from membership of occupations offering individual career mobility; and second, the self-perpetuating tendency within not merely the nuclear but the extended middle-class family to encourage maximisation of benefits on capital no less than income account. It is true that one result of this may be to deepen the 'eighteen-year trough' between the time when the mother in a two adult/two child household gives up work and the time when the second child leaves school.[28] But then there is also evidence for the importance of extended family aid during this period, typically channelled from father, or sometimes father-in-law, to son, and covering careers, housing and children.[29] In general, there is likely to be both a relatively stronger tradition and a relatively greater expertise among middle-class families in dealing with the opportunities and restrictions concerning the use of credit, the avoidance of tax and the management of expenditure. The many working-class families who are financing their acquisition of consumer durables by hire purchase are paying a far higher price for the money than the many middle-class families who are borrowing by way of a building society mortgage or a personal bank loan.

To contrast in this way the households of the best-paid manual workers with an undifferentiated 'middle class' is admittedly to ignore some important distinctions within the latter. But these distinctions perhaps suggest not so much that skilled manual workers are now accumulating as much 'net economic power' over their careers as clerical, technical, sales and professional workers as that some of the latter have (as they always have had) to be bracketed with the third rather than the second of my four suggested classes – those, that is, for whom net accumulation is, although not impossible, not easy, and who are no more likely to manage it, even if the comparison is made over a career or a lifetime, than skilled manual workers. The 'proletarianisation' of sections of the traditional middle class has been a recurring theme in the literature of European sociology. But from the standpoint of economic life-chances, it is more plausible to argue that a minority of salaried employees are no more favoured than some categories of wage-earners than that the traditional differences are about to be obliterated altogether by the fact of common subordination to the labour markets of advanced capitalist society. It may be that the mere fact of white-collar unionisation in some sense indicates 'a major break from normal, accepted middle-class values'.[30] But even if so, it is not a break which diminishes the significance of the differences which are the concern of this paper. On the contrary: white-collar unionisation is more likely to perpetuate than to undermine traditional economic differentials, and there seems no reason to suppose that conventional middle-class attitudes to savings and investment will be modified as a result of a recognition of the advantages to be gained from collective bargaining over common terms of employment.

The same is true, I suspect, for the self-employed as well as for salaried employees. The situation of the small shopkeeper, for example, is apt to be described in such terms as 'growing marginality',[31] and it is no doubt true that many small shopkeepers are increasingly conscious and resentful of the success of the large retail chains in capturing a progressively larger share of the total market. But it does not follow from this that the net economic advantages of owning a small business are any less than they ever were. Indeed, it is noticeable that the study which I have just cited contains no information whatever about the income or assets of those whose class position it sets out to describe.[32] The category of 'small business' covers a very wide range, and whatever the shape of the distribution within it the span is very broad; a foyboatman on the river Tyne who is technically a proprietor since he owns his own boat and gear has in practice little chance of significant accumulation and relies for improvement in his income on rates negotiated on his behalf by the Transport and General Workers Union; a mini-cab driver who is technically an employee may turn out to be using a car which isn't his to earn a tax-free £30 a day (if the London Taxi Drivers' Association is to be believed) as a 'pirate' touting inside the terminal buildings at Heathrow. But despite the almost complete lack of information about the true economic life-chances of the great majority of the self-employed, there can be little doubt that there is a value in proprietorship and exemption from PAYE which constitutes a substantial potential advantage in terms of post-tax income and capital gains. We know about as little about abuse of chargeable expenses among the middle class as about pilferage among the working;[33] but it seems plausible to suppose that opportunities for the first are on the whole more valuable than the second. Once we switch our attention from the level of weekly earnings to net accretion of economic power over years or decades, it becomes much harder to find reasons for supposing that self-employment has lost its attractions (even if it has at the same time retained its risks).

It will be apparent by now that any substantive conclusions which might be suggested are no better than guesses as to what would turn out to be disclosed by detailed empirical research of a kind which has not yet taken place.[34] But it may still be worth restating in summary what my guesses would be. There are four of them: first, that detailed information about representative household heads would support the suggestion that a division into four classes is the most appropriate once economic inequality in all its aspects is being considered over career and life-span; second, that representative heads of households in the skilled working class would be found to have a potential, but a significantly limited one, for net accumulation; third, that a minority of heads of households in the lower ranges of non-manual occupations would be found to belong in the third rather than the second of the four suggested classes even when their typical expectations for the future had been taken into account; fourth, that the traditional differences between 'middle' and 'working' class households still serve to perpetuate differentials to the relative advantage of the non-manual household head. I am fully aware, in making these guesses, that the pattern of economic inequality is constantly changing, both in the sense that individual households are rising and falling and that the overall system which determines the nature and extent of these movements is itself bound to change in ways that cannot be predicted in advance. But if there is a conclusion suggested by the experience of the past two generations, it is that despite any curbs imposed on the top class or welfare benefits channelled to the bottom class, and whatever may have been the changes to relative earnings among the two classes in the middle, there are strong constraints not only of a structural but also of a cultural kind which tend to perpetuate the overall pattern.[35]

There is a final conclusion of a methodological kind. Sociologists who are (quite rightly) dissatisfied with assessments of economic inequality based on statistics for the distribution of income and wealth are apt then to argue as though economic inequality ought not to be expressed in monetary terms at all.[36] This is unconstructive and misleading. It is perfectly true that a proper assessment of economic inequality will involve analysis of the overall pattern of economic relationships within which a person's receipts and expenses and net accumulation or depreciation of assets work themselves out over the course of his career and retirement. But the point of such an analysis is not to abandon the attempt to measure economic inequality in favour of purely qualitative distinctions in terms of life-style or class-consciousness or relationship to the means of production or the authority structure of large-scale industry. It is rather to incorporate all these in such a way that their actual effect on representative households is reflected in whatever measures and calculations are used. If research is ever carried out which makes this possible, it will certainly require more skills than those of the economist and the statistician. But these further skills will include those not only of the ethnographer but also, and no less importantly, of the accountant.

NOTES

[1] For a discussion of the limitations of survey data see Chapter 2 and Chapter 3. For a full discussion of the limitations of the statistics of income distribution see Chapter 2 this volume.

[2] Children are the most obvious example. As is shown by Margaret Wynn, *Family Policy* (London, 1970), citing data from several western countries, in the absence of specific governmental provision the cycle of household expenditure, and thus of formation and depreciation of assets, is crucially determined by number, age and therefore cost of children. But it can always be argued that nobody is unable to avoid having children in the way that they may, for example, be unable to avoid living in a climate which imposes a direct cost in the form of domestic heating. See also Chapter 2 p. 49 and Chapter 3 footnote 9 this volume.

[3] Chapter 2 this volume contains a discussion of the shape of the income distribution in Britain in the post-war period.

[4] In addition to the studies analysed in detail in Chapter 1 this volume may be added Dorothy Cole Wedderburn, 'Poverty in Britain Today – the Evidence', *Sociological Review*, N.S. Vol. 10 (1962), pp. 257–82; Tony Lynes, *National Assistance and National Prosperity* (London, 1962); Peter Townsend (ed.), *The Concept of Poverty* (London, 1970); and David Bull (ed.), *Family Poverty* (London, 1971).

[5] As Titmuss and others have remarked upon, there is not even a register of discretionary trusts, which together with gifts *inter vivos* constitute the most powerful agent for the transmission of large personal fortunes from one generation to the next. R. M. Titmuss, *Income Distribution and Social Change* (London, 1962). Journalistic sketches such as Peter Wilsher's

'Introduction' to Ferdinand Lundberg, *The Rich and the Super-Rich* (London, 1969) cannot claim to be offering representative figures.

[6] In 1971 the Treasury estimated that £350m would be raised by a 3 per cent tax on personal wealth over £50,000 (*Hansard*, Written Answers, Vol. 810, col. 262).

[7] For a discussion of redistribution of income see Chapter 3 this volume. The Inland Revenue's calculation for the distribution of wealth in 1960 gives a coefficient of 76 per cent which though dropping slightly in the following years was still 68 per cent in 1968.

[8] This point was acknowledged, although only in passing, in the PIB's Report No. 107, *Top Salaries in the Private Sector and Nationalised Industries* (Cmnd. 3970, 1969), pp. 6–7.

[9] Borrowing the now familiar phrase used by the Minority Report on the Royal Commission on Taxation (see the *Report*, Cmnd. 9474, 1955, p. 8).

[10] See Chapter 2 this volume, p. 45.

[11] Guy Routh, *Occupation and Pay in Britain 1906–60* (Cambridge, 1966) gives some interesting statistics showing the strength of differentials over a fairly long period. The familiar pattern of rising earnings in occupations where there is a premium on experience and falling earnings where capacity and competence decrease with age is discussed, e.g. by George J. Stigler, 'Determinants of the Distribution of Labor Incomes', in Edward C. Budd (ed.), *Inequality and Poverty* (New York, 1967). It is noticeable also that the ratio between retirement pensions and earnings since the coming of the 'Welfare State' has remained virtually constant (*Poverty*, Winter 1971, p. 14).

[12] For an illustration, see B. J. McCormick, *Wages* (Penguin Books, 1969), pp. 24–5.

[13] Cf. the 'Postscript' to W. G. Runciman, *Relative Deprivation and Social Justice* (2nd ed.; Penguin Books, 1972), pp. 382–99.

[14] See Chapter 2 this volume, pp. 44–5.

[15] Once adequate data were available, it would always be possible to show the relative positions of households of different composition.

[16] For example: Mr John Rowse, a London Transport driver for 32 years, died in January 1972 leaving an estate valued at £62,388. But he had no children, he never took a holiday and on the testimony of his brother-in-law (*The Times*, 29 February 1972) he and his wife 'just had the bare necessities'.

[17] John H. Goldthorpe and David Lockwood, 'Affluence and the British Class Structure', *Sociological Review*, N.S. Vol. 2 (1963), pp. 145–8.

[18] Josephine Klein, *Samples from English Cultures* (London, 1965), I, pp. 193–7.

[19] Runciman, *Relative Deprivation and Social Justice*, Ch. 2.

[20] J. H. Goldthorpe *et al.*, *The Affluent Worker: Industrial Attitudes and Behaviour* (Cambridge, 1968) p. 143. Contrast with this, e.g. the findings reported in J. E. Gerstl and S. P. Hutton, *Engineers: the Anatomy of a Profession* (London, 1966), p. 102: among the sample studied, 'virtually no one' under 35 and only 7 per cent of those between 35 and 44 felt themselves to have attained their 'top position'; among those between 45 and 54 the proportion rose to 19 per cent; and among those aged 55 and over, to 53 per cent (which the authors still describe as 'only' 53 per cent).

[21] If the interviews reported by Jeremy Bugler in *The Observer*, 11 January 1970, are representative, it may be that vehicle-builders, perhaps because they are more often recruited from outside a traditional working-class community, are more likely to adopt conventional middle-class standards of saving and consumption than dockworkers. But again, no evidence drawn from sufficiently representative samples is available.

[22] Frank Parkin, *Class, Inequality and Political Order* (London, 1971), p. 56.

[23] For the post-war period, compare the rise in the retail price index between 1951 and 1970 from 69.1 to 140.2 with the rise in the average weekly earnings

of adult male manual workers aged 21 and over from £8.30 to £28.05 during the same period (*Social Trends*, 1971, Tables 27 and 28). For the cost of living during the 1930s, see *Annual Abstract of Statistics* No. 84, Table 302, and for real incomes, A. R. Prest, 'National Income of the United Kingdom; 1870–1946', *Economic Journal*, Vol. 58 (1948), Table 2.

[24] Runciman, *Relative Deprivation and Social Justice*, Chs. 4 and 10.

[25] For a discussion of the effects of taxation, allowances and mandatory expenditure over the life-cycle of the household, Wynn, *Family Policy*, Chs. 5 and 6.

[26] This, too, has been more or less true over a long period, from the craft unionists of the Victorian 'aristocracy of labour' (see e.g. Geoffrey Best, *Mid-Victorian Britain 1851–75* (London, 1971), p. 77) to the skilled and even semi-skilled workers of the Depression, who were less than half as likely to be out of work in 1931 as the unskilled (see Colin Clark, *National Income and Outlay* (London, 1937), Table 19), while clerical unemployment, although lower overall, was not significantly so for the unspecialised clerk as against the artisan (see David Lockwood, *The Blackcoated Worker* (London, 1958), pp. 55–7).

[27] The household expenditure tables published in the Department of Employment's Family Expenditure Survey contain some figures tabulated by occupation of household head and income of household for payments on mortgages or purchases of savings certificates; but there is nothing approaching the information which would be necessary to answer the questions raised in this paper and even the breakdowns by income/occupation are not cross-tabulated against those by income/household composition. Some fascinating discussion of middle-class budgets may be found in correspondence published in the *Guardian* in February 1969 under the heading 'Money and the Middle Class', but no reliable generalisations could possibly be drawn from it.

[28] See Wynn, *Family Policy*, p. 149 and Table 9 (p. 136).

[29] See Colin Bell, *Middle Class Families: Social and Geographical Mobility* (London, 1968), Ch. 4. Bell's general conclusion is that 'the middle-class extended family performs functions that the working-class extended family cannot through financial inability rather than differences in sentiment' (p. 91).

[30] Kenneth Prandy, *Professional Employees* (London, 1965), p. 42.

[31] See Frank Bechhofer and Brian Elliott, 'Small Shopkeepers and the Class Structure', *Archives Européennes de Sociologie,* Vol. 9 (1968), p. 196.

[32] It would be a mistake to suppose that the self-employed are declining even in percentage, let alone in absolute, terms: cf. the conclusion of David C. Marsh, *The Changing Social Structure of England and Wales, 1871–1961* (London, 1965), p. 153, that 'Workers on own account have steadfastly maintained their place in the economic system despite the advance of mass production and the limited company.'

[33] As remarked by H. A. Clegg, *The System of Industrial Relations in Great Britain* (Oxford, 1970), p. 287: 'An even more delicate area of unacknowledged custom and practice [than discipline] is the pilfering common in a number of British industries, an aspect of industrial relations which has not yet been the subject of academic study.' The same could equally well be said of tax evasion and avoidance, although these are considered, e.g. by Titmuss, *Income Distribution and Social Change*, Ch. 8., so far as any relevant published evidence permits.

[34] The reader may, for that matter, want to ask what is the point of writing this paper at all instead of collecting some data from which substantive conclusions might be drawn. The answer is that I applied to the Social Science Research Council for funds which would allow fifty selected households to be interviewed in depth on these topics and the relevant calculations made,

but the application was rejected; and even had the research been done, there would have been no way of estimating how far the households interviewed were representative. For this, only a large-scale, elaborate and very expensive research design would have even a chance of success.

[35] For a discussion of the stability in the distribution of original income see Chapter 2 this volume, pp. 66–8.

[36] See for example the invocation of Marx's remark in the *Deutsch-Französicher Jahrbucher* (1844) that 'vulgar common sense turns class differences into differences in the size of one's purse' by Geoffrey Ingham, 'Social Stratification: Individual Attributes and Social Relationships', *Sociology*, Vol. 4 (1970), p. 105.

Case studies in poverty and relative deprivation

5

A critique of the concept of 'compensatory education'

BASIL B. BERNSTEIN

Since the late 1950s there has been a steady outpouring of papers and books in the USA which are concerned with the education of children of low social class whose *material* circumstances are inadequate, or with the education of black children of low social class whose *material* circumstances are chronically inadequate. An enormous research and educational bureaucracy has developed in the USA financed by funds obtained from Federal, State or private foundations. New educational categories have been developed – the culturally deprived, the linguistically deprived, the socially disadvantaged – and the notion of compensatory education has been introduced as a means of changing the status of children in the above categories. Compensatory education issued in the form of massive pre-school introductory programmes, large-scale research programmes and a plethora of small-scale 'intervention' or 'enrichment' programmes for pre-school children or children in the first years of compulsory education. Very few sociologists were involved in these studies because until this point education had been a low status area. On the whole, they were carried out by psychologists. The focus of these studies was on the child in the family and on the local classroom relationships between teacher and child but in the last few years one can detect a change in this focus. As a result of the movements towards integration and the opposed movement towards community control (the latter a response to the wishes of the various Black Power groups) more studies are being made in the USA of the *school*.

Work in England has been almost limited to the effects of streaming. Rosenthal's study *Pygmalion in the Classroom* drew attention to the critical importance of the teaching expectations of the child. In England we have been aware of the educational problem since the writings of Sir Cyril Burt before the war. His book *The Backward Child* is probably still the best descriptive study we have. After the war a series of sociological surveys and public enquiries into education brought this educational problem into the arena of national debate, and so of social policy. Now in Wales there is a large research unit, financed by the Schools Council, concerned with compensatory education. Important research of a most significant kind is taking place in the University of Birmingham into the problems of the education of Commonwealth children. The Social Science Research Council and the Department of Education and Science have given £175,000 in part for the development of special pre-school programmes concerned to introduce children to compensatory education.[1] One University Department of Education offers an advanced diploma in compensatory education. Colleges of Education also offer special courses under the same title. It is therefore important to consider the assumptions underlying this work and the concepts which describe it, particularly as my own writings have sometimes been used (and more often abused) to highlight aspects of the general problems and dilemmas.

To begin with I find the term 'compensatory education' a curious one for a number of reasons. It is difficult to understand how we can talk about offering compensatory education to children who, in the first place, have as yet not been offered an adequate educational environment. The Newsom Report showed that 79 per cent of all secondary-modern schools in slum and problem areas were materially grossly inadequate, and that the holding power of these schools over the teachers was horrifyingly low. The same report also showed very clearly how much lower were the reading scores of children in these schools compared with those of children at school in areas which were neither problem nor slum. This does not conflict with the findings that on average for the country as a whole there has been an improvement in children's reading ability. The Plowden report was rather more coy about all the above points, but there is little reason to believe that the situation is much better for primary schools in similar areas. Thus a large number of children, both at the primary and secondary level, are offered materially inadequate schools and unstable teaching staff, and further a small group of dedicated teachers are expected to cope with this situation. The strain on these teachers inevitably produces fatigue and illness and it is not uncommon to find in any week, teachers having to deal with doubled-up classes of eighty children. It is small wonder, then, that very early in their educational life the children display a range of learning difficulties. At the same time, the organisation of schools creates delicate overt and covert streaming arrangements which neatly lower the expectations and motivations of both teachers and taught. A vicious spiral is set up with an all too determinate outcome. As yet there is clear failure to provide on the scale required an *initial* satisfactory educational environment.

The concept 'compensatory education' serves to direct attention away from the internal organisation and the educational context of the school, and focus it upon the families and children. The concept 'compensatory education' implies that something is lacking in the family, and so in the child. As a result the children are unable to benefit from schools. It follows then that the school has to 'compensate' for the something which is missing in the family and the children become little deficit systems. If only the parents were interested in the goodies offered; if only they were like middle-class parents, then we could do our job. Once the problem is even implicitly seen in this way, it becomes appropriate to coin the terms 'cultural deprivation', 'linguistic deprivation' and so on. And then these labels do their own sad work.

If children are labelled 'culturally deprived' it follows that the parents are inadequate and that the spontaneous realisations of their culture, its images and symbolic representations, are of reduced value and significance. Teachers will have lower expectations of the children, which the children will undoubtedly fulfil. All that informs the child, that gives meaning and purpose to him outside of the school, ceases to be valid or to be accorded significance and opportunity for enhancement within the school. He has to orient towards a different structure of meaning, whether it is in the form of reading books (for example, Janet and John) in the form of language use and dialect, or in the patterns of social relationships. Alternatively, the meaning structure of the school is explained to the parents and imposed upon, rather than integrated within, the form and content of their world. A wedge is progressively driven between the child as a member of a family and community, and the child as a member of a school. Either way both the child and his parents are expected to drop their social identity, their way of life and its symbolic representation, at the school gate. For, by definition, their culture is deprived, and the parents are inadequate in both the moral and skill orders they transmit. I do not mean by this that no satisfactory home–school relations can or do take place. I mean rather that the parents must be brought within the educational experience of the schoolchild by doing what they can do, and can do with confidence. There are many ways in which parents can help the child in his learning which are within the parents' sphere of competence. If this happens, then the parents can feel adequate and confident both in relation to the child and the school. This may mean that the contents of the learning in school should be drawn much more from the child's experience in his family and community.

So far I have criticised the use of the concept of 'compensatory education' because it distracts attention from the deficiencies in the school itself and focusses upon deficiencies within the community, family and child. A third criticism can be added. The concept of 'compensatory education' points to the overwhelming significance of the early years of the child's life in the shaping of his later development. Clearly, there is much evidence both to support this view and its corollary that an extensive nursery school system is needed. However, it would be foolhardy to write off the post seven-years-age educational experience as of little influence. What is required initially is to consider the whole age period up to the conclusion of the primary stages as a unity. An approach at any one age would then be seen in the context of the whole of the primary stage. This implies a systematic, rather than a piecemeal, approach. Thus the unit for analysis or for policy formation is not a particular period in the life of the child (for example, three to five years, or five to seven years), but rather a stage of education which is the primary stage. Emphasis is then placed upon the sequencing of learning and the development of sensitivities within the context of the primary stage. In order to accomplish this the present social and educational division between infant and junior stages must be weakened, as well as the insulation between primary and secondary stages, otherwise gains at any one age in the child may well be vitiated by losses at a later age. We should stop thinking in terms of 'compensatory education' and consider instead, seriously and systematically, the conditions and contexts of the educational environment.

The very form research takes tends to confirm the beliefs underlying the organisation, transmission and evaluation of knowledge by the school. Research proceeds first by assessing criteria of attainment which schools hold and it then measures the competence of different social groups in reaching these criteria. Two groups of children are selected, one known beforehand to possess attributes favourable to school achievement, and the second known beforehand to lack these attributes. One group is then evaluated in terms of what it *lacks* when compared with another. In this way research, unwittingly, underscores the notion of *deficit* and confirms the *status quo* of a given organisation, transmission and in particular, *evaluation* of knowledge. Research very rarely challenges or exposes the social assumptions underlying what counts as valid knowledge, or what counts as a valid realisation of that knowledge. There are exceptions in the area of curriculum development, but even here, the work often has no built-in attempt to evaluate changes. This holds particularly for the educational Priority Areas 'feasibility' projects.[2] Finally, we do not face up to the basic question: *What is the potential for change within educational institutions as they are presently constituted?* A lot of activity does not necessarily mean *action*.

I have taken so much space discussing the new educational concepts and categories because in a small way, the work I have been doing has inadvertently contributed towards their formulation. It might, and has been said that my research, through focussing upon the sub-culture and forms of familial socialisation, has also distracted attention from the conditions and contexts of learning in school. The focus upon usage of language has sometimes led people to divorce the use of language from the sub-stratum of cultural meanings which are initially responsible for the language use. The concept 'restricted code' has been equated with 'linguistic deprivation', or even with the non-verbal child. I want first to start with the notions of elaborated and restricted speech variants. A variant can be considered as the contextual constraints upon grammatical-lexical choices. Sapir, Malinowski, Firth, Vygotsky, Luria have all pointed out, from different points of view, that the closer the identifications of speakers the greater the range of shared interests and the more probable that the speech will take a specific form. To illustrate, let us take a specific example.

Imagine a husband and wife have just come out of the cinema, and are talking about the film 'What do you think?' 'It had a lot to say' 'Yes, I thought so too – let's go to the Millers, there may be something going there'. They arrive at the Millers. who ask about the film. An hour is spent in the complex, moral, political, aesthetic subtleties of the film and its place in the contemporary scene. Here we have an elaborated variant, the meanings now have to be made public to others who have not seen the film. The speech shows careful editing, at both the grammatical and lexical levels, it is no longer context tied. The meanings are explicit, elaborated and individualised. Whilst expressive channels are clearly relevant, the burden of meaning inheres predominantly in the verbal channel. The experience of the listeners cannot be taken for granted. Thus each member of the group is on his own as he offers his interpretation. Elaborated variants of this kind involve the speakers in particular role relationships, and *if you cannot manage the role, you can't produce the appropriate speech.* For as the speaker proceeds to individualise his meanings, he is differentiated from others like a figure from its ground. The roles receive less support from each other. There is a measure of isolation. Difference lies at the basis of the social relationship, and is made verbally active, whereas in the other context it is consensus. The insides of the speaker have become psychologically active through the verbal aspect of the communication. Various defensive strategies may be used to decrease potential vulnerability of self and to increase the vulnerability of others. The verbal aspect of the communication becomes a vehicle for the transmission of individuated symbols

The 'I' stands over the 'We'. Meanings which are discreet to the speaker must be offered so that they are intelligible to the listener. Communalised roles have given way to individualised roles, condensed symbols to articulated symbols. Elaborated speech variants of this type realised universalistic meanings in the sense that they are less context-tied. Thus individualised roles are realised through elaborated speech variants which involve complex editing at the grammatical and lexical levels and which point to universalistic meanings.

A second example may be given. Consider the two following stories which Peter Hawkins[3] constructed as a result of his analysis of the speech of middle-class and working-class five-year-old children. The children were given a series of four pictures which told a story and they were invited to tell the story. The first picture showed some boys playing football, in the second the ball goes through the window of a house, the third shows a woman looking out of the window and a man making an ominous gesture, and in the fourth the children are moving away.

Here are the two stories:

1. Three boys are playing football and one boy kicks the ball   and it goes through the window   the ball breaks the window   and the boys are looking at it   and a man comes out and shouts at them because they've broken the window   so they run away   and then that lady looks out of her window   and she tells the boys off.

2. They're playing football   and he kicks it and it goes through there   it breaks the window and they're looking at it   and he comes out and shouts at them   because they've broken it   so they run away   and then she looks out   and she tells them off.

With the first story the reader does not have to have the four pictures which were used as the basis for the story, whereas in the case of the second story the reader would require the initial pictures in order to make sense of the story. The first story is free of the context which generated it, whereas the second story is much more closely tied to its context. As a result the meanings of the second story are implicit, whereas the meanings of the first story are explicit. It is not that the working-class children do not have in their passive vocabulary the vocabulary used by the middle-class children. Nor is it the case that the children differ in their tacit understanding of the linguistic rule system. Rather, what we have here are differences in the use of language arising out of a specific context. One child makes explicit the meanings which he is realising through language for the person he is telling the story to, whereas the second child does not to the same extent. The first child takes very little for granted, whereas the second child takes a great deal for granted. Thus for the first child the task was seen as a context in which his meanings were required to be made explicit, whereas the task for the second child was not seen as a task which required such explication of meaning. It would not be difficult to imagine a context where the first child would produce speech rather like the second. What we are dealing with here are differences between the children in the way they realise in language use what is apparently the same context. We could say that the speech of the first child generated universalistic meanings, in the sense that the meanings are freed from the context and so understandable by all, whereas the speech of the second child generated particularistic meanings, in the sense that the meanings are closely tied to the context and would be only fully understood by others if they had access to the context which originally generated the speech. Thus universalistic meanings are less bound to a given context whereas particularistic meanings are severely context bound.

It is important to stress that the second child has access to a more differentiated noun phrase, but there is a restriction on its *use*. Geoffrey Turner, linguist in the Sociological Research Unit, shows that working-class, five-year-old children in the same context examined by Hawkins, use fewer linguistic expressions of uncertainty when compared with middle-class children. This does not mean that working-class children do not have access to such expressions, but that the eliciting speech context did not provoke them. Telling a story from pictures, talking about scenes on cards, *formally framed* contexts, do not encourage working-class children to consider the possibilities of alternate meanings and so there is a reduction in the linguistic expressions of uncertainty. Again, working-class children have access to a wide range of synthetic choices which involve the use of logical operators, 'because', 'but', 'either', 'or', 'only'. The constraints exist on the conditions for their *use*. Formally framed contexts used for eliciting context independent universalistic meanings may evoke in the working-class child, relative to the middle-class child, restricted speech variants, because the working-class child has difficulty in managing the role relationships which such contexts require. This problem is further complicated when such contexts carry meanings very much removed from the child's cultural experience.

In the same way it is possible to show that there are constraints upon the middle-class child's use of language. Turner found that when middle-class children were asked to role play in the picture story series, a higher percentage of these children, compared with working-class children, initially refused. When the middle-class children were asked 'What is the man saying', or linguistically equivalent questions, a relatively higher percentage said 'I don't know'. When this question was followed by the hypothetical question 'What do you think the man might be saying?' they then offered their interpretations. The working-class children role played without difficulty. It seems then that middle-class children at five need to have a very precise instruction to hypothesis in that particular context. This may be because they are more concerned here with getting their answers right or correct. When the children were invited to tell a story about some doll-like figures (a little boy, a little girl, a sailor and a dog) the working-class children's stories were freer, longer, more imaginative than the stories of the middle-class children. The latter children's stories were tighter, constrained within a strong narrative frame. It was as if these children were dominated by what they took to be the *form* of a narrative and the context was secondary. This is an example of the concern of the middle-class child with the structure of the contextual frame, a view which can be supported with further evidence.

A number of studies have shown that when working-class black children are asked to associate to a series of words, their responses show considerable diversity, both from the meaning and form-class of the stimulus word. Following the analysis offered above this may be because the children are less constrained. The form-class of the stimulus word may have reduced associative significance and so would less constrain the selection of potential words *or* phrases. With such a weakening of the grammatical frame a greater range of alternatives are possible candidates for selection. Further, the closely controlled middle-class linguistic socialisation of the young child may point the child towards both the grammatical significance of the stimulus word and towards a tight logical ordering of semantic space. Middle-class children may well have access to deep interpretive rules which regulate their linguistic responses in certain formalised contexts. The consequences may limit their imagination through the tightness of the frame which these interpretive rules create. It may even be that with five-year-old children, the middle-class child will innovate more with the arrangements of objects (i.e. bricks) than in his linguistic usage. His linguistic usage is under close supervision by adults. He has more autonomy in his play.

A further example may be offered. When one mother controls her child she may place great emphasis upon language because she wishes to make explicit and to elaborate for the child, certain rules and the reasons for the rules, and their consequences. In this way the child has access through language to the relationships between his particular act which evoked the

mother's control, and certain general principles and reasons and consequences which serve to universalise the particular act. Another mother
may place less emphasis upon language when she controls her child and
may deal only with the particular act and will not relate to general principles and their reasoned basis and consequences. Both children learn that
there is something they are supposed, or not supposed to do, but the first
child has learned rather more than this. The grounds of the mother's acts
have been made explicit and elaborated, whereas the grounds of the second
mother's acts are implicit, they are unspoken.

Our research shows just this. The social classes differ in terms of the
contexts which evoke certain linguistic realisations. Mothers in the
middle class compared with those in the working class (although it is
important to add that this is not true of all, by any means), place greater
emphasis upon the use of language in socialising the child into the moral
order, in disciplining the child and in the communication and recognition
of feeling. Thus the middle-class child is oriented towards universalistic
meanings which transcend a given context, whereas the working-class
child is oriented towards particularistic meanings which are closely tied to a
given context and so do not transcend it. This does not mean that working-
class mothers are non-verbal, only that they differ from the middle-class
mothers in the *contexts* which evoke universalistic meanings. They are *not*
linguistically deprived, neither are their children.

It is possible to generalise from these two examples and to say that
certain groups of children, through the forms of their socialisation, are
oriented towards receiving and offering universalistic meanings in certain
contexts, whereas other groups of children are oriented towards particularistic meanings. The linguistic realisation of universalistic orders of meaning
are very different from the linguistic realisation of particularistic orders of
meaning, and so are the forms of the social relation (e.g. between mother
and child) which generate these. We can say then that what is made
available for learning, how it is made available and the patterns of social
relation are also very different.

When the child is considered in the context of the school there is likely
to be difficulty. For the school is necessarily concerned with the transmission
and development of universalistic orders of meaning. The school is concerned with making explicit and elaborating through language, principles
and operations as these apply to objects (science subjects) and persons
(arts subjects). One child, through his socialisation, is already sensitive to
the symbolic orders of the school, whereas the second child is much less
sensitive to the universalistic orders of the school. The second child is

oriented towards particularistic orders of meaning which are context bound, in which principles and operations are implicit, and towards a form of language use through which such meanings are realised. The school is necessarily trying to develop in the child orders of relevance and relation as these apply to persons and objects, which are not initially the ones he spontaneously moves towards. At one level the problem of educability, whether it is in Europe, the USA or newly developing societies, can be understood in terms of a confrontation between the universalistic orders of meaning and the social relationships which generate them, of the school, and the particularistic orders of meanings and the social relationships which generate them, which some children bring with them to school. Orientations towards meta-languages of control and innovation are not made available to such children as part of their initial socialisation.

The school is attempting to transmit un-commonsense knowledge, that is, public knowledge realised through various meta-languages. Such knowledge may be called universalistic. However it is also the case that the school both implicitly and explicitly is transmitting values and their attendant morality which affect educational contexts and contents of education. It does this by establishing criteria for acceptable pupil and staff conduct. Further, these values and morals affect the content of educational knowledge through the selection of books, texts, films and through examples and analogies used to assist access to public knowledge (universalistic meanings). Thus the working-class child may be placed at a considerable disadvantage in relation to the total culture of the school. It is not made for him; he may not answer to it.

Now I have suggested that the forms of an elaborated code give access to universalistic orders of meaning in the sense that the principles and operations controlling object and person relationships are made explicit through the use of language, whereas restricted codes give access to particularistic orders of meaning in which the principles and operations controlling object and person relationships are rendered implicit through the use of language.[4] I have also tried to explain the cultural origins of these codes and their change.[5] If we now go back to our earlier formulation we can say that elaborated codes give access to universalistic orders of meaning, which are less context bound, whereas restricted codes give access to particularistic orders of meaning which are far more context bound, that is, tied to a particular context.

Because a code is restricted it does not mean that a child is non-verbal, nor is he in the technical sense linguistically deprived, for he possesses the same tacit understanding of the linguistic rule system as any child. It simply means that there is a restriction on the contexts and on the conditions which will orient the child to universalistic orders of meaning, and to making those linguistic choices through which such meanings are realised and so made public. It does not mean that the children cannot produce at any time elaborated speech in particular contexts. It is critically important to distinguish between speech variants and a restricted code. A speech variant is a pattern of linguistic choices which is specific to a particular context as for example, talking to children, a policeman giving evidence in court, talking to friends at a cocktail party when the rituals are well known or talking in train encounters. Because a code is restricted it does mean that a speaker will not in some contexts, and under specific conditions, use a range of modifiers or subordinations and so on, but it does mean that where such choices are made they will be highly context specific. On the other hand, because a code is elaborated it does not mean that in some contexts, under specific conditions, a speaker will not use a limited range of modifiers, subordinations, etc., but it does mean that such choices will be highly context specific. For example, if an individual has to produce a summary such as a précis, then it is likely that it will affect his linguistic choices.

The concept code refers to the transmission of the interpretative rules of a culture or sub-culture – the core meaning structure. Codes on this view make substantive the culture or sub-culture through their control over the linguistic realisations of contexts critical to the process of socialisation. Building on the work of Professor Michael Halliday we can distinguish analytically four critical contexts.[6] First, the regulative contexts which are the authority relations where the child is made aware of the moral order and its various backings. Second, the instructional contexts where the child learns about the objective nature of objects and acquires various skills. Third, the imaginative or innovating contexts where the child is encouraged to experiment and re-create his world on his own terms and in his own way. Fourth, the inter-personal contexts where the child is made aware of affective states – his own and others. In practice these are inter-dependent, but the emphasis and contexts will vary from one group to another. I am suggesting that the critical orderings of a culture or sub-culture are made substantive and palpable through the form of its linguistic realisations of these four contexts – initially in the family. If these four contexts are realised through the pre-dominant use of restricted speech variants pointing to particularistic, that is relatively context-tied, meanings, then I infer that the deep structure of the communication is controlled by a restricted code. If these four contexts are realised predominantly through elaborated speech variants, which point towards relatively context independent, that is universalistic meanings, then I infer that the deep structure of the communication is controlled by an elaborated code. Because the code is restricted it does not mean that the users do not realise at any time, elaborated speech variants, *only that such variants will be used infrequently in the process of the socialisation of the child in his family.*

The concept code involves a distinction similar to the distinction which linguists make between surface and deep structure of the grammar. Thus sentences which look superficially different can be shown to be generated from the same rules. In the same way, although the linguistic choices involved in a summary will be markedly different from the linguistic choices involved in a self-conscious poem, which in turn will be markedly different from the linguistic choices involved in an analysis of physical or moral principles or different again from the linguistic realisation of forms of control, they may all, under certain conditions, point to the underlying regulation of restricted or elaborated codes.

Now because the sub-culture or culture through its forms of social integration generates a restricted code, it does not mean that the resultant speech and meaning system is linguistically or culturally deprived, that the children have nothing to offer the school, that their imaginings are not significant. Nor does it mean that the children have to be taught formal grammar and their dialect interfered with. There is absolutely nothing in the dialect as such, which prevents a child from internalising and learning to use universalistic meanings. But if the contexts of learning, the examples, the reading books are not contexts which are triggers for the children's imaginings on their curiosity and exploration in their family and community, then the children are not at home in the educational world. If the teacher has to say continuously 'Say it again Johnny, I didn't understand you', then in the end the child may say nothing. If the culture of the teacher is to become part of the consciousness of the child, then the culture of the child must be in the consciousness of the teacher. This may mean that the teacher must first be able to understand the child's dialect, rather than deliberately attempting to change it. Much of the contents of our schools are unwittingly drawn from aspects of the symbolic world of the middle class and so when the child steps into school he is stepping into a symbolic system which does not provide for him a linkage with his life outside.

It is an accepted educational principle that we should work with what the child can offer: why don't we practice it? The introduction of the child to the universalistic meanings of public forms of thought is not compensatory education – *it is education.* It is not, in itself, making children middle class. How it is done through the implicit values underlying the form and content of the educational environment might make them so. We need to distinguish between, on the one hand, the principles and operations, which it is our task as teachers to transmit and develop in the children, and, on the other hand, the contents we create in order to do this. Our starting point should be that the social experience the child already possesses is valid and significant, and it should be reflected back to him as being valid and significant. It can only be reflected back to him if it is a part of the texture of the learning experience created for him. If as much time was spent thinking through the implications of this as is spent thinking about the implications of the Piaget developmental sequences, then possibly schools might become exciting and challenging environments for parents, children and teachers.

Over and beyond the issues raised so far stand much larger questions such as what counts as having knowledge, what counts as a valid realisation of that knowledge, and what kind of organisational contexts are to be created for educational purposes; and for each of these questions can be added in relation to what age of the children? I have deliberately avoided extending these questions to include 'in relation to what ability group?' because even if such a question were to become relevant at some point, the answer to it depends upon the answers to the earlier questions.

The social assumptions underlying the organisation, distribution and evaluation of knowledge call for examination for there is no one single valid answer to the questions posed above. The power relationships created outside of the school penetrate the organisation, distribution and evaluation of knowledge through the social context of their transmission. The definition of educability, is itself at any one time an attenuated consequence of these power relationships. To ask these questions is not to eschew the past, is not to foreshorten one's perspective to the strictly contemporary, it is rather to invite consideration of Robert Lynd's question: knowledge for what?

Finally, we do not yet know what a child is capable of, as we have no theory which enables us to create sets of optimal learning environments and even if such a theory existed, it is most unlikely that resources would be made available to make it substantive on the scale required.

E

NOTES

[1] See Chapter 6 this volume and A. H. Halsey (ed.), *Educational Priority* (London, 1972) published after this chapter was written.
[2] See Chapter 6 this volume.
[3] P. R. Hawkins, 'Social Class, the Nominal Group and References', *Language and Speech*, Vol. 12, Part II (1969).
[4] B. Bernstein, 'Linguistic Codes, Hesitation Pheomena and Intelligence', *Language and Speech*, Vol. 5 (1962), p. 31.
B. Bernstein, 'A Socio-Linguistic Approach to Social Learning', *Social Science Survey*, ed. J. Gould (London, 1965).
[5] B. Bernstein and D. Henderson, 'Social Class Differences in the Relevance of Language to Socialisation', *Sociology*, Vol. 3 (1969).
B. Bernstein, 'A Socio-Linguistic Approach to Socialisation: with some references to educability', in J. Gumperz and Dell Hymes, (eds), *Directions in Sociolinguistics* (New York, 1970).
[6] M. A. K. Halliday, 'Relevant Models of Language' in ed. A. M. Wilkinson, *Educational Review*, Vol. 2 (1969).

6

Government against poverty in school and community

A. H. HALSEY

President Johnson's declaration in 1964 of 'unconditional war on poverty in America' inaugurated a plethora of legislation, governmental programmes and social science literature. British Government and British social science have followed a parallel course. A new generation has rediscovered poverty. But the new partnership of politicians and social scientists is no guarantee that poverty, especially the racial conflict in America now and in Britain in the future for which 'poverty' increasingly serves as a euphemism, will be banished from these rich societies. On the side of Government the Democratic and Labour parties have held and lost office, leaving behind no dramatic victories. On the side of the social sciences, conceptual debate remains more distinguished by volume than clarity. And, as Daniel P. Moynihan has pointed out, 'it is the persisting "social fact" of this literature that it not only involves a discussion by individuals who are successful about individuals who are not, but also representatives of unusually successful *groups* dissecting unusually unsuccessful ones'.[1]

My task in this chapter is to comment on the British educational priority area and community development programmes which began, respectively, in 1968 and 1969.[2] But at the outset it is important to underline that it is not revealed truth that poverty (however defined) can be abolished by the methods we are to discuss, under the Governments we serve or with ourselves and our colleagues in the social services as instruments. It may be so, and the success of the Education Priority Area and Community Development Programmes projects depends upon determination that it is so. Nevertheless it can be argued that no serious changes are possible in the present structure of rewards and opportunities without revolutionary advances in both social science theory and the structure of government. It can be more plausibly argued that intellectuals have never conducted a successful social revolution, though they have often played a crucial part in undermining belief in the legitimacy of political orders which are subsequently overthrown. It can more plausibly still be argued that the apparatus of social administration constitutes a large vested interest in the *status quo*. The young and impecunious family caseworker will not easily see herself as the agent of an exploiting class. Nevertheless we cannot ignore the power of the interests of those who run the bureaucracies of welfare – power which expresses itself ideologically if not materially in the shaping of policy and practice. It must be asked how far the established interests of professional social workers carry with them incapacities and ideological barriers to effective work on the abolition of poverty. How effectively can professional social workers communicate with members of the sub-working class? Advances in training methods have undoubtedly been made from this point of view in recent years. Nevertheless, despite the laudable drive towards professionalisation of the social services, it has to be recognised that trained incapacities and vested interests are also involved. Thus experience in the American poverty programmes has shown that in some circumstances trained sub-professionals may be more successful than professionals. For example, Frank Reissman, in describing the 'home-maker' element in the Mobilisation for Youth Programme (which uses sub-professionally trained lower-class mothers to help others with their family problems) offers the following quotation from a middle-class social worker who is comparing the professional with the ancillary worker:

> Indigenous people could teach professional staff a great deal if the latter were willing to learn . . . they don't perceive people as problems, or at least disagree with professionals about what constitutes a problem . . . Somehow, Mrs Smith was less forbidding to the home-maker than the caseworker, who was frightened of her. She was well-meaning, easily misunderstood, and temperamental. But she wasn't 'paranoid, rejecting, abusive'. Mrs Casey was 'a fine person who cared for her children' and that was the main thing even if she had four illegitimate offspring. To the social worker she was depressed, practically ego-less, 'so self-destructive'.[3]

And later he again quotes the social worker on quality of communication between professionals and their 'clients':

> The lack of felt, in contrast to actual, social distance between home-maker and client is evident in the results from several factors. I sometimes feel like an inhibiting influence when I go along to introduce a home-maker to a client. When I leave, they break out into their own language and vernacular . . . empathy rather than sympathy sometimes comes more naturally to the home-maker than the professional social worker.[4]

These problems are by no means exclusively American. Class and status impede relationships, even the relationships of those who are professionally committed to overcoming status barriers.

Other examples relating to the effectiveness of social work in this particular context appear in an unpublished study of some of the problems of immigrants in England[5] which shows that many statutory and professional workers are extremely ignorant of the special difficulties experienced by immigrants and by coloured people who are British-born and some are prejudiced and unsympathetic towards coloured people.

> Mrs Brown was another West Indian whose problems elicited little sympathy from the various social workers who knew her. She was struggling to bring up five children in two rooms on 'the assistance' with the aid of a succession of men-friends. Her health was poor, and whenever she went into hospital the children had to go into care. Then Mrs Brown would continue drawing her social security benefits and children's allowances, finding out too late that she had spent or sent to Barbados money she should never have received in the first place. Now, because the relations she had left them with had died, and they were in orphanages, she wanted to bring her four older children to Britain. This wish no one seemed to regard seriously, and Mrs Brown has so far been unable to get the most basic information about how it could be realised. The health visitor, for example, had promised to 'make enquiries' of a missionary recently returned from the Caribbean, but admitted that she had so far forgotten to do anything about this. The headmaster of the children's school had also once promised to help, but time had passed, and he now supposed her distress must have abated, and he laughed and said 'Oh, you don't want to worry about her, she's had that problem for two years.' Meanwhile, two of the children have passed their sixteenth birthdays and were no longer eligible to come to Britain as dependants.

The negligent lack of sympathy described here is certainly not typical of all those engaged in social work. Such an example does, however, remind us that we cannot assume the existence of a perfect instrument of official social policy in the existing staff of the social services. There are, in any case, much more formidable obstacles to the welfare society – i.e. the society in which there is no poverty: and not least among these is the existence of the welfare state itself.

However, what we have to consider is the development of governmentally inspired and financed programmes against poverty which are posited on the assumption that the welfare society may be attained through the legitimate use of the existing political structure. This assumption may, of course, prove historically to have been the most interesting facet of the educational priority area and community development projects: as a basis for the abolition of poverty it may turn out to have been nothing more than a shibboleth of liberal society in decline.

Experimental social administration

However, within the limits of this political assumption easily the most interesting feature of these programmes is that they postulate a new relation between social science and social policy. They assert the idea that reforms may be seriously conducted through social science experiment. The traditional political mode of reform is to announce a nostrum which is held to be certain in its cure of the social ills to which it is addressed. Here instead there is the promise of a new style in politics and administration – a commitment to enquiry rather than an assumption of omniscience. The idea is that among possible policies about which little is known, a rational plan *A* seems to be the most viable. The politician commits himself to trying plan *A* in an experimentally devised situation, but at the same time commits himself to abandoning it if evaluation by the most valid social science techniques show that it does not work and ought therefore to give way to plan *B*.

The emancipation for administrative civil servants which is implied by this idea can scarcely be exaggerated. It could and should mean for them a quite new relationship with Ministers, a substitution of positive for negative responsibility of a kind which they have seldom been challenged to enjoy in the past. It also implies a strengthening of partnership with social scientists in the universities – a development of intellectual exchange from which both may hugely profit.

The role of the social scientists in these projects is crucial. There is no space here to consider the technical problems of evaluating social action. It must suffice to remark that only in a loose sense can these projects be described as experimental and to point summarily to the immense difficulties involved. The laboratory is, by definition, natural and not experimental. There are, for example, political as well as academic determinants of localities chosen for action research. The desired outcomes of action are often imprecisely defined and in any case resistant to clear measurement. The in-puts are not completely controlled and the relation between in-put and out-put is to that extent indeterminant. We have neither the intellectual tools nor the qualified social scientists demanded by the task. Nevertheless, the challenge is irresistible. It is to become seriously involved in the development of social policy, its definition of ends, its planning and allocation of means and its measurement of results. The task in the case of the EPA and CDP projects is to produce a theory of poverty and to test it in the very real world of the urban twilight zones.

The theory of poverty

What then is a viable explanation of poverty? First, poverty is not adequately conceived in the singular, either in its manifestations or its causes. Multiple and related causes must be recognised, with the implication that a war on poverty is indeed a war and not a single battle. Thus a panel of the Social Science Research Council recently produced a discussion of current research in which six types of poverty are delineated:

(*a*) crisis poverty;

(*b*) long-term dependency;

(*c*) life-cycle poverty;

(*d*) depressed area poverty;

(*e*) down-town poverty; and

(*f*) 'the culture of poverty'.[6]

The complex typology recognised by the expert committee, and the fact that the six types are not clearly distinguishable in practice, must be borne in mind in considering the EPA and CDP projects which address themselves primarily to the fifth type, 'down-town' poverty, and assume the validity of a description of the poor which permits effective intervention using 'communities' or local administrative units as the appropriate arena of battle. On this view the problem is formulated as one where modern urban conditions tend to concentrate social deprivation geographically, especially in the decaying inner ring of conurbations, in such a way as to reduce the quality of environmental service and opportunity. All local institutions, it is argued, are consequently defective – the family, the school, the welfare agencies, the job market and the recreational organisation. Moreover the situation is seen as self-perpetuating; those most capable of doing so move out to take advantage of the opportunities provided elsewhere, be they residents moving to better jobs or better houses or be they school teachers or social workers who live in more salubrious districts and are concerned with this alien territory only in their professional capacities. And the least capable move in, those most in need of and least able to avail themselves of education, housing, jobs and other publicly provided amenities and opportunities (e.g. immigrants and the downwardly mobile). Thus the inhabitants of the priority or development areas are thought of, correctly or incorrectly, as a sub-working class formed out of selective migration with a distinctive set of economic, social and cultural attributes.

The theory of 'down-town' poverty begins with an elaboration of this description. Its factual base is surprisingly little explored in Britain. In America the description is heavily influenced by concern with the social conditions of negro ghettoes in the northern industrial cities, and the question must therefore be raised as to its applicability to British cities, either generally or more particularly to the districts inhabited by immigrants whose origins and characteristics cannot be exactly equated with those of American negro migrants from the southern cities. It is significant that the label given to this kind of poverty by the SSRC panel is clearly a transatlantic importation: and though Americans have, in the past few years, begun to produce a description of their version of the sub-working class,[7] to transplant the description without careful enquiry could be disastrous for both analysis and remedy.

On the basis of a review of American social science literature, Rossi and Blum have summarised the characteristics of the poor as follows.

> 1. *Labour-Force Participation.* Long period of unemployment and/or inter-mittent employment. Public assistance is frequently a major source of income for extended periods.
> 2. *Occupational Participation.* When employed, persons hold jobs at the lowest levels of skills, for example, domestic service, unskilled labour, menial service jobs, and farm labour.
> 3. *Family and Interpersonal Relations.* High rates of marital instability (desertion, divorce, separation), high incidence of households headed by females, high rates of illegitimacy; unstable and superficial interpersonal relationships characterised by considerable suspicion of persons outside the immediate household.
> 4. *Community Characteristics.* Residential areas with very poorly developed voluntary associations and low levels of participation in such local voluntary associations as exist.
> 5. *Relationship to Larger Society.* Little interest in, or knowledge of, the larger society and its events; some degree of alienation from the larger society.
> 6. *Value Orientations.* A sense of helplessness and low sense of personal efficacy; dogmatism and authoritarianism in political ideology; funda-mentalist religious views, with some strong inclinations towards belief in magical practices. Low 'need achievement' and low levels of aspirations for the self.

As a general description of the poor in any advanced industrial society this summary would command the assent of most social scientists. However the description of down-town poverty which has developed during the 1960s in relation to the American poverty programme is more proble-matical. It is well expressed by H. Gans, who distinguished between a working class and a lower class.

> The former is distinguished by relatively stable semi-skilled or skilled blue-collar employment and a way of life that centres on the family circle, or extended family. The lower class is characterised by temporary, unstable employment in unskilled – and the most menial – blue-collar jobs and by a way of life equally marked by instability. Largely as a result of a man's instability, the lower-class family is often matrifocal or female-based. This is most marked among the negro population, in which the woman has been the dominant figure since the days of slavery, but it can also be found in other groups suffering from male occupational instability. Although this type of family organisation had some stable and positive features, especially for its female members, the hypothesis has been suggested that it raises boys who lack the self-image, the aspiration, and the motivational structure that would help them to develop the skills necessary to function in the modern job market. Also it may prevent boys from participating in a 'normal' family relationship in adulthood, thus perpetuating the pattern for another generation. These conditions are, of course, exacerbated by racial and class discrimination, low income, slum and overcrowded housing conditions, as well as illness and other deprivations which bring about frequent crises.[8]

The matrifocal family is also described in English studies, for example Madeline Kerr's *Ship Street*, but the essential point here is the juxtaposition of uncertain occupational opportunities with an unstable family structure. In this connection S. M. Miller has drawn the contrast between W. F. Whyte's *Street Corner Society* which described men in an Italian slum in Boston in the late 1930s and Elliott Liebow's *Tally's Corner* (1967) which offers a vivid portrait of a Washington negro ghetto in a blighted section of the inner city in the early 1960s.

> Whyte's men were unemployed casualties of the Depression, and members of strongly-knit families. Most of them went on later to employment. On Tally's Corner the men have much less favourable relationships with each other and with their families; their hopes for a different and better future are constantly frustrated. The shift in these two books from the emerging Italian temporarily blocked by an economic depression to the thwarted negro of the affluent society captures the change in the social issues facing American society.[9]

The theory is then, that of a vicious cycle of lack of opportunity and lack of aspiration, so that the 'pathologies' of rejection of the world and the search for gratification in alcohol and drugs, the apathy, drifting and dependence on public aid, are to be seen as adaptations to a life of exclusion from the main stream of society.

It is an open question as to how far British city slums resemble either those of Boston in the 1930s or Washington D.C. in the 1960s, though the signs that coloured immigrants are developing into a 'thwarted social stratum' are clear enough in E. J. B. Rose's *Colour and Citizenship*. But whether or not the theory can be properly applied to the British scene, it corresponds in many respects to the SSRC's sixth type – the 'culture of poverty' – and as such has been the subject of a developing debate in America during the 1960s. There is consensus that the poor are different. But the explanation of these differences by those who insist on a situational rather than a cultural theory have profoundly different implications for the strategies of action against poverty.

The culture of poverty approach[10] insists in its simplest form that the poor are different not primarily because of low income but because they have been habituated to poverty and have developed a sub-culture of values adapted to these conditions which they then pass on to their children. It was this definition of the problem which dominated the war on poverty in America and the provisions of the Economic Opportunity Act of 1964 – hence the emphasis on community action and social work rather than on employment policies and the redistribution of income.[11] Recent contributors, however, have returned in one form or another to a situational approach, and this is reflected in the essays put together by Moynihan, by anthropologists like Walter Miller or sociologists like H. Gans or O. D. Duncan. Thus Duncan asserts that 'if there were any chance that the slogan-makers and the policy-builders would heed the implications of social research, the first lesson for them to learn would be that *poverty is not a trait but a condition*'.[12]

Out of this debate something like a constructive synthesis seems to have emerged which makes it clear that the 'poverties' to which urban industrial populations are prone must be understood to have their origins in both situational and cultural characteristics of those minorities which suffer disadvantage and discrimination and to have its cures in both economic and cultural reform, not only at the local or community level but also in the total structure of society.

Community

In attempting to apply the theory of poverty to social action in the context of the EPA and CDP projects, it must be recognised that both the American war on poverty and the transatlantic theorising which we have discussed rely heavily on the idea of community. This word is of ancient usage in sociology. Unfortunately it has so many meanings as to be meaningless.[13] Of course the locality can be a useful natural laboratory for the exploration of sociological hypotheses, as Margaret Stacey recently argued. But she is surely right, too, in concluding that 'it is doubtful whether the concept "community" refers to a useful abstraction'. All attempts to give this concept a precise empirical meaning have failed and certainly in complex societies there is no total social system, that is a social network in which the whole of one's life may be passed, which is also a local territorial unit.

The interest of the concept is fourfold in relation to our present purposes. First, it contains the persistent residue of a romantic protest against the complexity of modern urban society – the idea of a de-centralised world in which neighbours could and should corporately satisfy each other's needs and legitimate demands for health, wealth and happiness. There may perhaps even be a special attractiveness in this idea for the administrator of welfare who is simultaneously guilty about his role in the perpetuation of large-scale bureaucracy and at the same time oppressed by the complex technical and human difficulties in the way of pursuing samaritan goals through impersonal means.

The second aspect is more mundane. Americans seem to use the word 'community' out of traditional every-day usage to refer to the small local settlement, typically placed on the frontier of civilisation and remote from the settled centre of government, which has to face the problem of creating and maintaining an ordered social life in the context of commitment to the values of individual freedom and especially freedom from arbitrary central authority. These two aspects together spell paradox for a governmentally managed programme of social action. They seem somehow to call for an administration which is dedicated to get rid of itself; and in this sense the idea is parallel with the Marxist hope that the state will wither away with the creation of a communist society.

The third, and perhaps most interesting, aspect of the contemporary idea of community is its anarchism. I do not mean to refer here to the familiar and traditional suspicion and hostility of local groups to distant government – though this is not to say that either Welsh or Czech nationalism are of no significance. I have in mind Edward Shils' discussion of student unrest.[14] He points to the significance of affluence for the first generation of its full beneficiaries. It is precisely among the socially selected body of university students that the world's problems can be most plausibly interpreted in terms of social as opposed to economic relations, psychological as opposed to physical un-freedoms, status as opposed to class. Theirs is the first generation to be brought up under the illusion that society is possible without authority. 'In a variety of ways this was the uniquely indulged generation. Parents who were in a state of unprecedented prosperity were persuaded of the merits of hedonism and were capable of giving some reality to its precepts in the raising of children.' For some, therefore, the future holds not 'the danger of death by starvation, but the danger of death by boredom'.

Of course, as Shils points out,

> These views of life, society and the university are not by any means shared by the entire generation of students today in the Western countries. Most of the students in most of the universities still share in the older culture. None the less, the new 'communitarian', 'participatory' culture – which is really the romantic hunger for Gemeinschaft on a more grandiose scale – pervades a substantial minority of the intelligent, sensitive and hyper-active students.

Is it too far-fetched to suggest that this kind of sentiment has also found its way into the new fashions of social work which we are discussing? It is detectable among some of the social work students, including some of the most able. It is one of the elements in the ideology of some of the voluntary community workers in Notting Hill and elsewhere. It may even have some affinity with the vulgarised Freudianism which is sometimes expressed in theories of social casework.

Fourth, the community is attractive as a framework for social action in that it is a territorial unit in which both political and economic functions are performed. The social services, housing and education, are under the direct control of local government authorities and it would therefore seem to make sense that if something can be done about these political units an appreciable impact on the problem of poverty could be achieved. But the apparent directness of the community approach may be misleading. As Peter Rossi has argued,

> The reasons for social pathology lie in the past and present operations of the total social system of the nation or at least region. The best one can do with social services is to equip a few individuals with enough in the way of skills and knowledge to be able to make their way out of their ghettoes. The opening up of employment opportunities, the achievement of a more equitable distribution of income, and the overcoming of very real barriers of discrimination on a large scale are goals which cannot be pursued success-fully within a territory of residence.[15]

It is for this reason, Rossi argues, that the American community action programmes which started out to be mainly the co-ordination and supple-mentation of existing social services, often ended up in practice as providing the basis for parapolitical and political organisations.

> This is also the reason for the failure of social action programmes directed at changing the quality and quantity of social services delivered to localities. No amount of upgrading of skills or increased quality of education is going to make a dent in a society which does not need the newly skilled workers and derives at least some status benefit from maintaining a depressed group in the society . . . We all gain from poverty: the occupational system has a supply of underpaid workers to do the dirty work of the society; the respectable working class have the joy of a comparatively higher status; and the health, welfare and education industries have clients to fuss over.

Nevertheless despite these limitations we are dealing now on both sides of the Atlantic with an amalgam of rhetoric and reality under the heading of community action programmes. These are defined in the USA under Title II of the *Economic Opportunity Act* of 1964 as

> a programme which mobilises and utilises, in an attack on poverty, public and private resources of any urban or rural or combined urban and rural geographical area (referred to in this Title as 'community') . . . to give promise of progress towards an elimination of poverty through developing employment opportunities, improving human performance, motivation and productivity and bettering the conditions under which people live, learn and work.

Similarly the British Home Secretary, in announcing in Parliament on 16 July 1969 the names of the first three local authorities (Coventry, Liverpool and Southwark) who had agreed to take part in the Community Develop-ment Project, described it as 'a neighbourhood-based experiment aimed at finding new ways of meeting the needs of people living in areas of high social deprivation: by bringing together the work of all the social services under the leadership of a special project team and also by tapping resources of self-help and mutual help which may exist among the people of the neighbourhood'.

The double objective, with its underlying conflict, should be noticed in both cases. Resources from Central Government are recognised as necessary, but the main emphasis is put on tapping local and private 'community' resources. There is a drive towards reducing the burden on the national exchequer as well as towards the promotion of local autonomy. As a *Guardian* reporter put it when the British scheme was first announced in January 1969, 'the problem is not just one of shortage of welfare funds. People need to be helped to find solutions in their own way, and to create community services at a neighbourhood level. Otherwise the fear is that welfare payments are merely poured down a bottomless pit.'[16] But surely participation and the growth of consciousness among the organised poor will also generate demand for more resources from Government over and above whatever new energies for community self-help or regeneration are produced by the action projects?

Application of the theory

In social action research theory is applied in a political context. Within the framework of the theoretical discussion of poverty there are large political implications according to whether the emphasis is put on the structure of opportunities or the raising of levels of motivation. Clearly the EPA and CDP projects are so conceived – in being confined to small geographical areas and endowed with very limited resources – that they have to focus mainly on the second alternative. A basic assumption of the EPA programmes is that the most advantageous point at which to break into the vicious poverty circle is in early childhood, in the primary school or in the pre-school period: and this approach tends to lead to considerable emphasis on work with families, thus raising fundamentally the question of limits to the right of the State, through its agencies to intervene in the relation between parents and children.

But quite apart from this fundamental issue there are three partial interpretations of the general theory which may be distinguished and which have political consequences. On a first view, the cause of poverty is 'cultural deprivation' in the sense of inadequate social parenthood, and the cure consists of improved socialisation with the implication that the main thrust must be towards family casework. In the EPA context this means that the sub-working-class family is held to be the major villain of the piece, failing to provide the early training in literacy, numeracy, and acceptance of work and achievement habits which constitute the normal upbringing of the middle-class child and which prepare the child to take advantage of the opportunities provided in school.[17] An example and an elaboration of this point of view directed towards the more pathological aspect of 'cultural deprivation' would be Sir Alec Clegg and Barbara Megson's *Children in Trouble*, with its description of parental neglect, cruelty and workshyness.

The second interpretation focusses on the other socialising institution – the school. It is the theory that the cause of poverty is educational deprivation. The blame is transferred here to the school teacher who fails to provide adequate educational stimulus to the sub-working-class child.

Although they both concentrate on the socialisation process these two interpretations of the theory are often opposed in practice, at least in their emphases. Perhaps it is worth pointing out, given the tremendous stress put by many of the American programmes on the 'community' factors, that evidence for the second type of interpretation is strong. As Gans points out, Kenneth Clark's studies of negro children in Harlem show that the longer these children stay in school the poorer is their performance and the negro children who begin by being equal with white children in attainment and intelligence when they first enter the primary school, fall further and further behind in the higher grades. Such studies indicate that whatever the effects of the sub-working-class home, additional deprivation is contributed by the school experience itself: and the reasons are not mysterious when class sizes, teacher turnover, age of buildings, etc., are taken into account.[18]

On the other hand these two interpretations have been linked in the British EPA projects which emphasise both pre-schooling and the development of the so-called community school. Pre-schooling is a possible key to unlock community support for improved education: to reverse the process whereby the deprived child is one who has been prepared not for learning but for failure. Here is one of Clegg's infant school head-teachers:

> We have children starting school for whom the words 1, 2, 3, 4, 5 represent a new language, children who are so unawakened to the world around them that the meaning of the colour words, red, blue, etc., is not known. Of the 19 children admitted in September this year there are eight who could not fit red to a red jersey or blue to a blue bead. Looking at a book, having someone read a story from it, or talk to them about it, is a new experience, as is the handling of a pencil or crayon. For some, communication by speech is an art to be acquired in school, toilet training has not been established, and the handling of cutlery needs to be taught. . . .

Playgroups, nursery classes and nursery schools can directly repair these deficiencies; and the effect can multiply. If there is forbearance from the professional teachers and charity from their trade unions, then parents can learn to teach and the primary schools can begin their own task without a crippling handicap of ineducability among their five year olds.

The key to a still larger house is the community school. It is typical that contacts in slum schools between parents and their children's teachers are either non-existent or farcical. At worst the teacher drives through enemy-occupied territory at 9 am to withstand siege until the 4 pm withdrawal. At best the occasional 'open evening' attracts the respectable and aspiring Mum, sometimes accompanied by an embarrassed Dad, to a ritual and uncomprehending inspection of the pupils' exhibits while they queue for an inhibited account of Johnny's progress from the class teacher. Odd exceptions here and there suggest that it is possible to overcome this travesty of partnership between parent and teacher. The Plowden Committee found one school in its National survey where 'there is after-school activity on almost every evening during the year when groups of children meet voluntarily for pottery, drama, recorder playing, gardening ... football, athletics, jumping and agility work. Parents are welcome.' *Genuine* participation could provide the multiplier here. The traditional isolation of school from community reflects the uneasy relation between, on the one hand, the legally protected autonomy of the family and, on the other, the political state committed to the provision of individual opportunity through selective education. Within the traditionally isolated school, chances could be given to the exceptionally able or highly motivated individual, but all too often by subversion of the family (a process as rare as it is inefficient).

The community school holds out the promise of peace and co-operation between teacher and parent. The first dove must be flown by the teacher, especially one who is appropriately trained. The development of courses designed for teachers intending to go to EPA schools and their link to community oriented curriculum change has been one of the most successful innovations of the EPA projects. But the teacher cannot reconstruct the community unaided. If he is successful at all, the needs of the neighbourhood for health, housing, employment and other services will be found to impinge directly on his teaching tasks. The implication is clear: educational priorities must be integrated into community development, or the EPA must become the CDP. The EPA school is impotent except in the context of a comprehensive organisation of social services in the community.

The third interpretation, however, puts the emphasis on the opportunity structure of society and in this sense is opposed to both of the first two interpretations. On this view, high achievement orientation and performance on the part of the sub-working class child would be irrational until the structure of opportunities for jobs, and indeed all the other elements of citizenship in the affluent society, are provided equally for all, independently of their social familial and racial origins. There is very little that can be done directly in order to apply this side of the theory within the framework of an EPA action programme. All that can be said is that no amount of success with work on either the cultural poverty of the home or the educational poverty of the school will result in anything but frustration if socialisation cannot be translated into opportunity at the end.

All these three interpretations are at the same time explanations of poor school performance. A parallel can, however, be drawn with independence or dependence on the social services. The view may be taken first, that cultural deprivation leads to both dependency on and incapacity to use the social services intelligently. For example, failure to take up the statutory entitlements may be regarded as a failure on the part of the individuals concerned. A second view, equivalent to the educational deprivation view, regards these services as inadequate for the needs of slum dwellers, for example, the gap between need and supply is interpreted as a failure of comprehension and communication on the part of the welfare bureaucracies. Another example would be that housing services are too narrowly defined, concerning themselves with the letting of council tenancies and not with the search for accommodation, mortgages, etc., in the private as well as the public market. Then the third and radical interpretation would suggest that social services are no more than a palliative while the structure of opportunity, especially opportunities for employment and discrimination against coloured immigrants, continue. This third point of view may be taken to the point of seeing the whole apparatus of both EPA and CDP as a diversion of genuine egalitarian policy into the obscurities of unnecessary research.

The initial aims and objectives of the CDP programme[19] assert the validity, or at least partial validity, of the first (cultural) and second (social services) interpretations of the theory of poverty, but they largely leave aside the implications of the third (structural) approach.

The idea is to involve the people living in the area in community schemes flowing from their own perceptions of need, and translated into action with their participation. It is not assumed that the correct response to a need defined by the project team is for the team to communicate it to the Town Hall, and for the Town Hall to offer a ready-made solution. For example, it is likely that the organisation of pre-school play groups will attract high priority in the plans for many areas. But the most constructive way of developing this kind of activity is held to be one where play groups are requested by the people themselves, and where the Town Hall then provides only such resources as will enable a neighbourhood to run a preschool group largely by its own efforts, or possibly supported by a voluntary agency.

The underlying general aim of social action is to create a more integrated community, supported by services more integrated in their concepts and practices (even though some of them will remain separately organised). It includes measures to relieve the statutory services by developing voluntary social welfare activity and mutual help amongst the individuals, families and social groups in the neighbourhood, supported by the voluntary agencies providing services within it (some of which are known to be conscious of their lack of relevance to present-day needs, and may be expected to welcome an opportunity to find a new role).

All this assumes the possibility of a degree of consensus about the appropriate standards of living and the proper extent and quality of the public services which may prove unattainable. The ambitions and expectations engendered by an effective CDP programme directed to encouraging people to recognise and define their needs may well give rise to demands which cannot be met locally. The stimulation of deprived communities to improve their situation may lead to demands for more radical changes in social policy aimed at national redistribution of income and opportunities. And it is in this sense – in the awakening of political consciousness and the development of political processes which local institutions cannot contain – that the CDP programme may, albeit unintentionally, be the means of directing public attention to the third or structural approach to poverty.[20] Whether the result would be more redistributive policies or suppression of further experiment must be a matter of conjecture.

Meanwhile it is not to be expected that social action in the experimental areas will mean introducing facilities which are large, expensive or wholly new in conception. The projects cannot, for example, hope to set up new comprehensive schools or to re-house the whole neighbourhood; nor can they hope to invent some panacea which will make good in a few years the effects of long standing social deprivations, some of which extend over several generations. It is not the purpose of the projects to do so. Large-scale remedies are assumed to belong to the steady evolution, as resources and politics permit, of familiar general policies. The CDP programme will depend for its success on the cumulative effect of a large number of individually small but carefully co-ordinated initiatives, few of which will be wholly new. But all will be designed to remedy whatever can be remedied without large-scale redevelopment, and to do so in a way which progressively builds up the capacity of the neighbourhood to express its needs and wishes, of the statutory services to respond with effective understanding of the inter-dependence of all forms of social action, and of both to cooperate with voluntary agencies in establishing networks of communication and co-operative effort. Given this beginning, a substantial multiplier effect might then be expected as deprived people reach the head of the queue for the large-scale remedies.

I have argued that the third or 'structural' interpretation of the theory of poverty is difficult to apply within the framework of the community programmes: if action develops along these lines it will represent an unpremeditated consequence rather than an integral part of the projects. They therefore afford no serious opportunity of experimenting with alternative forms of the hypothesis that the abolition of poverty is possible by large-scale redistribution of national resources.

Conclusion

British administrators and social scientists have embarked, in the wake but also in the light of American experience, on a new programme of evaluated social action against the type of poverty which is characteristic of some of the inner districts of conurbations. Some elements of a theory of poverty are available, though by no means fully explored and heavily reliant on translation across the Atlantic. There is a clear need for better theory based on empirical research. It could be an important product of the EPA and CDP programmes. Meanwhile we are in effect applying theories in the new style of experimental social administration. There are difficulties – political and administrative – in our path, some of which have been discussed. They complicate the search for both more developed theory and effective application. Nevertheless the experiments may well throw new light on approaches to amelioration of poverty and deprivation as manifested particularly in the blighted districts of city redevelopment. They may generate unplanned political movements towards large-scale national reform of the distribution of resources and opportunities in a rich but unequal society.

NOTES

[1] D. P. Moynihan (ed.), *On Understanding Poverty* (New York, 1969), p. 28.

[2] For a general account of the three year Educational Priority Area projects in London, Birmingham, Liverpool and the West Riding see A. H. Halsey (ed.), *Educational Priority* (London, 1972).

[3] In P. Lazarsfeld *et al.* (eds), *The Uses of Sociology* (New York, 1967), p. 454.

[4] *Ibid.*

[5] Judy Bainbridge, 'Race Relations and Racial Friction', Diploma thesis, University of Oxford, 1969.

[6] SSRC, *Research on Poverty* (London, 1968), p. 9.

[7] See the essays by P. H. Rossi and Z. D. Blum, Oscar Lewis, H. J. Gans, L. Rainwater and W. Miller in Moynihan's *On Understanding Poverty*. See also H. Gans, 'Urban Poverty and Social Planning' in Lazarsfeld, *The Uses of Sociology*.

[8] Gans, 'Urban Poverty and Social Planning'.

[9] S. M. Miller, 'Invisible Men', *Psychiatric and Social Science Reviews*, Vol. 2 (1968), p. 14.

[10] See Oscar Lewis, 'The Culture of Poverty' in Moynihan, *On Understanding Poverty*.

[11] Thus in presenting the case for the Economic Opportunity Act to Congress in 1964, Sargent Shriver argued that 'being poor . . . is a rigid way of life. It is handed down from generation to generation in a cycle of inadequate education, inadequate homes, inadequate jobs and stunted ambitions. It is a peculiar axiom of poverty that the poor are poor because they earn little and they also earn little because they are poor.'

[12] Otis Dudley Duncan, 'Inheritance of Poverty or Inheritance of Race' in Moynihan, *On Understanding Poverty*, p. 88.

[13] See Margaret Stacey, 'The Myth of Community Studies', *British Journal of Sociology*, Vol. 20 (1969).

[14] See Edward Shils, 'Of Plenitude and Scarcity', *Encounter*, Vol. 32 (1969).

[15] Peter H. Rossi, unpublished paper at an Anglo-American conference on the evaluation of social action programmes at Ditchley Park, October 1969.

[16] Jonathan Steele, 'Multi-Million Attack on Twilight Areas', *Guardian*, 15 January 1969.

[17] See also Chapter 5 this volume.

[18] See also Chapter 5 this volume.

[19] The Community development projects will eventually cover ten or twelve slum areas or 'communities' of between 3,000 and 15,000 population. Inter-service teams are being set up, addressing themselves in a co-ordinated way to the total personal needs of families and of the community as a whole by bridging the gap between the street and the offices of the various departments of welfare.

[20] See Chapter 9 this volume.

7
Relative deprivation in work
DOROTHY WEDDERBURN and CHRISTINE CRAIG

The theme running through the contributions to this volume is that inequality and deprivation are multi-dimensional. Nowhere is this more apparent than in the work situation. Employers and employed stand in different and unequal relationships to one another both of power and of command over resources. This results in the more obvious inequalities – those of wealth and income – between capital owners and employees. And if this appears to beg the question of who are the 'owners' or 'employers' in modern capitalist society it cannot be denied that there is a vast gulf between the wealth and power of top managers and lower level employees. In fact, the employing enterprise is a hierarchy where income differences are paralleled by other dimensions of economic inequality which may extend to differences in the regularity and dependability of income, and in the nature and extent of fringe benefits. There are also less tangible inequalities which relate to the content of work, to the kind of social relationships which people are involved in at work, and to the exercise of power. There are varying degrees of constraint imposed by the rules which govern working life. Jobs vary widely in their degree of interest and responsibility, they vary in the opportunities afforded for the development of individual potentialities and in the opportunities which they provide for upward mobility.

Some of these inequalities lend themselves easily to documentation and measurement, others less so. Few attempts have been made to relate one dimension of inequality to another, or to examine how far deprivation in one sphere is accompanied by deprivation in another. Yet because of the importance of work in our society these inequalities permeate many other aspects of an individual's life. In what follows we first review the data which is available about inequality at work. Second we discuss the extent to which people are aware of these inequalities. Finally we consider how far some of these factors are changing and the significance of such changes for aspects of social class.

The range of inequalities at work

Official studies in the sixties suggested that there had been some improvement in the position of manual workers compared with non-manual workers in respect of fringe benefits such as occupational pension schemes and the provision of sick pay by employers, which can be viewed as part of the total package of remuneration. Yet there remained wide differences between occupational groups, and between the public and the private sector. In 1971 it was estimated that 87 per cent of male non-manual workers were members of occupational pension schemes compared with only 56 per cent of manual workers (in fact, a decline in manual worker membership since 1967, when it was 64 per cent).[1] Moreover, there were considerable differences in the basis of treatment under these schemes. Any scheme which calculates benefits as a percentage of 'normal' earnings will, of course, reflect existing earnings' differentials between different occupational groups. But 59 per cent of the occupational pension schemes for manual workers provided a pension calculated as a fixed sum per year of membership of the scheme. In contrast, 85 per cent of the non-manual schemes were salary service schemes and provided pensions based upon final salary or salary in the last years of service.

Such surveys, however, did not examine differentiation within the very broad headings of manual and non-manual. Moreover, they were carried out across industries or occupational groups so they did not cast any light on the differences in the position of different occupational groups employed by the same employer. More data is now available which does enable some such comparisons to be made over a diverse range of employment conditions. There are two main sources. The first is an enquiry carried out at the Department of Applied Economics, Cambridge, into the differences in the terms and conditions of employment of manual and non-manual employees in manufacturing industry.[2] Secondly data are available from the Department of Employment's New Earnings Survey which has been conducted annually since 1968.[3] The following discussion draws on both these sources.

The Cambridge study was carried out in two stages. First, in 1968, a postal questionnaire was sent to a random sample of establishments which employed more than one hundred workers, in manufacturing industry. (This is henceforth referred to as the 1968 postal enquiry.) The sample was stratified by industry group, size of establishment and region. Information was collected about the formal employment conditions of 'typical' male employees aged between 35 and 40, with five years service, in each of the following six categories:

1. Semi-skilled or production worker (operatives).
2. Foreman in the plant or works, or plant supervisor.
3. General routine clerical worker.
4. Draughtsman, or technician of similar grade.
5. Professionally qualified employee, a member of middle management.
6. Work's manager or member of senior management.

The main object was to discover differences between these categories. Standardisation in respect of age and length of service was introduced to overcome any problems which might arise from the fact that employment conditions are frequently related to these two variables. For example, entitlement to sick pay or holidays may increase with length of service. These six occupational categories were selected to represent the broad strata in the occupational hierarchy of firms, where, it was hypothesised, there would be a greater homogeneity of employment conditions within the strata than between them. The enquiry covered most terms and conditions of employment other than the level of pay; for example, hours, holidays, sick pay, pension schemes, attendance, length of notice of dismissal, disciplinary measures and promotion opportunities.

The replies to this postal enquiry described the formal (or official) terms and conditions of employment, i.e. those which were part of the firms' written rules and agreements. But there is considerable scope for variation in the interpretation of formal rules. There are areas where management discretion plays an important part, for example, in the granting of time off for domestic reasons, and the period for which sickness absence with pay is granted. In the case of such things as disciplinary measures and promotion possibilities, even where formally agreed procedures exist, custom and practice have considerable influence. Such matters cannot be studied by means of a postal questionnaire. Supplementary data was therefore obtained from case-studies of 26 companies which had participated in the postal enquiry – (henceforth referred to as the case studies). These suggested that the manual/non-manual gap is certainly wider than is shown by a study of official terms and conditions.

Table 7.1 presents a summary of some of the main findings from the postal enquiry which relate to formal terms and conditions of employment. In all these areas there is a sharp contrast between the manual workers (operatives) on the one hand, and non-manual grades on the other, and in every case the manual conditions are less favourable. The sharpest contrast

Table 7.1: *Terms and conditions of employment* (percentage of establishments where the condition applies)

Selected conditions of employment	Operatives	Foremen	Clerical workers	Technicians	Management Middle	Senior
Formal sick pay scheme available	46	65	63	65	63	63
Sick pay provided for more than 3 months	49	58	55	57	65	67
Coverage by formal pension scheme	67	94	90	94	96	95
Pension calculated as fixed amount per year of service	48	18	16	14	13	12
Holidays, excluding public holidays, of 15 days or more a year	38	71	74	77	84	88
Choice of time at which holidays taken	35	54	76	76	84	88
Time off with pay for domestic reasons	29	84	84	86	92	93
Period of notice of dismissal in excess of statutory requirements	13	29	26	29	53	61
Clocking on to record attendance	92	33	24	29	2	4
Pay deduction as penalty for lateness	90	20	8	11	1	—
Warning followed by dismissal for frequent absence without leave	94	86	94	92	74	67

Source: Craig, Men in Manufacturing Industry.

is between operatives and senior management. Only 35 per cent of operatives had any choice about the time when they took their holiday, compared with 88 per cent of senior management. Only 29 per cent of operatives were likely to be given time off with pay for domestic reasons such as a death in the family, or illness of a wife compared with 93 per cent of senior management. On the other hand, 46 per cent of operatives were covered by a formal sick pay scheme compared with 63 per cent of senior management. There is in fact, overall, a greater similarity of treatment between the grades in respect of the more purely 'economic' aspects of the terms of employment, such as sick pay and pension schemes, than in aspects controlling working hours and behaviour such as holidays, attendance recording and certain disciplinary penalties.

But there is also evidence of some differentiation within the non-manual strata. It is small in respect of the traditional fringe benefits, but there is a discernible break in respect of other items like periods of notice, choice of holiday time and disciplinary measures. Here foremen, clerical workers and technicians have less favourable conditions than management grades. In one or two areas even, like record attendance and choice of holiday time, the conditions of foremen are rather closer to those of operatives than to other non-managerial grades, presumably reflecting both the physical proximity of the foremen and operatives on the production process and also the demands of production itself. But by and large the findings suggest that the terminological distinction which many firms make, between 'operatives' (hourly paid), 'staff' and 'management' do reflect objective differences of employment. Because of this we shall in further discussion mostly reduce our six categories to the three of 'manual workers', 'staff' and 'management'. At the same time we should note that the *big* divide in employment conditions still falls between operatives or manual workers on the one hand, and non-manual grades, staff and management, on the other.

Table 7.1 shows some of the main differences in the kind of treatment given to the different occupational groups across industry, but does not show the extent to which employers gave equality of treatment to the different groups within their own firms. Table 7.2 shows that uniformity was the exception, and that in all cases where there was differentiation, the manual workers had the least favourable conditions. The postal enquiry (a reasonably representative sample of manufacturing industry) did not produce a single firm where all occupations were treated uniformly for all terms and conditions. The subsequent case studies suggested that the true picture was of even greater inequality. For example, although 42 per cent of establishments stated on their questionnaires that the canteen facilities

Table 7.2: *Summary of the degree of uniformity of treatment of different occupational groups*

	Percentage of establishments where the condition of employment is the		
	Same for all grades	Least favourable for operatives: Same for non-manual grades	Least favourable for operatives and differences between non-manual grades[b]
Sick pay schemes	16	49	27
Pension schemes	31	52	10
Holidays	19	27	41
Canteen facilities[a]	42	11	33
Penalties for lateness	6	52	33
Penalties for bad time keeping	17	23	50

[a] 'Least favourable' in this context means 'separate'. No data was available to judge the quality of the canteen.
[b] Some establishments could not be fitted into these three categories and have been omitted.
Source: Craig, *Men in Manufacturing Industry.*

were the same for all grades, we found in the case studies that in many firms it was customary for different occupational groups to use different facilities; and among the firms where penalties for bad time-keeping were officially the same for all (17 per cent of the establishments), there were certainly many where the penalties were less likely to be enforced for non-manual workers.

Evidence from both the postal enquiry and the case-studies led to the conclusion that manual workers were in every case more closely bound by discipline than were staff. Sometimes this was because of the exigencies of the production system itself, but it also reflected a widespread belief among management that manual workers were less responsible than staff and less identified with the company. Discipline, therefore, tended to be stricter for manual workers than for staff, immediate penalties more severe, and the amount of discretion allowed both to the employees and their supervisors much more limited. In the case of discipline there was a heavy reliance upon the 'rules' to control manual workers; for staff, there was personal consideration, even in some cases counselling and guidance. Even where formal disciplinary agreements existed for all grades, they were more frequently invoked for manual workers and at earlier stages. Precisely because there was more flexibility and discretion for staff recourse to formal procedures was less necessary. But, where both operatives and categories of staff were organised in trade unions and had procedure agreements, the use of the procedure was seen as more advantageous to the manual workers than to the staff. The case studies do suggest, however, that this position might be changing with the growth of white-collar trade unionism among some grades, a point to which we return below.

Control of attendance and standards of required behaviour is one aspect of the employment situation where a very sharp line is drawn between manual and non-manual workers. Physical working conditions are another. It requires little documentation to establish that manual workers as a group are exposed to worse noise levels, extremes of temperature, noxious smells, and enjoy lower standards of amenities such as lavatories and canteens. A very important consequence of the conditions in which they work is the greater physical risk to which manual workers are exposed. To the risk of loss of life or severe disablement from accidents at work must be added the risk of contracting industrial disease.

Manual workers also spend much longer in these less favourable physical conditions. They have, on average, shorter holidays and a longer working week than most non-manual workers, and are more likely to have to work 'unusual' hours. Data from the Department of Employment's New Earnings Survey (henceforth referred to as the NES) show that whereas in 1970 60 per cent of non-manual grades were working less than 38 hours a week, more than 65 per cent of manual grades were working more than 40 hours; and a quarter were working more than 50 hours a week including overtime. The NES also showed that no less than 22 per cent of manual grades received shift payments compared with only 4 per cent of non-manual workers. Shift working interferes with normal family and social life. It may be, as the National Board for Prices and Incomes Report argued, that manual workers select themselves in such a way that for those who work shifts the advantages of, for example, higher pay and free time during the day more than compensate for the disadvantages.[4] But this only serves to underline the relative deprivation of manual workers many of whom have to make this kind of choice between various desired ends when non-manual workers are not forced to.

The 1968 postal enquiry and the NES data on the make-up of pay provide a vivid illustration of another dimension of inequality between manual and non-manual workers. This is in the extent to which earnings are predictable and dependable. The Cambridge postal enquiry (Table 1) showed that while 90 per cent of manual workers suffered deductions from pay if they were late to work, only a minority of staff and virtually no

Table 7.3: *Make up of pay^a by occupational group – Men* (percentages)

| | All manual occupations | | Some non-manual occupations | | | | All non-manual occupations | |
| | | | Managers | | Technicians | | | |
	Of total pay	Of employees paid this way	Of total pay	Of employees paid this way	Of total pay	Of employees	Of total pay	Of employees paid this way
Basic pay	69.1	97.6	91.5	99.8	93.0	100.0	91.3	99.4
Overtime pay	16.4	63.6	0.7	6.1	4.8	27.5	2.8	19.0
Shift and other premium payments	3.0	21.7	0.1	0.6	0.6	5.0	0.3	3.6
Payment by result	6.9	18.7	—	0.2	—	0.2	0.1	0.2
Bonus	3.3	31.4	4.5	32.6	0.9	15.8	2.2	21.4
Commission	0.2	1.3	2.8	9.9	0.1	0.5	2.5	7.6

^a Excluding holiday, sick pay and miscellaneous pay.
Source: Department of Employment, *New Earnings Survey*, 1970 (HMSO, 1971).

management were treated in this way. It also showed that if there are, for example, domestic emergencies and time has to be taken from work, the vast majority of manual workers would lose pay while the great majority of non-manual workers would not. In the NES survey 16 per cent of all manual workers had lost money, i.e. been paid for less than their basic hours compared with only 3 per cent of the non-manual grades. This included loss of pay as a result of voluntary absenteeism, which is heavier among manual than non-manual workers and where it might be argued the manual worker is deliberately making a choice. As we have seen, however, in the advent of domestic crisis he has no choice but to be absent and lose pay. The manual worker is also far more dependent upon overtime and payment by results which are also important in making earnings irregular and fluctuating. In 1970 only 70 per cent of the total take-home pay of manual workers was derived from their basic pay compared with over 90 per cent of the pay of non-manual workers.

Actual level of earnings is of course central to any discussion about occupational differences, and earnings capacities do still vary greatly despite a widespread belief that differentials between manual and non-manual groups have narrowed considerably in the post-war period. Routh's

Table 7.4: *Distribution of earnings by industry and occupation, April 1970* (full-time men paid for a full week)

Selected occupations	Median earnings £ per week	As percentage of the median			
		Lowest decile	Lower quartile	Upper quartile	Highest decile
Manufacturing industry					
Manual	28	69	83	120	142
Non-manual	32	65	80	127	170
All industries and services					
Unskilled worker	22	69	82	123	149
Semi-skilled worker	26	69	82	121	144
Skilled worker	27	71	83	121	145
Foreman or supervisor	31	72	85	118	137
Clerk – routine or junior	19	76	86	120	144
Clerk – intermediate	23	75	86	117	138
Technician – laboratory	26	67	80	128	156
Draughtsman	31	74	87	116	131
Engineer – mechanical	37	61	78	125	154
Accountant	40	48	73	130	163
Works, production, manager	40	67	80	126	156
Marketing, advertising, sales manager	49	62	80	127	161

Source: Department of Employment, *New Earnings Survey*, 1970 (HMSO, 1971).

historical survey has, in fact, established a remarkable stability over a fifty year period,[5] but data from the 1970 NES shed some light on why the popular view persists. As Table 7.4 shows, in 1970 the median earnings of adult male non-manual workers in manufacturing industry were some 17 per cent higher than those of all manual workers. In all industries (that is both service and manufacturing) the median earnings of most of the specific occupations within the non-manual group were also higher than those in the manual group. Foremen, draughtsmen, mechanical engineers and managers all had higher earnings than even skilled manual workers. But the median earnings of a routine male clerical worker were only £19 a week compared with the £27 of a skilled manual worker, and a laboratory technician was earning the same as a semi-skilled worker. If we examine not only the dispersion of earnings *between* occupational groups, but also *within* them, it is clear that the spread of earnings among non-manual workers was much greater than among manual workers (see the decile and quartile intervals in Table 7.4). It is therefore not difficult for *some* non-manual workers to find *some* manual workers earning more than themselves, even though this is not typical of the groups as a whole.

But Table 7.4 data relate to the averages of all workers in an occupational group irrespective of age or length of service. There are other aspects of life-time earnings which suggest that manual workers may be even more relatively deprived, for the earnings progression of the two categories of workers is very different[6] (Table 7.5). The manual worker typically has a longer working life. He leaves school earlier. It is the case that compared with a young non-manual worker, age for age, he may earn more in his early years partly because the young non-manual worker may be employed

Table 7.5: *Median earnings by age, April 1970* (Full-time men paid for a full week. All industries and services: £ *per week*)

Age group	Manual	Non-manual
15–17	8.9	8.6
18–20	16.5	13.7
21–4	23.7	21.9
25–9	26.0	28.4
30–9	27.4	34.4
40–9	26.9	35.6
50–9	24.8	34.0
60–4	22.6	28.9
65 and over	19.4	23.1
All ages	24.8	30.3

Source: Department of Employment, *New Earnings Survey, 1970* (HMSO, 1971).

in training positions (so, too, of course will the manual worker serving an apprenticeship), but also because the young manual worker can exert effort to increase his earnings through working overtime or extra piece-rate payments. Non-manual occupations, however, are typically associated with payment systems carrying with them increments paid at least over a salary range, even though the content and nature of the job do not change. This type of progression is particularly common in public employment. It also exists in private industry but there it is more usual to award pay rises as 'merit' increases, so that the level of pay is determined by management's judgement of the quality of the individual.[7]

Such pay progression is relatively rare for manual workers, who are more likely to find their earning abilities declining after the mid-forties because they are less able to expend the physical effort required to sustain them. Nor can manual workers expect much pay progression as a result of promotion to higher positions in a career structure whereas this is quite typical of the experience of a non-manual worker. For manual workers we can say, then, that higher pay over time comes in the main from increased effort or longer hours. In the short run it is seen to come, most importantly, from the results of collective action through membership of a trade union. Higher pay for the non-manual worker is in the main the result of incremental salary scales, personal assessment of his merit by the employer and by the possibilities of a 'career' – that is promotion to more responsible, highly paid, positions (although, as we note below, this situation may be changing).

The case-study material underlined the fact that few manual workers have opportunities to progress in the sense of crossing the manual/non-manual line. In certain kinds of production processes it may be possible to move from jobs with lesser to greater skill, but all would lie within the same general spectrum of manual work. The most common promotion would be to that of the position of foreman. Increasingly, however, the opportunities for promotion, where they exist, lie with the technically qualified men and the case-studies show some examples of the replacement of the traditional shop floor foreman by a technically qualified man. In other words, the opportunities for upward mobility for the manual worker are being narrowed even further. But promotion prospects in non-manual occupations also vary. Foremen of the traditional kind promoted from the shop floor cannot expect to go much further, and the case-studies also revealed extremely limited career opportunities for routine clerical workers.

Other surveys have quantified the extent to which overall security of employment differs for different occupational groups.[8] This situation may be changing somewhat. It certainly appears that in the 'shake-out' of labour in 1971–2 companies were concerned to reduce overheads as much as they were to cut back on immediate production costs, although the unemployment rate for non-manual workers remained lower than for manual workers. Technological change, in particular computers, may also have some long-term impact on white collar employment, by reducing the number of routine clerical jobs. These are trends which should be watched for the future. In the meantime, manual and non-manual occupations remain fairly sharply differentiated both in respect of security and in the periods of notice given when dismissal does occur. The law specifies minimum periods of notice which are the same for all grades of worker, but the 1968 postal enquiry revealed that in only 13 per cent of establishments were operatives normally entitled to more than the legal minimum period of notice, compared with a quarter where clerical workers, and a half where other non-manual grades received more than the legal minimum. Thus despite the laying down of a legal minimum floor which is the same for all, old inequalities are reasserting themselves.

The Cambridge enquiry was one of the first to try to document systematically inequalities in the relational aspects of work. But the information it obtained about the application of disciplinary procedures and promotion prospects can do little more than indicate a vast area of inequality which deserves further attention. In particular it is important to know more, first, about the way in which the actual work task itself is experienced and second about the experience of power.

It does not require very sophisticated analysis to see that the job of a surgeon, or even of a production manager is more intrinsically interesting and rewarding than that of a lathe operator or of an oven-man on a biscuit production line. But there are no systematic methods yet available by which jobs may be ranked according to the degree of interest afforded. How can one compare the interest of the work of an invoice clerk with that of a panel operator? It is possible to identify characteristics of the work task which are valued, such as variety, autonomy, freedom from mechanical or physical constraints, high levels of informational and judgemental inputs.[9] But no scaling system has been devised to embrace the total range of occupations in modern society. And to ask workers to rate their own jobs according to the degree of interest afforded confounds the problem because their judgements can be seen to depend upon their initial expectations.

One possible approach to an objective measure at the moment is to ask people whether they would choose the same kind of work if they were beginning their life over again, or if they would continue in the same kind of job if they inherited enough money to live comfortably. Blauner summarises the results of a number of such studies which show:

> Higher percentages of satisfied workers are usually found among professionals and businessmen. In a given plant, the proportion satisfied is higher among clerical workers than among factory workers, just as in general samples it is higher among middle class than among manual working-class occupations. Within the manual working-class, job satisfaction is highest among skilled workers, lowest among unskilled labourers and workers on assembly lines.[10]

Equally important, but no less difficult to establish is the experience of power in the work situation. The Cambridge study certainly indicated that there was a hierarchy running from manual workers to management, in which rules governing behaviour at work became progressively more relaxed. The opportunity to exercise discretion in the performance of the work itself also varies, although here the manual/staff distinction, at least, is certainly too crude, because craftsmen are likely to have far more discretion than routine clerical workers. But there is also the dimension of power to influence decisions or to control the actions of other people in the organisation. Studies such as those of Tannenbaum based on people's perception of power again suggest a familiar hierarchy from manual workers through various levels of management.[11] But with the complexity of modern organisations this hierarchy is no longer a simple pyramid and one is left asking uncomforatable questions about whether the position of the routine clerical worker in a sales department is very different in respect of 'power' from that of the production worker.

Lockwood has distinguished between 'market situation'

> that is to say the economic position narrowly conceived, consisting of source and size of income, degree of job-security, and opportunity for upward occupational mobility

and 'work situation'

> the set of social relationships in which the individual is involved at work by virtue of his position in the division of labour.[12]

Together, he argued, these two situations comprise what Marx understood as class position. This review of the current position in Britain suggests that manual workers' 'market situation', despite some changes, remains inferior in most respects to that of most non-manual workers. The non-manual group, however, is extremely heterogeneous and there are some occupations where security of employment, and opportunities for promotion seem more akin to those of manual workers. Similarly in respect of the 'work situation' – that is the nature of the work task, the experience of work constraints and the experience of power – it is possible to generalise and say that non-manual workers are better off than manual workers, but there are many differences within the non-manual group. To summarise it might be said that the overall picture is one of considerable inequality in all aspects of the employment relationship; where the traditional dividing line between manual and non-manual occupations still represents a fairly sharp break in conditions: but where some differentiations within the non-manual group are also important.

Awareness of inequalities

In the face of such inequalities it is surprising that greater resentment is not expressed by those workers who are deprived. It is more surprising, perhaps, than the parallel lack of awareness and resentment about society-wide inequalities of wealth and income for two reasons.[13] Many of these occupational groups are working for the same employer and although there may be physical segregation between works and offices, there is still closer proximity between occupational groups in the same establishment than between different social groups in life outside of work. Second, manual worker trade unions might have been expected to use the superior employment conditions of their non-manual colleagues as a reference point for bargaining. Had such a basis been used individual members might have become conscious of their deprived position. There are however, few examples of such a bargaining stance. Indeed, it has been the other way round, and it has been the non-manual unions who have pointed with concern to the narrowing of differentials between their members and manual workers.

One of the most remarkable features of the bargaining record of manual worker trade unions has been the narrowness of the range of working conditions with which they have concerned themselves. Pay levels, guaranteed fall back pay, hours and holidays have been the major negotiable items at national level. The extension of occupational pensions and sick pay schemes noted earlier have come, in the main, not because of pressure from trade unions, but as a result of employer initiative. Some trade unionists would argue that their first priority should be to use their bargaining position to achieve good comprehensive state social security benefits rather than to become involved with what is essentially competition from the private sector. But it is not altogether clear that these two policies are mutually exclusive. As for negotiations about physical working conditions, security of employment and discipline, these have tended to take place *ad hoc* on specific issues as they arise.

Work discipline provides a good illustration of the basic assumption of conflict of interest which underpins the approach of most manual worker trade unions. Looking at the evidence from the Cambridge study many manual worker trade union leaders might argue – plausibly – that they can obtain a better deal for their members by agreeing disciplinary procedures, using those procedures where they exist and by exerting pressure with strike threats if necessary. This, they might say, would be a more effective defence than any non-manual worker will obtain as a result of 'management discretion'. The issue is, thus, between the advantages of collective action and individual negotiation. There are considerable implications in the growth of non-manual trade unions which are discussed below. But the point of importance is that manual worker trade unions have been concerned to defend their members within management's rules rather than to question the assumptions upon which those rules are based. These unions have not, therefore, played an important part in articulating awareness of relative deprivation among their members.[14]

One small-scale study in two companies suggested that, even when asked specifically, as many as a third of manual workers might be unaware of, or believe that there were *no* differences between their employment conditions and those of non-manual workers.[15] The two-thirds who were aware of differences concentrated particularly on the 'market situation', security, the length of notice, guaranteed wages and sick pay and pension schemes. They were also conscious that staff had more money and shorter hours of work. Relatively few people referred to differences of working conditions or of status, although when they did their comments were expressive:

> They have a cushy job, sitting down all the time, (but I wouldn't like it). They don't have so many gaffers, or have to work in bad conditions.
>
> They don't have the messing around and moving machines. They have offices and can come in cars and suits; they have air conditioning.
>
> There is a parking space for Dr so-and-so, and if he goes there it is all right; if you go there you are for it.
>
> They have more and better toilet facilities.

The references to differences of treatment on matters like discipline were also few. When asked specifically about attitudes to time recording or 'clocking on', over a half of the sample of manual workers were indifferent and as many were in favour as against the practice, because it was felt to be a necessary discipline, or for some, a safeguard which provided an impartial record of hours worked.

In both of the companies in which these attitudes were explored, management were considering the introduction of schemes of 'staff status' for manual workers although for very different motives and in very different settings. The response from the manual workers to the idea of staff status was correspondingly varied. In one company two-thirds were in favour of staff status, but only just over a third in the other. The main reasons for favouring staff status in both companies was, however, a generalised one, that all should be treated alike and 'be equal', rather than any particularised value being placed upon specific aspects of staff conditions of employment. Yet in the context of replies to other questions it was clear that the majority of workers valued sick pay and pension schemes, and regularity and predictability of weekly wages. In other words, it appears that improvements in employment conditions of this kind would be welcomed for themselves, rather than because the manual workers had any awareness of particular conditions enjoyed by their non-manual counterparts to which they aspired.

The non-manual workers interviewed in these two companies were those closest in the hierarchy to manual workers. They included foremen and lower staff grades (technicians and routine clerical workers). The majority of this group were in favour of staff status for manual workers, interpreting this in terms of what they saw as their own more advantageous position in respect of security, pension and sick pay arrangements:

> We are all equal in old age.
>
> It's important for human relations. If they are anything like me with children and a home they must need the money when they are sick.

None the less, some of the staff, and the foremen in particular, saw their better employment conditions as 'privileges', owed to their status. They stressed the importance of time recording and the inferior provisions in regard to sick pay for manual workers as necessary constraints for disciplining an otherwise irresponsible labour force.

The two companies were very different in size and history. One had only recently emerged from being a family concern where there had been considerable emphasis upon face to face relations among all employees. This could well be a situation where status enhancement was important for junior members of staff, and where they would feel the need to have outward and visible signs of their superior position compared to manual workers. The manual workers in this company, on the other hand, were concerned with immediate and pressing issues like bad physical working conditions, inadequate shift differentials and, among the craftsmen, the heavy overtime they were expected to work. The second company was a large multi-national concern with a bureaucratic staff structure, and formal procedures for promotion. Here the junior staff seemed at least as conscious of a gulf between themselves and other grades of staff as of any other differences, and they were more in favour of staff status for the manual workers. Interestingly, the craftsmen, in this company, were distinguished from the other manual workers by using wider reference groups. They *did* compare themselves with staff and management on the one hand and felt on the other hand that it was the unskilled workers who had a particularly bad deal. This egalitarianism was linked to their sense of their own craft worth, their sense of independence of their particular employer and their own importance in the production process.[16]

This evidence adds further support to the view that most manual workers use a restricted frame of reference for judging their position. Indeed, the evidence is now overwhelming for seeing the response to employment as a *process*

> by which the worker's aspirations, his hopes and desires come to terms with the reality of working class life.[17]

This applies also in the area of the intrinsic interest of work. It appears that with the exception of craftsmen most manual workers experience a lowering of expectations of what work could be like. If expectations are not high, objectively uninteresting jobs can be rated as 'satisfying' or 'interesting'. Or alternatively there may be a tendency always to stress those features of a job which can possibly be represented as positive and satisfactory. It is interesting to speculate about whether, for certain non-manual occupations, there may be parallel upward adjustment of expectations as experience provides newer and wider opportunities through the promotion opportunities discussed earlier. If this indeed occurred there would be a compounding of inequalities.

There is considerable evidence that the ordering of expectations from work varies for different occupational groups. Manual workers look first to such market factors as the level of pay, security of employment and good physical working conditions. The higher up the non-manual group one goes, towards managerial and professional occupations, the more emphasis is placed upon the interest of the work, and the 'prospects'.[18] These different orderings clearly reflect the reality which confronts different class groups.

As Ralph Miliband has said:

> Moreover, classes, including the working classes do not only reproduce themselves physically, but mentally as well, and tend to instil in their children the consciousness, expectation and mental habits associated with their class. Of all the socialisation functions which the family perform, there is none which is more 'functional' than this one; for in the present context, it means that the working class family tends to attune its children into a multitude of ways to its own subordinate status.[19]

The future of workplace inequality

Differentiation in the objective terms of employment, and in subjective terms of status within the employing organisation between different occupational groups, has a long history. In origin it was economic – the need to buy the loyalty of workers who were to be assistants to the entrepreneur, who were to be 'l'homme de confiance' or the 'employer's substitute'. There was a relative shortage of suitably educated people and a need to purchase their loyalty to their employer.[20] This employer/employee relationship was predicated on the assumption that the employee shared his employer's interests and his definition of responsibilities. The nature of the employment differentiation between manual and non-manual workers is amazingly similar in many capitalist countries and in some European countries is even enforced by law.[21] But although, as we have seen, the basic inequalities remain, there are forces making for change, of which we shall discuss three. The first is the change in the composition and character of the non-manual labour force. The second are shifts in employers' attitudes towards differentials, which it might be argued are related in part, at least, to the change in the character of the non-manual labour force. Third, there are changes in trade union organisation.

Discussions of changes in the occupational structure have been bedevilled by the breadth of coverage of what has been called 'non-manual' or 'white collar' employment. It is not uncommon to find sales and service workers, clerical, administrative, technical, professional and managerial workers all grouped together.[22] But lower level sales and service employees have the same market situation as manual workers, and although there are some differences in the work situation (they tend to be freer from immediate constraints of supervision, and to have an important relationship with a third party, the customer) they are mostly differences of degree. If it were not confusing because the term has been used in other contexts, Dahrendorf's suggestion that they constitute the 'new working' or 'service' class is a useful one.[23]

But if these categories are excluded non-manual employment still increased from 13 per cent of the total occupied population in Britain in 1911, to 30 per cent in 1961. One of the fastest growing groups was clerks who represented 5 per cent of the labour force in 1911, but nearly 13 per cent in 1961. Over 40 per cent of the total increase in non-manual employment was accounted for by the increased use of clerks.[24] Yet the character of the clerk changed dramatically between 1911 and 1961. Whereas in the first of these years only one clerk in four was a woman, by 1961 it was two out of three. Moreover, it would be no exaggeration to say that there have been such changes in the division of labour that the clerk of 1961 is not only of a different sex, but even if male, is doing work of a different character.

There have been other significant occupational shifts among foremen and technicians, particularly in a more recent period. In the ten years between 1951 and 1961 the number of foremen increased absolutely by some 15 per cent but relatively very little (from 2.6 per cent of the labour force to 2.9 per cent) while technicians increased absolutely almost 50 per cent, and relatively from 4.7 per cent to 6 per cent. This is a global indication of the narrowing of promotion opportunities for manual workers, and of the increasing importance of technical qualification which was discussed earlier. Moreover future manpower forecasts suggests that this trend will continue, while the growth of clerical employment is likely to slow down.[25]

In this rapidly expanded, heterogeneous group of non-manual workers, there are many who bear little resemblance to the employer's man, whose work is routine, and who have few career prospects. In the face of such developments it is small wonder that the continued sharp differentiation between manual and non-manual workers in terms of market situation – pay, regularity of earnings, fringe benefits, hours, holidays, etc., has begun to be questioned. As the first section of this paper showed, such questioning has so far had relatively little effect. But none the less a few major companies have publicly committed themselves to a narrowing of differentials. One or two trade unions in their evidence to the Donovan Commission, the report of the Donovan Commission itself, the Labour Government in 'In Place of Strife', have all spoken with approval of the desirability of narrowing differences.[26]

Employer motivation is mixed. Certain kinds of capital intensive technology, where production depends only to a limited extent upon the individual efforts of manual workers, lend themselves particularly well to the introduction of an annual guaranteed salary, eliminating piece rate and bonus systems. But there are also employers who hold a unitary[27] view of the enterprise and believe that by extending staff conditions of employment to manual workers they may produce in those manual workers a 'non-manual' attitude to work, by which they mean greater 'flexibility' and identification with company objectives. Such a change of attitude would express itself in a willingness to work overtime or extra shifts, when production demanded, without necessarily receiving extra payment, because a guaranteed annual salary has been provided; a willingness to accept flexibility of job and of work content, so that changes become not, as in the past, the subject of continuous negotiation and bargaining, but are accepted as a *quid pro quo* for the regularity of income and improved fringe benefits.[28]

The response of workers and their trade unions to such employer initiatives can only be understood in terms of their total class position, that is their relative deprivation in both 'market' and 'work situation' terms. As the review of the evidence has shown, they are at the bottom of a hierarchy both of economic and power inequality. They have traditionally sought redress through collective action ranging from formal collective bargaining to informal shop floor action to modify or evade the constraints of rules governing work behaviour. The continuous experience of conflict over the 'wage-effort' bargain is fundamental to a rejection of the kind of ideological assumption of a shared identity of interest with employers which underpins many a non-manual worker's relationship with his employer.

But is there now a gap emerging between the objective facts of the 'market' and 'work' situation of some non-manual workers which would call in question the ideological assumptions of shared interests with employers? The evidence reviewed in this chapter does not support the view that class differences across the manual/non-manual line are disappearing.[29] But it does point to shifts of importance in some aspects of the employment situation facing certain groups of non-manual workers. Such shifts have been accompanied by a rapid growth of white collar unionism, significantly most rapid in private employment and in such hitherto untouched areas as insurance and the City.[30] It could be, of course, that this kind of non-manual membership will impose its own meanings upon the concept of collective action. Of more significance, we would suggest, however, than whether or not non-manual worker trade unionists accept the 'values' of trade unions (by which is generally meant the socialist-political affiliation) is whether they begin to develop a consciousness of a conflict of interest, a distinction between 'management' and 'us'. The fastest growing white-collar unions show every sign of attempting to underline such a distinction both in their propaganda and in their style of work. It is then reasonable to ask whether this is the beginning of a replacement of middle-class individualism by instrumental collectivism.[31]

But whilst such activity may have the effect of rupturing the 'shared values' basis upon which the 'work situation' of non-manual groups has developed, it may also widen even further the market differentials between manual and non-manual groups. That is unless the manual unions extend their bargaining position to encompass more aspects of the market situation and also broaden their range of reference groups to include non-manual occupations.

Finally, to return to the present, if objective differences in the experience of and rewards from work do not generate deep feelings of resentment, are they of any sociological importance? To answer this we must consider the relationship between work experience and experience in the wider society. Work experience almost certainly serves to reinforce more general objective economic inequalities in a number of ways.[32] A clear example is the effect of differences in the pattern of life-time earnings upon spending and saving habits. It is easier for the man with a predictable income to enter into a regular saving commitment, like a mortgage, which ultimately affects differentially the rate of accumulation of wealth and affects the position of subsequent generations. But there may also be other, less obvious, consequences of a more psychological kind. The very concept of a 'career' which is meaningful only for certain non-manual occupations, involves a *future* perspective, a concept of developing and growing possibilities over time; whilst insecurity of employment concentrates attention upon the present. It would be surprising if this work perspective did not have some influence upon other attitudes to time and to planning, for example, to the organising and planning of educational experience for children and even to the utilization of leisure.

It would again be surprising if the experience of the work task itself and of power relationships at work did not have some similar consequences. Work which provides the opportunity for self-fulfilment and development, which enables individuals to experience work as something which can be controlled, rather than as controlling, may well affect positively perceptions of one's ability to control other life situations. This in turn will influence both the perception of the choices available and the choices actually made. Such connections have previously been discussed philosophically in the context of 'alienation'. But a detailed empirical study of the consequences of work experience has not been undertaken. The greater ability of the middle class to deal with 'authority' in all its manifestations – whether it be the school, the local authority or entitlement to various social benefits – is almost certainly not simply a reflection of educational attainment but also a reflection of these differences in the expectations of what it is possible to control. If such consequences could be established they could form an important element in explaining why welfare measures have not been successful in modifying inequalities generated by the basic economic system.[33]

NOTES

[1] Ministry of Labour, *Sick Pay Schemes. A Report* (London, 1964). Government Actuary, *Occupational Pension Schemes, 1971*, Fourth Survey (London 1972). Data from the Department of Employment's earnings survey suggests that there has been an improvement in the coverage of manual workers by sick pay schemes over the last ten years. Department of Employment and Productivity, *New Earnings Survey*, 1970 (London, 1971).

[2] Christine Craig, *Men in Manufacturing Industry*, Mimeographed (Cambridge, 1969).
Christine Craig, 'Terms and Conditions of Employment of Manual and Non-Manual Workers: Final Report to S.S.R.C., unpublished (Cambridge, 1971).
Dorothy Wedderburn, 'Inequality at Work', *New Society*, Vol. 15 (1970).

[3] Department of Employment and Productivity, *New Earnings Survey, 1968* (London, 1970) and *New Earnings Survey 1970* (London, 1971). More recent data from the surveys of 1971 and 1972 are available but the analysis is not so full. Since the picture does not appear to have changed we have used the 1970 figures throughout this chapter.

[4] National Board for Prices and Incomes, *Hours of Work, Overtime and Shift Working* (London, 1970).

[5] G. Routh, *Occupation and Pay in Great Britain, 1906–60* (Cambridge, 1965), p. 148. '. . . as between managers, foremen, skilled and semi-skilled and unskilled manual workers, the structure was not much different in 1960 from what it had been in 1913'.

[6] For the consequences of this for the measurement of inequality see Chapter 2, pp. 45–6 and 65–6.

[7] National Board for Prices and Incomes, *Salary Structures* (London, 1969). This report shows that more than 80 per cent of employees in industry in managerial, executive, professional and technical staff (that is excluding clerical and routine technical staff) were appraised.

[8] S. R. Parker, G. C. Thomas, N. D. Ellis and W. McCarthy, *Effects of the Redundancy Payment Act* (London, 1971), p. 97.
A. I. Harris, assisted by Rosemary Clausen, *Labour Mobility in Great Britain* (London, 1966), p. 64.

[9] For a fuller discussion see Dorothy Wedderburn and Rosemary Crompton, *Workers' Attitudes and Technology* (Cambridge, 1972), pp. 65–7.

[10] R. Blauner, 'Work Satisfaction and Industrial Trends in Modern Society' in (ed.), R. Bendix and S. M. Lipset, *Class, Status and Power* (2nd. ed., London, 1967), p. 475.

[11] C. G. Smith and A. S. Tannenbaum, 'Organisational Control Structure: A Comparative Analysis' in A. S. Tannenbaum, *Control in Organisations* (New York, 1968).

[12] D. Lockwood, *The Blackcoated Worker* (London, 1966), p. 155.

[13] See Chapters 4 and 10.

[14] For a contrasting situation in Sweden see Chapter 10.

[15] Dorothy Wedderburn, 'The Conditions of Employment of Manual and Non-Manual Workers' in *Social Stratification and Industrial Relations*, mimeographed (Cambridge, 1969).

[16] See Wedderburn and Crompton, *Workers' Attitudes and Technology*, pp. 142–3.

[17] J. E. T. Eldridge, *Sociology and Industrial Life* (London, 1972), p. 20.

[18] J. H. Goldthorpe, D. Lockwood *et al.*, *The Affluent Worker in the Class Structure* (Cambridge, 1969), p. 57; Wedderburn and Crompton, *Workers' Attitudes and Technology*, pp. 145–50; D. E. Mercer and D. T. H. Weir, 'Attitudes to Work and Trade Unionism among White-Collar Workers', *Industrial Relations,* Vol. 3 (1972), pp. 51–2.

[19] R. Miliband, *The State in Capitalist Society* (London, 1969), p. 263.

[20] D. Lockwood, *The Blackcoated Worker*, pp. 18–35.

[21] L. Francois, *La Distinction entre Employés et Ouvriers en Droit Allemand, Belge, Francais et Italien* (The Hague, 1963).

[22] The traditional distinction between manual and non-manual occupations is a marxist one, based upon the concept of productive and non-productive labour, i.e. production of surplus value. The characteristic feature of the development of industrial societies has been the rapid relative growth of employment in the tertiary sector, service industries, public administration, banking and finance, and *within* manufacturing industry a growth in the relative importance of administrative, technical and clerical employment. The NES adopts a 'narrow' definition of non-manual even excluding foremen. Bain, in his study of white collar unionism, adopts a 'wide' definition 'where there is any doubt about whether an occupation was white-collar or manual (e.g. foremen and shop assistants) it has been included in the white collar group'. G. S. Bain, *Trade Union Growth and Recognition* (London, 1967), p. 3. But see a more general discussion of the problem of definition G. S. Bain and R. Price, 'Who is a White Collar Employee?', *British Journal of Industrial Relations*, Vol. x (1972).

[23] R. Dahrendorf, 'Recent Changes in the Class Structure of European Societies', *Daedalus*, Vol. 93 (1964).

[24] G. S. Bain, *The Growth of White Collar Unionism* (Oxford, 1970), Table 2.1.

[25] 'The Occupational Effects of Technological Change', *Ministry of Labour Gazette*, Vol. LXXVI (1967).

[26] See, for example, *Report of the Royal Commission on Trade Unions and Employers' Associations* (London, 1968), para. 322.

[27] A. Fox, *Industrial Sociology and Industrial Relations* (London, 1966).

[28] For example see the agreement concluded between I.C.I. and the signatory unions in 1969, known as the Weekly Staff Agreement.

[29] See, too, the arguments advanced in Mercer and Weir, 'Attitudes to Work and Trade Unionism Among White-Collar Workers', p. 60.

[30] Bain argued that up to 1964 there was no boom in white-collar unionism, 'In spite of the phenomenal growth of some white-collar unions, white-collar unionism in general has done little more than keep abreast of the increasing white-collar labour force and the density of white-collar unionism has not increased significantly during the post-war period.' He also argued that the 'future growth of white-collar unionism in Britain is largely dependent upon government action to encourage union recognition'. Bain, *The Growth of White-Collar Unionism*, p. 37 and p. 188. It seems that such a shift in employer attitude has occurred and has combined with a more aggressive approach to recruitment by the unions with economic pressures 'with the result that white-collar union density rose dramatically from 29 per cent to 38 per cent' (in the period 1964–70). G. S. Bain and R. Price 'Union Control and Employment Trends in the U.K. 1964–70' *British Journal of Industrial Relations*, Vol. x (1972).

[31] J. H. Goldthorpe and D. Lockwood, 'Affluence and the British Class Structure', *Sociological Review*, Vol. 11 (1963).

[32] See Chapter 4 this volume.

[33] For an argument for a similar sort of connection see the foreword to the English edition of Marienthal where Lazarsfeld says:
'We devoted much attention to the problems of working class youth who at that time started work at the age of fourteen. We tried to show that as a

result "proletarian youth" was deprived of the energizing experience of middle-class adolescence. Consequently, the working-class man never fully developed an effective scope and could therefore be kept in an inferior position.' Marie Jahoda, Paul F. Lazarsfeld, Hans Zeisel, *Marienthal* (London, 1972), pp. xiii-xiv.

8

Disability and deprivation

MAVIS MACLEAN and MARGOT JEFFERYS

Although individuals with serious physical and mental handicaps commonly arouse pity and have become the objects for private philanthropy in most industrial societies, they have never been in a good position to exert economic pressure on Governments to improve their economic and social status in the community.[1] It is not surprising, therefore, that little time or money has been devoted to finding out systematically about the prevalence of severe handicaps in the population, or about their economic, social and psychological consequences for the handicapped or for the family and other units in which they live.

Governments, reflecting the state of the public conscience, have been content to supply handicapped individuals with financial resources, or to give powers to statutory authorities to provide a range of supportive rehabilitative services; but until recently these measures have been either hedged around with restrictive clauses which are likely to have had a deterrent effect on those needing help, or they have been permissive rather than obligatory so far as the local authorities' responsibilities were concerned.

Since 1970 there have been some important new developments, notably the passage of the Chronically Sick and Disabled Persons Act 1970, and the National Insurance (Old Persons' and Widows' Pensions and Attendance Allowance Act) 1970. There has also been more research into the problem.[2] It is still too early to assess the significance of the contribution which these measures will make to the welfare of disabled persons; but it seems clear that the Government responsible for them was at least partly galvanised into action by the persistent public campaigning of pressure groups, among whom associations led by certain disabled interest groups were prominent. Professions involved with the medical or social care of handicapped people, with a few notable exceptions, have played only a small part in the campaign to improve services for the severely disabled. Work in the specialities and institutions serving the physically and mentally handicapped have generally had a low status within the professions of medicine, nursing and social work, and in a period of labour shortage there have been constant difficulties in attracting and retaining adequately trained staff. These workers have lacked both funds and other resources and the support of their professional colleagues in other specialities. In these circumstances it is not surprising if many become apathetic and limit their objectives. Another reason for the inertia among professionals may be that until recently they shared the prevailing ideological assumption that the severely handicapped did not require active therapeutic intervention, whether this was perceived in physiological, psychological or social terms, but did need humane custodial care or 'management'.

This widely held assumption began to be undermined during and immediately after the Second World War when sizeable numbers of young healthy adults were seriously disabled as a result of the bombing of civilians or of injuries sustained in the Armed Forces. Public sympathy ensured that a few outstanding men in physical medicine and orthopaedics, such as Sir Ludwig Guttman at Stoke Mandeville, were given the resources and encouragement to employ aggressive therapeutic measures of a predominantly physiological kind aimed at restoring as much residual function as possible. In order to achieve the necessary motivation for physiological improvement a covert rather than overt form of psycho-therapy was established, which sought to persuade (rather than coerce) the patient into identifying with the aims of the rehabilitating collectivity, the underlying assumption being that in doing so the disabled person would increase his own potential.

The relatively high general level of employment of the immediate post-war years prompted a more active policy of drawing disabled people also into employment. Government-sponsored Remploy Factories were set up and the Disabled Persons Act of 1944 required firms employing twenty or more people to employ a quota of workers from the Disabled Persons Register. The task of finding work for individuals with disabilities was given to Disablement Resettlement Officers. Unfortunately these officers, despite recent recommendations, are not necessarily 'specialists' in the work since their posts are regarded as a step in the normal career of civil servants. Thus many spend only a few years as DROs before promotion to more senior positions elsewhere.

Despite these measures the continuing pervasiveness of a passively custodial humanitarian approach rather than an aggressively therapeutic one underlies the provision for the disabled and has restricted the development of positive attitudes towards, provision for, and knowledge about disabled people. Social work has largely been called upon to deal with the more aggressive or threatening forms of deviance within society, such as law-breaking, violence and feckless parental behaviour. The physically disabled do not constitute the same kind of threat to society. At the same time, the thought or sight of severe handicap may be disturbing and frightening to 'normal' people, and may lead to a desire to avoid the severely disabled person thus tacitly excluding him from the activities of the human groups to which he would normally be attached. There has, therefore, been a tendency to hand over responsibility for the physically disabled to medical and custodial institutions, and to give little help or encouragement to families or kin to care for them in the community.

Since the early 1960s, however, concern for the disabled has been steadily increasing with the growing realisation both in this country and in other countries such as the United States, that increasing affluence does not, in itself, provide the basis for a solution to the problems of disadvantaged groups within the community. Public interest in the inadequacies of State financial provision for the disabled has been stimulated by the work of the Disablement Income Group founded in 1965, which has pressed continuously for a special disablement allowance. It has been pointed out that current social security benefits, based primarily on the concept of loss of earnings and insurance contribution records, have ignored the special costs usually associated with disability, and particularly the cost of replacing, with an employed person, the work of an unpaid housewife should she become disabled.[3]

The extent and character of material deprivation of disabled persons

Evidence concerning the relative deprivation experienced by particular groups of disabled people in material terms is gradually accumulating. For example, Peter Townsend and Sally Sainsbury in 1964 examined the housing, employment and income characteristics of a sample of those registered in the 'general classes' of the physically handicapped, (i.e. excluding the blind and deaf), in three local authority areas.[4] Townsend concluded: 'There is no doubt that a disproportionately large number of the disabled are in poverty or on its margins.' In 1967, 9 per cent of those on the then Ministry of Labour's Disabled Persons Register were unemployed, compared with the national average of 2 per cent.[5]

This picture of deprivation was confirmed when information was obtained by the Social Research Unit, Bedford College in July 1969 from a special study of a homogeneous group of disabled people. The group concerned was an unselected sample of persons with spinal injuries of sudden onset resulting in paraplegia or tetraplegia. It included all National

Health Service patients aged 18 and over first admitted to a spinal injury centre during 1966 and 1967 who left it with a residual motor impairment. Private patients and men from the Armed Services were excluded. The average length of stay in hospital was seven months, so that individuals in the sample all had at least a year since leaving hospital in which to adjust to their new situation.

The study aimed to measure the effects of the onset of disability on the social and economic circumstances of the ex-patients.[6]

A total of 230 postal questionnaires were sent out followed by a reminder in cases where no reply had been received within the first fortnight. Altogether 150 people answered, yielding a final response rate of 60 per cent. Although ex-patients were expected to be highly motivated to respond, it was appreciated that many might have difficulty in doing so. A comparison of respondents with non-respondents using data from hospital records failed to show any significant difference between the two groups in respect of age, sex, type of spinal condition or length of stay in hospital.

There were three times as many men as women in the sample and whilst the age range was considerable the great majority were of working age.

In fact, of the 150 respondents, 100 were working immediately before they were admitted to hospital. The two largest groups among the remainder were housewives and people already sick.

The onset of disability produced considerable changes in both employment and social status. Of 100 who were working immediately before admission to hospital only 45 were working at the time of the enquiry. Using the Registrar General's classification of occupations it was possible to indicate the degree of social mobility occurring as a result of the onset of disability. Table 8.1 shows the percentage of members of each former social class who maintained the same class, changed to an occupation

Table 8.1: *Changes in social class and employment status after onset of disability*

Pre-admission social class	Number of cases[a]	Social class after discharge				
		Per cent in:				
		Same	Higher	Lower	Not working	Total
I	16	75	–	–	25	100
II	22	33	–	–	66	100
III	30	23	10	7	60	100
IV and V	26	29	7	–	64	100

[a] Excludes six cases working before admission to hospital but whose occupation was not known.

in a higher or lower class, or were no longer working at the time of the enquiry.

The majority of those who were in Social Class I occupations before admission were both able to continue work and were still in an occupation of a similar social class status. Among manual workers (Social Classes III, IV and V) some marginal mobility occurred in both directions; but the most marked feature of their position as of the Social Class II patients, was that three out of every five individuals were not working at all at the time of the enquiry.

Clearly both sex and age were associated with re-employment after disability. Thirteen of the women in the sample were in employment before admission to hospital and only four of them had returned to work. The numbers are small, but they suggest that less than one woman in every three returned compared to half the men. Increasing age also reduced the chances of a return to work, but not it seems before the age of fifty. More than half those in their twenties, thirties and forties got jobs again but only a third of those aged fifty or more.

Information was obtained on household as well as personal levels of weekly income before and after the onset of disability, because it was felt that while the disability might affect the income of the individual concerned a re-organisation of work roles within the family might help to maintain the level of household income.

Among the 117 individuals whose personal income range for both pre-

Table 8.2: *Personal weekly income of men and women before admission and at the time of inquiry* (whole numbers)

	At time of inquiry					
Before admission	Up to £5	£6–15	£16–30	Over £30	Not known	Total
Men						
Up to £5	2	2	1	–	4	9
£6–15	5	16	1	–	1	23
£16–30	8	20	10	–	1	39
Over £30	2	3	7	11	1	24
Not known	4	2	1	–	10	17
Total	21	43	20	11	17	112
Women						
Up to £5	9	–	–	–	–	9
£6–15	6	9	–	–	2	17
£16–30	–	–	3	–	–	3
Over £30	1	1	–	–	–	2
Not known	3	1	1	–	2	7
Total	19	11	4	–	4	38

admission and post-discharge periods was known, 51 per cent had incomes within the same range on both occasions; only 3 per cent had incomes in a higher range and 46 per cent had incomes in a lower range. It is interesting to compare this with respondents' subjective estimates of whether their personal weekly income had risen or fallen since the onset of their disability. Of the 84 who replied, 16 per cent said their income had increased, while 84 per cent said they had had a fall in income, over a third estimating that the fall in their income had been more than £10 a week. There is not necessarily a discrepancy between the subjective estimates and those calculated by comparing the pre-admission and post-discharge figures since the latter were concerned with ranges rather than actual incomes which could well rise or fall within a range.

When total *household* weekly incomes were examined, 108 patients supplied information for both pre- and post-admission periods. The household income showed a greater tendency to change than the individual income and in a downward direction. Only 18 per cent had income in the same range; 14 per cent had increased their income but as many as 68 per cent had suffered a drop in income to a lower income range.

Information about sources of personal income after leaving hospital was sought in the survey. However, there was a good deal of confusion in the minds of the respondents who answered this question. For example, National Insurance Sickness Benefit cannot be claimed while National Insurance (Industrial Injuries) Act benefits are being received; yet nine individuals claimed to be receiving National Insurance Sickness Benefits together with National Insurance Injuries Benefits. The unreliability of the information supplied by informants is in itself of interest. It might be due to the difficulties of responding to a postal enquiry, but it might also reflect the complexity of the benefit system which makes it difficult for the individual concerned to have any clear picture of what he is entitled to receive.

As might be expected the most important sources were Sickness Benefit and Supplementary Benefit. Only 10 per cent of the sample had received lump sums of money in compensation; five of this group had received sums less than £5,000, four between £6,000 and £20,000 and six over £20,000.

The leisure activities of people who suffered disability were very much affected. Of the 59 respondents who had been active members of clubs before going into hospital, only 29 were still active at the time of the enquiry; however, ten respondents, who had not previously belonged to clubs, had become members of special associations for the disabled. A disabled person's activities outside the home depend to a great extent on the availability of transport. Forty-three per cent of the respondents were members of households which owned a normal car, and 26 per cent had the single-seater Invacar, which, while giving them some personal mobility, does not permit the disabled person to travel with other people, but no less than 31 per cent were members of households which possessed no motorised transport.

Current social policy emphasises care within the community, and at the time of the enquiry, 53 per cent of the respondents said they were being seen occasionally by a local authority welfare officer. Respondents were asked how they had been getting on since leaving hospital, and to give their ideas about the position of disabled people in society. One hundred respondents made comments which could be classified and by far the largest group, over a half, said they were actively working to help the disabled in society. Twenty-eight of these mentioned specifically that they were trying to persuade the Department of Health and Social Security to change its policy of providing disabled persons with Invacars to one of providing them with modified minicars. The isolation of the Invacar driver which made family outings impossible, the high incidence of breakdowns, and its conspicuous nature were frequently criticised. Another large group mentioned the need for better designed appliances and improved access to public and private buildings. Housing problems were mentioned by fifteen respondents; they had had to wait a long time before being rehoused or obtaining adaptations which were sometimes unsatisfactory when completed. Nearly a third mentioned financial difficulties arising they felt from the low level of benefits to which they were entitled. Most of the respondents stressed the increase in their necessary expenses which sprang from their disability. Sixteen respondents described emotional difficulties, particularly depression, and a reluctance to see other people. Seventeen respondents, on the other hand, claimed to be well and happy, and without any particular difficulties.

In general, therefore, this group which, in respect of the medical and rehabilitation services received in hospital, is likely to be among the most privileged of severely disabled people, had suffered substantial deprivation in the way of loss of earning power, lower incomes and reduced facilities for leisure activities, and had experienced serious problems in relation to transport and housing.

Community attitudes to the disabled

The physically disabled are not the only disadvantaged group in the community; others with certain ascribed or pre-disposing characteristics, for example, black people, women and those in certain unskilled manual occupations, have along with the physically disabled been unable to improve their relative economic position at a time of generally increasing living standards. The inability of all these groups to extract a larger relative share of an increasing national product can be mainly ascribed to certain factors which they have in common. First, to a greater or lesser extent they all possess little in the way of training or skills which would enable them to exact a better economic return for their labour. In the case of the severely disabled, their numbers and the marginality of their possible contribution to the national economy is greater than that of most other disadvantaged groups. Second, all these groups, possibly for different reasons, have not developed sufficiently powerful organisations for collective action to put pressure on employers or the government for an improvement of their economic position and social status.[7] In the case of the severely disabled, the absence of a single organisation to press claims for higher wages and social security benefits and for more community services is probably a reflection both of the relatively small numbers affected, and the fact that most of the associations concerned with their needs have dealt only with the problems of those disabled in a particular way – for example, by polio, multiple sclerosis, cerebral palsy, spasticity, blindness or deafness. The recently formed Disablement Income Group is a notable exception. Although the membership is relatively small, it has been conspicuously successful as a pressure group.

While many of the problems which the disabled face are therefore due to their inability to bring effective pressure to bear on employers or the Government, there is also some evidence that significant numbers of disabled people who could make use of services provided for them do not do so. One reason may be the reluctance of disabled people to identify themselves as disabled, a step which is essential if they are to legitimise their request for most forms of service. Denial or concealment may be a way, albeit an ineffective one, of avoiding the stigma associated with the acknowledgement that one is different from and, in the last resort dependent upon, 'normal' members of society.

The possible reluctance of disabled people themselves to invite identification may either lead to, or stem from, a reluctance on the part of both those closely connected with the disabled and the public generally to label individuals in a way which underlines their inadequacies. If there were such a general reluctance it could paradoxically compound the difficulties of the disabled since many of them are dependent on their families in any approach to the helping services.

A first indication that a number of severely handicapped, dependent people were not being recognised as disabled became apparent in a study of the feasibility of investigating the prevalence of severe motor impairment on a national scale, undertaken by the Social Research Unit at Bedford College for the Department of Health and Social Security.[8] In reply to a postal screening enquiry aimed at identifying the possibly impaired, 86 per cent of the households randomly approached indicated that there were no severely impaired individuals living there. But it was found that 10 per cent of them did contain individuals with severe motor impairments who were not capable of performing independently one or more of the basic activities of daily living.[9] On further investigation the respondents were found to be thinking of the individuals concerned as 'just old' rather than as 'disabled'. In short, they appeared to see the impairments as the natural accompaniment of increasing age, and to be unwilling to classify them as disabled.

The results of this enquiry prompted the Social Research Unit to choose the use of the term 'disability' and the attitude to it as the focus of a research and teaching exercise undertaken by staff and students at Bedford College in July 1969. The study was designed to investigate whether a sample of the general public would acknowledge certain kinds of severe physical impairments as disabling in individuals whom they knew with varying degrees of intimacy, ranging from friends or neighbours, fellow workers, non-household kin, through to household members. Each respondent who indicated that he knew someone with severe sight or hearing impairments or restricted mobility was asked to say whether or not he thought of that individual as being disabled in any way, and to give reasons for his answer. He was also asked whether he knew anyone else whom he thought of as disabled. For a number of reasons the sample was not a fully random one, in particular being biased towards women. None the less the replies from the 613 interviews have considerable interest.

The incidence of contact of the respondents with disabled people was measured using two kinds of definition of disability; first a functional definition based on some limitation of hearing, sight or mobility and a second subjective definition offered by the respondent.

Half our respondents reported knowing someone with impaired hearing, 10 per cent of these having a household member with this condition. Almost a third of the respondents had some contact with a blind or partially sighted individual, while 3 per cent had a household member in this category. Almost half had contact with someone of limited mobility, 8.5 per cent having such a person within their household.

Altogether three-quarters of the respondents had contact with at least one functionally impaired individual. When asked, however, whether the impaired individuals they named were disabled or not and to name other people whom they considered disabled, there appeared to be a reluctance to label those with severe impairments as disabled. Only 53 per cent reported contact with people who they themselves described as disabled compared with the 75 per cent who acknowledged contact with at least one functionally impaired person. Moreover the reluctance appears to extend to individual adults of any age and not to be confined to the elderly.[10] Such a finding suggests that efforts to identify those with severe difficulties, requiring community intervention and help, would reveal only a proportion of such individuals if the general public were required to label themselves, or people known to them, as disabled. For example, if all those who had functional difficulties and were known to the respondents had been considered disabled, 18 per cent of the respondents would have known four or more disabled persons, whereas the actual percentage of respondents who were willing to label four or more of their contacts as disabled was only 7 per cent.

Table 8.3: *Attitudes to the integration or segregation of disabled people in work, leisure activities and housing*

Percentage of respondents favouring:	In work	In leisure activities	In housing
Integration	53	53	71
Segregation	37	30	8
D.K. or 'it depends'	10	17	21
Total N = 100 per cent	613	613	613

In spite of all the known difficulties involved in measuring attitudes,[11] particularly without skilled interviewers, it was still considered interesting in this study to explore attitudes towards disabled people. A non-directive vignette was used to elicit some information about the extent to which people generally considered segregation or integration for the disabled as the desired norm in the field of housing, leisure activities and occupation. Respondents were asked to imagine a man of working age, confined to a wheelchair but not otherwise ill, and to say whether they thought he would be better off working, spending his leisure and living among other disabled people or with non-disabled people.

Very few respondents felt that the paraplegic man of the vignette should live away from his own home and family, but approximately a third felt that he would be better off working and spending his leisure time with other disabled rather than non-disabled people. One of the most interesting findings was that the reasons given for the particular opinion offered (whether integration or segregation was favoured) contained four times as many references to the behaviour of 'normal' people as they did references to the behaviour or needs of the disabled person himself. In short, it appeared that the majority of respondents were more concerned with the probable reaction of non-disabled people to disabled individuals, than with whether or not disabled people themselves would benefit. An alternative explanation might, however, be that the sample saw the ability of disabled people to manage, as dependent primarily on the reactions of non-disabled people to them.

One of the hypotheses of the research was that the views expressed in response to the vignette would vary according to whether or not the respondents were in personal contact with disabled persons. Thus it was expected that those who had personal contacts with disabled people would be more likely to express integrationist as opposed to segregationist views than would those with no contact. This view was examined in relation to both the subjective definition of disablement, and the objective functional impairment definition used.

Table 8.4: *Percentage of respondents with and without contact with functionally impaired and subjectively defined disabled favouring segregation for the paraplegic*

	Functionally impaired		Subjectively defined disabled	
Percentage definitely favouring segregation	Some contact	No contact	Some contact	No contact
At work	25	25	20	33
In leisure	29	27	27	33
In housing	8	19	10	13
Total N = 100 per cent[a]	385–323	146–127	268–243	245–210

[a] The percentages are based only on respondents who gave either a clear segregationist or a clear integrationist answer to each question. Those answers with reservations or unclear were not included.

In relation to work, there was no difference between the proportions of those who had and those who had not had contact with objectively defined functionally impaired people expressing integrationist attitudes, when the 10 per cent whose answers were neither clearly integrationist nor segregationist were excluded. When the respondents were asked about their contacts with people they described as disabled, however, those with contact were more likely to favour integration than those who had no such contacts. A similar pattern, although rather less marked, emerged with respect to leisure activities. Although the overall proportion of respondents definitely favouring segregation in housing was considerably smaller than in the areas of work and leisure, there was a tendency for more people without personal contact, on either definition of disability, to favour segregation. Little difference was found between the attitudes of men and women towards segregation in leisure activities and housing, but men were considerably more likely than women to accept disabled people in the normal work situation. It was expected that those with the most intimate contact with disabled people, that is, those with disabled people in their own households, would be the most likely to hold integrationist views. In fact this was not the case. A significantly higher proportion of those with a disabled person in their own household than of those without such a close contact favoured segregation of the disabled in at least two out of the three spheres of activity. In the sample as a whole, 15 per cent of all respondents predominantly favoured segregation, compared with 27 per cent of the respondents who had a physically impaired member in their household, and 33 per cent of those with a household member whom they themselves defined as disabled. This conclusion was supported by the additional finding that a significantly higher percentage of respondents with a physically impaired person within their household, than of the total sample, favoured segregation rather than integration for the disabled in housing and in leisure activities, though not in work.

The reason for this unexpected finding cannot be found in the survey itself. It may be that some of those who were intimately involved with seriously disabled persons were more aware than others of their 'special' needs. The finding, however, is a salutory reminder that, for whatever reason, relatives may not be automatically willing to countenance measures aimed at integrating disabled people into the 'normal' economic and social activities of the society. Such attitudes may well spring from the experiences which such families have had in supporting their disabled relatives, and, to overcome them, it will be necessary to design policies which help families as much as the disabled themselves.

Finally there was further disturbing evidence in this study that the general public may be willing to accept a low standard of living as an inevitable accompaniment of disability, in the finding that 67 per cent of the respondents thought that the disabled people whom they knew were not in need of any further help from outside their families and considered that 'enough was being done' for them.

Emotional deprivation in disability

The psychological aspects of the interaction between the disabled and the non-disabled have formed the subject of observation and detailed experimental research in the United States. Erving Goffman postulated that a person who differs in a negatively valued way from the norms of his society tends to experience social and emotional deprivation in that society.[12] He claimed that such a person elicits responses from his social environment which are consistently stereotyped, inhibited and over-controlled, and so will find difficulty in developing sensitivity and skill in human relationships. Kleck has supported this thesis by experimental work,[13] comparing the amount of eye contact, which is held to be an important indicator of the quality of inter-personal communication, which occurred in social interaction between two non-disabled people, and the amount which took place when one of the subjects, unknown to the other, simulated disability by sitting in a specially constructed wheelchair. He found significantly less eye contact in this latter situation than in the former one.

Goffman suggested that this kind of stereotyped response of 'normals' to any class of 'deviants' increases the social distance between them, the stereotyping acting as a self-perpetuating phenomenon. Kleck found, however, that when apparently disabled and non-disabled persons were involved in teaching situations, although the non-disabled teacher initially appeared to over-praise the work of disabled pupils significantly more than that of non-disabled pupils, the distortion diminished over time. The apparent contradiction between Goffman and Kleck's findings may be a result of the latter's use of simulated disability in the experiments, since those taking part in the disabled role would have no prior experience of behaviour in this role and consequently no history of deprivation in social interaction. The Social Research Unit finding, reported above, that close and continuing contact with a disabled person appears to be related to segregationist attitudes about disability, would lend support to Goffman's thesis rather than to Kleck's.

Kleck's experiments, however, suggest that in interactions between non-disabled and disabled people a process of 'labelling' or responding to another individual on the basis of selecting only one of his infinitely numerous characteristics is taking place. It is hardly surprising that the physically disabled should resent such a process which denies their individuality.[14]

Problems of social distance and negative self-evaluation may be even more acute when the disability is congenital, or acquired during early childhood rather than in adult life. Richardson[15] studied the attitudes of various groups of children towards disability in other children, comparing different races and nationalities and including both disabled and non-disabled children. His research subjects were shown pictures of children of their own age each with a different kind of disability, as well as a picture of a child with no disability, and were asked to rank the pictures from most preferred to least preferred playmate. Richardson described his findings as 'the emergence of an attitude', since almost all the subjects including the disabled children themselves, produced very similar rank preference orders, in which the non-disabled child emerged as the most preferred playmate. This implies that not only are children with disabilities likely to encounter negative attitudes; they are also likely to share these attitudes themselves.

Using information collected at summer camps attended by both disabled and non-disabled children Richardson also described the effects of physical disability on child socialisation. He found that at the first meeting between a disabled child and a group of non-disabled children, the non-disabled child who was most isolated from his classmates, was the most likely to become the friend of a disabled child. A similar phenomenon was observed by Davis in the social relationships formed by a group of children leaving hospital with residual impairment after contracting polio.[16] The loss to the child in terms of impeding the development of social skills is cumulative.

Conclusion

The studies reported in this paper have demonstrated the considerable material deprivation experienced by disabled people in our society, as well as the limitations imposed on their leisure activities and full participation in the affairs of the community. In addition to physical difficulties they are also likely to experience emotional deprivation.

The studies have also indicated the difficulties of achieving far-reaching change because they show that in interaction between the disabled and non-disabled diffidence and anxiety occur on both sides. 'Normal' people find difficulty in accepting the disabled fully, while the disabled find difficulty in accepting the help which is available since it involves a process of self-labelling which may result in a loss of self-esteem. Any radical improvement in the conditions of the disabled in society requires, therefore, a concerted effort by the disabled themselves, by those who care for them and by public policy makers to study needs and to change the attitude of the general public.

NOTES

[1] See Chapter 9 this volume.

[2] A. I. Harris, *Handicapped and Impaired in Great Britain* (London, 1971). Judith Buckle, *Work and Housing of impaired persons in Great Britain* (London, 1971). Also studies in progress in the Social Research Unit, Bedford College.

[3] *The Economics of Disability*, Disablement Income Group, Paper No. 8. (London, 1968).

[4] Peter Townsend, *The Disabled in Society* (London, 1967).

[5] *Ministry of Labour Gazette*, Vol. LXXV (1967).

[6] The hospital authorities helped to trace these patients, and the director enclosed a covering letter with the postal questionnaire, explaining the purpose of the inquiry and urging them to respond.

[7] See Chapter 9 this volume.

[8] M. Jefferys, J. B. Millard, M. Hyman, M. D. Warren, 'A Set of Tests for Measuring Motor Impairment', *Journal of Chronic Diseases*, Vol. 22 (1969).

[9] S. Katz, *et al.* 'A new classification of functional status in Activities in Daily Living', *Journal of Chronic Diseases*, Vol. 9 (1959).

[10] Among cases reported with the listed conditions, the elderly (over 65 years) were as likely to be described by respondents as disabled as those who were under 65. That is, there were comparable proportions of elderly among both those acknowledged as impaired who were considered disabled and who were not so considered.

[11] L. S. Liss, 'Verbal attitudes and overt behaviour', *Social Forces*, No. 44 (1965).

[12] E. Goffman, *Stigma* (London, 1968).

[13] R. Kleck, 'Physical stigma and non-verbal cues emitted in face to face interaction', *Human Relations*, Vol. 21 (1968). 'Physical stigma and task oriented instructions', forthcoming.

[14] T. Dembo, G. Lavieu Leviton, B. A. Wright, 'Adjustment to misfortune – a problem of Social-Psychological Rehabilitation', *Artificial Limbs,* Vol. 3 (1956).

[15] S. A. Richardson, '*The Effects of Physical Disability on the Socialisation of a Child*'. Personal communication.

[16] F. Davis, *Passage through crisis* (New York, 1963).

Poverty and class consciousness

9

Politics and poverty

RALPH MILIBAND

In their recent study of poverty in Nottingham, Ken Coates and Richard Silburn have rightly noted that 'poverty has many dimensions, each of which must be studied separately, but which in reality constitute an interrelated network of deprivations'.[1] There is one element in this 'network of deprivations' which is crucial, and with which this paper will be concerned, namely the political element. On the whole, 'the politics of poverty', which has received a large amount of attention in the United States, has been largely neglected in Britain: too little effort has been made to situate it and analyse it in the context of the political system, and to 'conceptualise' it in political terms. In the vast and constantly growing literature on the subject of poverty, the phenomenon is commonly taken as an economic, social, cultural or psychological condition. But the concept of poverty needs to be extended to the political realm as well, and to include the notion of political deprivation.

Political deprivation is less immediately visible than other forms of poverty. On the surface, the poor are as much in possession of civic and political rights as anybody else: they are full citizens whose equality is expressed in their equal right of access to the ballot box and to all the other means of political pressure and redress available in the political system. In real life, however, and against the background of other forms of deprivation, this equal citizenship is, in political terms, very largely robbed of its meaning. For the deprived not only lack economic resources: they also, and relatedly, lack political resources as well. Economic deprivation is a source of political deprivation; and political deprivation in turn helps to maintain and confirm economic deprivation. In other words, the different elements of the 'network of deprivation' reinforce each other.

By 'the poor', I mean here those people whose total economic resources are so low that they live around or below the level corresponding to the poverty line defined by society, or rather by the relevant State agencies. Professor Atkinson discusses the various estimates of numbers involved elsewhere in this volume.[2] But even Sir Keith Joseph, then the Conservative

Shadow spokesman on social affairs, suggested before the General Election of June 1970 that between seven and ten million people lived on or below the poverty line, 'a fact', *The Times* recalled him as saying, 'that left no room for complacency'.[3]

Of course, all such figures are somewhat arbitrary, since they depend among other things upon the level at which the poverty line is fixed. Still, it is not now seriously to be argued (which does not mean that it is not often done) that a very substantial minority of the British people live 'in poverty', and are deprived of necessities and amenities which would now be generally regarded as minimal. In fact, this kind of formulation greatly understates the extent of poverty, without inverted commas. There is a lot of middle class hypocrisy about this. For on any kind of reckoning of what would be regarded as a reasonable 'style of life' by most people in the middle classes, not to speak of the truly rich, the figures would have to be greatly extended and would need to encompass a very substantial part of the British people indeed, including the larger part of the wage earning population.

For the purpose of the present discussion, however, the concept of poverty may be more narrowly construed. But it is nevertheless important not to overlook an essential characteristic of those officially designated as poor, namely their class membership. The tendency is to speak of the poor as the old; or as members of fatherless families: or as the chronic sick and the disabled; or as the unemployed and their families; or as the low paid. But old age, membership of fatherless families, sickness and disablement, and even unemployment are not as such necessarily synonymous with poverty. Some people in these categories are not poor at all: to be an old, ailing and an idle *rentier* may not be agreeable, but neither need it mean poverty. Nor even are some members of the middle classes who happen to be low-paid 'in poverty', since they may command a variety of private resources which enable them to live in reasonable comfort. Old age, disablement, low pay, unemployment, etc., become synonymous with poverty in so far as those involved are members of the working class – recruited, so to speak, from its ranks; and the point may be emphasised by reference to the fact that one of the largest categories of those living in poverty is made up of families whose head, though in full-time employment, *is* a member of the working class, at the lowest rung of the wage scale. Thus, Mr Giles Radice, summarising a TUC *Report on Low Pay*, notes that 'in September 1968, 8 per cent of full-time adult men workers (nearly a million) and 70 per cent of full-time adult women workers earned less than £15 a week. Almost two million men earned less than £17 a week';[4] and Professor Townsend has similarly noted that 'families in which the head is in full-time work but has either a relatively low wage or several children or both . . . is three million'.[5] The basic fact is that the poor are an integral part of the working class – its poorest and most disadvantaged stratum. They need to be seen as such, as part of a continuum, the more so as many workers who are not 'deprived' in the official sense live in permanent danger of entering the ranks of the deprived; and that they share in any case many of the disadvantages which afflict the deprived.[6] Poverty is a class thing, closely linked to a *general* situation of class inequality; and ultimately remediable, as will be argued later, in *general* class terms.

In the nineteenth century, 'the poor are always with us' was intended to suggest that, though help to the poor might be a charitable duty, poverty itself must be reckoned to be an inevitable, permanent part of the social landscape, a fact of nature. However, with the extension of the suffrage, the emergence of organised labour as a political force, and the spread of a democratic rhetoric, it became less and less fashionable for politicians to suggest, or to be thought to accept the view, that poverty must always be with us. In the twentieth century, and with ever greater emphasis, nothing less than a commitment to the complete eradication of poverty would do; and declarations of war against poverty, slum housing, and slum schools became the common currency of politics. Introducing his 1909 Budget, Lloyd George announced that 'this is a war budget for raising money to wage implacable warfare against poverty and squalidness'. 'I cannot help believing', he also said, 'that before this generation has passed away, we shall have advanced a great step towards that good time when poverty and the degradation which always follows in its camp will be as remote to the people of this country as the wolves which once infested its forests'.[7] Some twenty-five years later, Sir Hilton Young, the Minister of Health in the 'National Government' of Ramsay MacDonald, was reported as saying that 'twelve months hence the slums should be falling, according to present prospects, five times as fast, till the work reached its maximum speed two years hence. Five years was not an unduly long time in which to cure an evil which had been growing for a hundred.'[8] Twenty-two years later, Mr Duncan Sandys, the Minister of Housing in the Eden Government announced that 'the success of the house building drive has now made it possible for the Government to adopt a much more comprehensive housing policy. From now on, we attack on all fronts . . . we think there may be about a million slum houses. If this figure proves correct, I suggest we should aim at breaking the back of the problem within ten years.'[9]

By the 1950s, however, there had occurred a shift in attitude towards the 'problem' of poverty. While it was conceded that deprivation might not yet be a thing of the past, 'responsible opinion' was generally agreed that, because of the immense changes which were held to have occurred since the Second World War, and which were epitomised by the notion of the Welfare State, the 'problem' was well on the way to eradication. Indeed, those whose fate evoked the loudest laments in the late 1940s and 1950s were not the working-class poor, but the middle and upper classes, pitilessly ground down by a crushing tax structure. As Professor Lionel Robbins (as he was then) put it in 1955, in a phrase which deserves to live, 'relentlessly, year by year, it [i.e. the tax structure] is pushing us towards collectivism and propertyless uniformity';[10] and one of the most dismal features of that dismal epoch was the way in which a host of Labour 'revisionists' joined in the fabrication and dissemination of the myth that a massive redistribution downwards had occurred in Britain.[11]

In the perspective then prevalent, the poor were resolutely pushed out of view; and in so far as they remained in view at all, they were mostly considered as a cluster of special cases in otherwise ever more 'affluent' and 'post-capitalist' societies. The very concept of the 'affluent society', and the emphasis of its inventor that poverty *was* a matter of special cases,[12] helped to exile the poor to the outer periphery of society, as mere minorities which were either unlucky or in various ways inadequate, often even perversely and deliberately inadequate.

This crassly complacent but widely held view came under severe challenge in the late 1950s and early 1960s: before long, poverty had been 'rediscovered', in the United States and in Britain, not merely as a pimple on the otherwise smooth and smiling face of the 'affluent society', but as a major blight. Though it should not be exaggerated, this wider recognition of the existence and extent of poverty is an obviously positive fact, and much praise is due to academics like Titmuss, Abel-Smith, Townsend and others who, as far as Britain was concerned, contributed to that wider recognition. On the other hand, it is crucial to the understanding of the politics of poverty to appreciate that recognition, though very necessary, cannot by any means be taken as a guarantee that much will therefore be done about it. In 1959, Harold Wilson spoke of 'the burning desire among Labour Party members at all levels to end poverty and to advance far beyond the 1945–51 reforms to a much more real equality'; and he also then said that 'given a Labour victory, the test is this: will there be twelve months from now a narrowing of the gap between rich and poor, quite apart from any general upward movement there may be as a result of increased national production? That answer is, quite simply, that there will be.'[13] But eleven years later, six of them years of a Labour Government presided over by the same Harold Wilson, the argument was not whether poverty had been reduced, never mind eradicated, but whether it had *increased*, and even those who argued that it had not dared not advance the claim that much had been done about it.

What this points to is the basic fact that whether poverty is seriously tackled or not does not simply depend on its recognition – Lincoln was entirely wrong when he said that a society cannot live half slave and half free. It depends first and foremost on the respective strength of conflicting forces operating in society, some making for the persistence of poverty, and others working against its persistence; and the trouble, for the poor, is that the forces operating against them are very much stronger than those working in their favour. What is involved here is not recognition, or the discovery of the right policies, or the creation of the right administrative framework, or even the good will of power-holders. The matter goes deeper than that, and concerns the distribution of power in society.

Tackling poverty must be taken to mean two different things. It may mean more ample provision for the immediate improvement in the circumstances of the poor; and it may mean something much larger, namely the actual eradication of poverty. Both are fundamentally political questions, though of a very different order; and it is necessary to treat them separately.

Immediate improvement in the circumstances of the poor requires a variety of public measures, which involves vastly increased public expenditure for the purpose. But the first thing to note in this respect is that there are many other claimants upon public funds, with far more powerful and compelling voices, from large enterprises (which are voracious and effective applicants for public assistance) to the struggling middle classes. The simple fact of the matter is that the poor enter the pressure market, where they enter it at all, from the weakest possible position: that of course is one of the main reasons, if not *the* main reason, why they remain poor. Mr Ben Whittaker has observed that 'one of the difficulties in relieving poverty is that whereas other groups which are competing for a share of the national budget such as motorists, businesses or ratepayers have vocal and well organised lobbies, the poor are unseen and unheard'.[14] This, as will be shown later, requires some measure of qualification. But the general point is well taken. I have argued elsewhere that unequal competition is a general and inherent phenomenon in capitalist societies, which negatively affects not only the poor but the working class and the subordinate classes as a whole.[15] But it affects the poor most of all. They are, as I have suggested earlier, an integral part of the working class: but many of them constitute its inactive part, and are self-excluded from the defence organisations which organised labour has brought into being, and which have helped to improve its bargaining position. The point applies to the old, the very young, the chronic sick and the disabled. Nor of course are old age, chronic sickness and disablement conducive to autonomous, sustained and effective pressure.

As for the low-paid adult wage earners, many of them tend to be found in industries with a large number of small enterprises, with a contracting and ageing labour force, and often with an above average proportion of low-paid women workers[16] – though it is also worth noting that one-quarter of the lowest paid workers are public employees and that, as J. Edmunds and G. Radice have observed, low pay 'is present throughout the whole of the economy'.[17] The circumstances of low paid workers tend to discourage organisation, or have at least hitherto tended to discourage organisation – the matter is by no means beyond redress. At any rate, poorly paid workers have often been poorly unionised, although public employees are a notable exception.

This weakness of the poor in terms of the pressure they can exercise has a direct bearing on the attitude to poverty of what many people find it possible, apparently without irony, to call 'the community'. 'The community' is in fact strongly ambivalent about the poor. On the one hand, its political culture now incorporates a greater awareness of the existence of poverty and (probably) a greater degree of 'compassion' for the plight of the poor, or at least of some categories of the poor. It is proper to be moved by television programmes on slum dwellers, or the old, or deprived children. On the other hand, such emotions do not, in practice, have much concrete consequence. More important, there are also strong contrary emotions at work. Thus, there is a widespread suspicion, which affects all classes, that many people in poverty 'have only themselves to blame'; and there is a corresponding resentment that such people should be 'getting something for nothing'. Both the suspicion and the resentment are naturally much encouraged by official denunciation of 'scroungers' and 'layabouts'; and while such denunciations may be qualified by the suggestion that they only apply to small numbers of people, it may be surmised that it is the denunciation rather than the qualification which makes the impact. As Dwight Macdonald has also noted for the United States, but the point is of application to Britain, 'there is a monotony about the injustices suffered by the poor that perhaps accounts for the lack of interest the rest of society shows in them. Everything seems to go wrong with them. They never win. It's just boring'.[18]

More generally, the prevailing system of values legitimates enormous inequalities of income and property, and thus makes it acceptable that people earning £1,000 a month, or more, should tell people earning £1,000 a year, or indeed a good deal less, that their unreasonable demands are threatening the country with ruin. Such a moral (or rather immoral) climate works against the poor; and in so far as the poor themselves are affected by the prevailing culture, as they are, its character and tone greatly serve to foster acceptance of their condition. If there is any virtue at all in the notion of a 'culture of poverty', much of it must be seen as an *induced* culture, calculated to produce guilt and to reinforce passivity.

The administrative services of the 'Welfare State' are themselves part of this induced culture. In making contact with these services, the deprived 'citizen' enters a world which is alien, which is most likely to appear hostile, and in relation to which he feels himself on trial – as indeed he is. Professor Abel-Smith has noted that 'poor families are already caged in a very labyrinth of means tests'.[19] Mr Reddin also writes that 'the Ministry of Social Security operates at national level perhaps the most extensive means-tested system in the world. At local authority level means tested schemes are myriad'[20]; and he adds that 'the middle class versions of the means test, such as that for university grants, tend to be more civilized and socially acceptable devices than anything to be found among the lower income groups. An exploration of the range of means tests is akin to some voyage into the underworld – with snares on every side and confusion at either hand.' In this perspective, it is perhaps no great wonder that so many people do not take up the benefits to which they are entitled. Information about benefits is in any case inadequate. But even when it is available, the human cost may well be deemed by the recipient to be too high.

The point here is not that the agencies administering relief are necessarily staffed by heartless bureaucrats; but that the system they administer, and the role and responsibilities which they assume, have their own imperative requirements; and the requirements are such as to suggest to the poor that the war which is being waged is not against poverty but against them. In this war, they are also likely to feel that they are found to be the losers. Such a feeling is not conducive to effective anger.

Given the weakness of the poor, and their consequent inability to impose their needs upon the political culture, governments are under no great compulsion to pay close attention to these needs. Moreover, they are, as I have argued, under strong pressure to heed other and conflicting claims – and may in any case be disposed to do so. This imbalance is further increased in periods of economic difficulty and crisis (which means more or less permanently), when calls for cuts in public expenditure are loudly heard on all sides, and when such calls are powerfully reinforced by the pressure of international creditors. In such circumstances, and given these pressures, the poor stand by far the best chance of being sacrificed on the altar of the 'national interest'; whoever else may not suffer, they do.

This, however, is not the whole story: the poor are not altogether absent from the political system. For one thing, various categories of the deprived are spoken for by various organisations, which press their claims upon central and local authorities. But most of them are relatively weak pressure groups with no over-developed sense of deference to authority, such as patronage, which is not conducive to effective pushing. Even pressure groups with no over-developed sense of deference to authority, such as with Child Poverty Action Group, work within limits fairly narrowly circumscribed by slender resources. But there is more to it than slender resources. The experience of the Child Poverty Action Group indeed provides a good illustration of the limits of pressure exercised *on behalf* of the poor. The years of the Labour Government might have been thought to provide an exceptionally favourable climate for pressure by reasoned persuasion, or even to require very little pressure at all: after all, some of the leading figures of the CPAG had ready access to entirely sympathetic ministers. That they should not have been able to achieve more than they did[21] suggests clearly enough that such endeavours are most unlikely, by themselves, to have more than a marginal impact. Even this is better than nothing, particularly if it is translated, as it must be, into individual terms. But marginal it nevertheless remains; and the impact of such groups on a Conservative Government is more than likely to be even smaller, to put it at its best.

Social workers have also sometimes been considered as an actual or potential 'pressure group' on behalf of the poor, on an individual and local basis, or even on a national scale. This is possible, but needs to be seen in the context of a role which is profoundly ambiguous. On the one hand, social workers have responsibilities towards their 'clients', which may involve a strong commitment. On the other hand, they have responsibilities towards the authorities which employ them, and must work the system of which they are a part. The two roles, it should be obvious, are not necessarily congruent; and they may well be extremely incongruous. Much emphasis has been placed in recent years on the need for better trained, better equipped and better paid social workers; and for a more integrated social service. All this is no doubt desirable. But it would not remove the ambiguity of the place of social workers in the system, and it would not of itself turns them into more effective voices on behalf of the poor.[22]

In terms of pressure group politics, the most important of all such voices is – or could be – that of the trade union movement; and both individual unions and Trade Union Congresses have, in the last few years, shown much greater concern for low-paid workers and for the deprived generally than in earlier periods. Given the fragmentation of organised labour, its sectional divisions and its usually low level of solidarity, this must be reckoned as progress indeed. More important than the passage of resolutions on low pay or higher benefits or equal pay, however, is the general combativity of organised labour, and its rejection of policies of wage 'restraint'. In its attempts to foist such policies upon the trade union movement, the Labour Government often argued that such 'restraint' was necessary, *inter alia*, to raise the wages of the low-paid. All experience suggests that the low-paid do not gain from the 'restraint' of other wage earners. On the contrary, their chances of improvement are closely linked with the level of militancy of the trade unions, and upon the latter's determination to assert the claims of labour, not only in regard to wages but over the whole range of economic and social policy.

In the end, however, efforts on behalf of the poor need to be supplemented by action on the part of the poor themselves. In fact, the effectiveness of efforts on their behalf depends, in part at least, on the pressure generated by the poor. In this respect too, one of the few general laws of politics holds, namely that those who do not speak for themselves are not likely to be effectively spoken for by others.

For the poor, the obstacles are very great indeed. But they are not, in all cases, insuperable. For the low-paid workers in particular, militant trade unionism, with the support of other sections of the trade union movement, offers an avenue of improvement which more and more such workers have been taking up. And there have, in recent years, been many examples to show that at local level and on a variety of specific issues, such as housing, rent and amenities, many deprived people are not nearly so irremediably helpless as is sometimes suggested.[23] With the aid of outside helpers, often serving as catalysts of organisation and action, some of the deprived have shown that, by their own efforts, they could focus attention on their needs and grievances and force, at least at local level, a partial alleviation of their plight. Very slowly and fitfully, the lesson is being learnt that, in the words of one writer, 'conflict is the method most likely to achieve the stated objectives in deprived areas ... Only conflict strategy has any record of providing the forces which stimulate inhabitants to take control of their lives and redress the inadequacies of housing, play space, etc.'[24]

This 'conflict strategy', it should be noted, has to be planned and carried out outside the 'normal' channels of grassroots politics. Permanent insecurity and the daily battle against grinding want in any case discourage involvement in established, structured and routinised forms of political activity. Such activity tends to be the preserve of the well-fed. But the discouragement turns into a fatal inhibition by virtue of the fact that 'normal' political activity, in the present state of British party politics, is most likely to appear not only alien but irrelevant to the deprived. Coates and Silburn note that 'it is difficult to find any plausible reasons why anyone in St. Ann's [Nottingham] should believe that the organisations to which they could conceivably adhere might in some way assist them in solving any of their actual problems'.[25] The comment is bitter but accurate, and of much wider application than for St. Ann's; and it obviously is of most immediate application to local Labour parties. Individual members of such parties may play a role in the organisation of the deprived; and the parties themselves may engage in this or that form of charitable activity on behalf of people in need. But they are not likely to engage in 'conflict strategy'. In many cases, the conflict will be about action (or the lack of action) by Labour authorities, which local Labour parties are expected to support, not to oppose, or at least not to oppose with any sustained and systematic vigour. Equally or more important, most of these parties dwell in a world of politics from which conflict and direct action are excluded or frowned upon, as likely to give them a bad 'image', to be politically divisive and electorally damaging. In this perspective, the political 'apathy' of the poor is not simply to be attributed to their immediate circumstances, but also to a quite realistic awareness that their participation in routine politics is not likely to hold any serious promise of rapid amelioration; and this is what they require. This is not to argue that which party dominates a local council is necessarily a matter of no consequence to the poor; only that they cannot be expected to believe that direct involvement in local party activity is the effective channel for the achievement of immediate remedy.

At the same time action outside the confines of established and institutionalised politics, whether effective or not, would seem fated to remain spasmodic and localised. It has, on occasion, been suggested in recent years that what the poor need is not a Poverty Programme but a Poverty Movement; or rather that such a programme would only seriously be set in train if a sufficiently formidable movement of the poor forced it upon an otherwise complacent and even hostile political system. But such a movement has little chance of coming into being. The creation of a national and viable movement of any kind is a major enterprise; and the difficulties are, in this instance, enormously magnified by the total situation of the poor. Moreover, the poor are not a homogeneous and undifferentiated grouping, and the fact of deprivation is in itself insufficient to constitute the minimal unifying element which such a national movement requires. The poor certainly need to turn themselves into a considerable nuisance *vis-à-vis* 'the community', rather than remain an object of virtuous 'compassion'. But their best hope of doing so probably lies in local action, coupled of course with whatever pressure they and associations speaking on their behalf can bring to bear on relevant national organisations and the State itself.

This is not a comforting perspective. But even this perspective is in a crucial sense *too* comforting. For while various forms of pressure and action *can* achieve improvements for this or that section of the deprived, or even for the deprived generally, and are therefore eminently desirable, they will not 'abolish poverty', even on the present minimal definition of that term, and allowing the most generous reckoning of their possible impact. The reason for saying this is that 'abolishing poverty' in Britain requires very much more than a greater measure of concern for the poor, or stronger pressure on their behalf, or an 'overall social strategy', or a higher level of economic growth, or more public expenditure, or a sympathetic Government. All this may make an indent. But removing the blight requires the transformation of the economic structures in which it is embedded.

Mr C. A. R. Crosland has argued that 'growth is the essential condition for a civilised level of social spending'.[26] But essential or not, it is not a *sufficient* condition for the purpose. With this, Mr Crosland agreed, and noted that, given a satisfactory level of economic growth (itself problematic but let it pass), major political decisions remain to be made. But this is precisely the point at which the argument turns into obfuscation. For what is suggested is that a Government armed with good intentions, determination and the right social policies (i.e. a Labour Government – but let that pass too) *would* be able to eliminate poverty and much else as well. However, the implementation of the right social policies also requires the implementation of a whole range of fiscal and economic policies. This is not to be had without a massive extension of public control over economic life in general, and without genuine as opposed to rhetorical planning of the 1965 variety. The point here is not that there is nothing to suggest that a Labour Government, on any reasonable projection, would be prepared to embark on such an enterprise: it is rather that such an enterprise cannot be carried through in the context of a predominantly private enterprise economy, the 'commanding heights' of which are securely held by men whose concern is *not* with the right social priorities and all else this requires – as indeed why should they be? And their power, based upon their control of key areas of economic life, would be sufficient to cripple the purpose of Governments much more determined than any Labour Government is ever likely to be. In common with all his colleagues who now shape the Labour Party's orientations, Mr Crosland takes for granted, explicitly accepts as a datum, the indefinite perpetuation of the basic features of the present economic system. This being the case, talk of the 'elimination of poverty' is no more than an illusion or a deception. *Something*, to stress again a point made earlier, can be done by an even modestly reforming Government. But the truth – and it is a bitter truth – is that the abolition of poverty will have to wait until the abolition of the system which breeds it comes on to the agenda; and this is a question which far transcends the issue of poverty itself.

NOTES

[1] K. Coates and R. Silburn, *Poverty: The Forgotten Englishmen* (London, 1970), p. 45.

[2] See Chapter 2 of this volume.

[3] *The Times*, 9 September 1970.

[4] *New Society*, 5 March 1970.

[5] P. Townsend, 'Poverty, Socialism and Labour in Power' in W. Rogers (ed.), *Socialism and Affluence* (London, 1967), p. 47.

[6] 'Although it is true that poverty has been pushed away from the daily experience of a majority of working people, it is also true that it has been removed to only a short distance – the distance of a few weekly pay packets . . . Poverty is thus a condition to be anticipated by a much larger proportion of people than those who are poor at any one time, at some stage of their lives. Poverty is thus not merely a problem of special groups, or of other people, but an atmosphere in which large numbers of people live their lives, and which threatens at any time to assume a more concrete presence.' R. Williams (ed.), *May Day Manifesto* (London, 1968), pp. 22–3.

[7] Quoted in C. I. Waxman, *Poverty: Power and Politics* (New York, 1968), p. x.

[8] Quoted in *New Left Review* by Raphael Samuel, James Kincaid and Elizabeth Slater, 'But Nothing Happens', No. 13–14 (1962), p. 39.

[9] *New Left Review*, Nos. 13–14 (1962), p. 40.

[10] L. Robbins, 'Notes on Public Finance', *Lloyds Bank Review*, No. 38 (1955), p. 19.

[11] For which see J. Saville, 'Labour and Income Redistribution' in R. Miliband and J. Saville (eds.), *The Socialist Register, 1965* (London, 1965). For a discussion of the facts about redistribution of income see this volume Chapters 2 and 3.

[12] K. J. Galbraith, *The Affluent Society* (London, 1958), p. 254.

[13] *New Statesman*, 3 October 1959, quoted in Paul Foot, *The Politics of Harold Wilson* (London, 1968), p. 145.

[14] B. Whittaker, *Participation and Poverty* (London, 1968), p. 16.

[15] R. Miliband, *The State in Capitalist Society* (London, 1969).

[16] See J. Marquand, 'Which are the Low-Paid Workers?' in *British Journal of Industrial Relations*, Vol. v (1967).

[17] J. Edmunds and G. Radice, *Low Pay* (London, 1969), p. 7.

[18] D. Macdonald, 'Our Invisible Poor', in L. A. Ferman, J. L. Kornbluh and H. Haber (eds), *Poverty in America: A Book of Readings* (Ann Arbor, 1965), p. 18.

[19] *Social Services for All?* (London, 1968), p. 113.

[20] *Social Services for All?* p. 7. In December, 1968, Mr Whittaker noted that 'there are some 3,146 different forms of means tests in Britain; the Ministry of Social Security alone issued over 3,000 types of claims forms for various forms of benefit' (*ibid*, p. 19).

[21] For which see CPAG, *Poverty and the Labour Government* (London, 1970).

[22] For a useful discussion of the status and role of social workers, see A. Sinfield, *Which Way for Social Work?* (London, 1969).

[23] See, e.g. 'A Tenant's Notebook', *International Socialism*, No. 31 (1967–8).

[24] R. Holan, 'The Wrong Poverty Programme', *New Society,* 20 March 1969.

[25] K. Coates and R. Silburn, *Poverty: The Forgotten Englishmen,* p. 115.

[26] C. A. R. Crosland, 'The Price and the Prize of Sustained Growth', *The Times,* 26 September 1970.

10

Relative deprivation: a comparison of English and Swedish manual workers[1]

RICHARD SCASE

Recent studies of the British class structure suggest that the awareness of inequality, particularly among manual workers, is extremely limited. Runciman, for example, found that only a small majority of manual workers perceived that there were other occupational groups better off than themselves. When they were aware of inequalities, they made limited comparisons; they tended to mention either other groups of manual workers or individuals who could be compared with a specific aspect of their own personal situation.[2] Hence respondents referred to 'people with no children', 'people on night work', 'people with good health', and so on; comments which suggested that manual workers did not perceive of inequality as a structural feature of society, but rather as a consequence of personal effort and circumstance.

Goldthorpe and his colleagues came to similar conclusions in their study of 'affluent' workers in Luton.[3] They found that 54 per cent of a sample of manual workers conceived of the class structure in terms of a 'money' model, with a large central class consisting of most manual and white-collar workers, and one or more residual or 'elite' classes, differentiated in terms of wealth, income, and material living standards. As a result, Goldthorpe and his associates suggest that workers' perceptions of their position in the class structure were inconsistent with their roles in the productive process: roles characterised by deprivation in the spheres of decision-making, working conditions, fringe benefits, and status differentials. They argue that these attitudes were derived from social roles outside the work-place and that there was little awareness of inequality as a structural, and socially-organised feature of society.

Adopting a somewhat broader perspective, Inkeles has suggested that different industrial societies have not only similar institutional structures, but also relatively similar value systems,[4] and there are other writers who have claimed that all industrial-capitalist societies generate common ideologies and values which promote among workers 'false consciousness' and a restricted awareness of their *real* position within society.[5] In view of these suggestions it is interesting to consider whether workers in other industrial societies have similar attitudes towards inequality as they have in Britain.

This chapter investigates this issue in relation to the attitudes and opinions of manual workers in England and Sweden.[6] More specifically, the objective is to explore any similarities in the awareness of inequality and the experience of relative deprivation among manual workers in the two countries. If there are such similarities it would lend support to the claims that institutions of different industrial-capitalist societies have similar effects upon the political and cultural socialisation of manual workers; but if there are systematic differences it will be necessary to reconsider these claims.

Because practical difficulties prevented a comparison of random samples of manual workers in England and Sweden, a more restricted investigation had to be undertaken of two groups of English and Swedish workers who were matched according to a number of factors. Both were employed in factories which had several common characteristics.[7] In the first place the work processes of each factory involved converting iron and steel into a range of engineering goods and components. Secondly, the technology was similar except that the Swedish factory was more highly capitalised: consequently a number of the tasks and processes which were undertaken by machinery in the Swedish factory were done by physical labour in the English workshops. Thirdly, both factories produced goods for relatively static, or even contracting markets: there had been no expansion over recent years and there was little expectation among management and workers that this was likely to occur in the forseeable future. At the time of the investigation neither factory was confronted with the threat of redundancies, although there had been some lay-offs in the English factory during the 1950s: there was an assumption among both groups of workers that employment prospects were relatively secure.

While the two factories were similar in terms of these items – product, technology, and market situation – they were not in at least two other respects. Working and employment conditions, by *absolute* standards, were superior in the Swedish factory: this was so for heating, lighting, ventilation, sanitation, for regulations affecting industrial safety and the use of equipment, and for refreshment and recreation facilities. In addition, there were smaller differences in the Swedish factory in the treatment of manual and non-manual workers in such areas as dismissal procedures, systems of payment, and time off from work for personal reasons.[8] But secondly, there were differences in the sizes of the two factories; the Swedish employed 298 manual workers, compared with 972 in the English. Unfortunately it was impossible to select two factories of the same size which could also be matched according to other criteria.[9]

In terms of wage differentials, it was difficult to make precise calculations because in both factories earnings, particularly those of non-manual workers, varied according to age and length of service. Moreover, management, especially in the English factory, were reluctant to disclose detailed information about the structure of wages and salaries. However, they were prepared to give 'approximate' earnings. This information suggested that for the English factory the highest-paid manual workers (skilled) could earn approximately £30 a week, or £1,560 a year, 'senior clerical officers' up to £2,000 a year, and 'senior management' up to £4,500. In the Swedish factory the highest-paid manual workers (skilled) could earn about 3,000 Kr. a month, white collar employees 4,000 Kr., and senior managers up to 6,750 Kr. Thus it appears that in terms of the remuneration of highly-paid manual workers and senior management, there was less inequality in the Swedish workplace than in the English. The earnings of the Swedish senior managers were roughly two-and-a-quarter times more than those of highly-paid manual workers, while those of their English counterparts could be as much as three times greater. However, differences in the earnings of 'affluent' manual workers and white-collar employees were about the same in both workplaces; by the age of about 40, 'higher' white collar workers could be earning something like one-third more.[10]

The samples were limited to groups of workers between the ages of 25 and 54 in order to eliminate those whose careers had not yet been firmly established, and those who were approaching retirement.[11] The analysis also focussed almost exclusively upon married men who provided 85 per cent or more of both samples.

Can these workers be regarded as representative of all manual workers in England and Sweden? Because they were matched according to a number of variables, their general representativeness is extremely limited. They were chosen from industries which, like all industries, have characteristics peculiar to themselves; specific traditions of historical development, industrial conflict and technological change.[12] Factors such as these limit the degree to which it is possible to generalise findings derived from this study but they can be regarded as at least *indicative* of patterns in the two countries which need to be substantiated by more comprehensive investigations.

The data was collected by interviews in the spring and summer of 1970, using schedules printed in English and Swedish[13]; neither sample was aware of its part in an international comparison.[14] The response rate for the Swedish workers was 87 per cent and 73 per cent for the English. This provided 122 completed Swedish schedules and 128 English schedules upon which the present discussion is based.

The results of the enquiry

In his enquiry, Runciman asked respondents, 'Do you think there are any other sorts of people doing noticeably better at the moment than you and your family?' He found that 25 per cent of all respondents and 27 per cent of manual workers stated they could think of no other sorts of people.[15] A similar question was used in the present enquiry: 'Are there any people you can think of who are better off than workers like yourself?' Whereas less than one-tenth of the Swedish sample claimed that they could think of no other people, this opinion was held by more than one-fifth of the English workers.

It is difficult to make international comparisons of wage differentials because, among other things, of differences in the systems of classification

TABLE 10.1: *'Are there any people you can think of who are better off than workers like yourself?'*

	Swedish workers		English workers	
	No.	Per cent	No.	Per cent
Yes	98	80	91	71
No	10	8	28	22
Don't know	14	12	9	7
Total	122	100	128	100

Table 10.2: *Average earnings of occupational groups in Britain and Sweden* (expressed as multiples of average earnings of male unskilled labourers)

	Sweden (1963)	United Kingdom (1960)
Unskilled manual	1.0	1.0
Skilled manual	–	1.5
Foremen	1.4	1.9
Clerks	1.3	1.3
Lower administrative and professional staff	1.8	1.6
Higher administrative and professional staff	3.1	3.5

Source: Extracted from United Nations, *Incomes in Post-War Europe* (1967) Table 5.16

which are used. But Table 10.2, extracted from a United Nations enquiry, suggests that wage differentials between various occupational groups are certainly not fundamentally different in Sweden and the United Kingdom.[16]

In view of this, the difference in the opinions in the two samples suggests that the frequency of relative deprivation was greater among the Swedish respondents than among the English. All those workers who held that there were others better off than themselves were then asked 'What sort of people?'. Whenever possible, the responses were coded according to the actual terms used by workers.

Table 10.3: *'What sort of people?'*

	Swedish workers		English Workers	
	No.	Per cent	No.	Per cent
'Businessmen', 'Directors'	15	15	4	4
'Managers'	2	2	6	7
'Professionals', 'Professional people'	7	7	5	6
'Higher white collar workers'	5	5	–	–
'White collar workers' or specific non-manual occupation mentioned	15	15	3	3
'Educated people'	7	7	–	–
'The rich'	1	1	1	1
Specific manual occupation mentioned	43	44	69	76
Other, and non-classifiable responses	3	3	3	3
Don't know	–	–	–	–
Total	98	100	91	100

Table 10.3 shows that the Swedish workers were more likely to mention non-manual occupations than were the English sample. Indeed various non-manual occupational titles, together with 'educated people', and 'the rich', were mentioned by 53 per cent of the Swedish workers compared with only 21 per cent of the workers in the English sample. On the other hand, 76 per cent of the English respondents mentioned various manual occupations compared with only 44 per cent of the Swedish workers; a difference between the two samples of 32 per cent. In these responses, both samples stressed similar occupations – those in the car, steel and dock industries. The only major difference between the two groups was that the Swedish respondents gave greater emphasis to the earnings of building construction workers.[17]

Clearly the evidence indicates that the awareness of inequality was not the same for both groups of workers; in fact, the responses of the English workers were fairly consistent with those obtained by Runciman in his analysis. He found that only 19 per cent of his sample of manual workers who claimed that there were other people better off than themselves, mentioned non-manual workers.[18] The present enquiry confirms Runciman's contention that English manual workers make highly restricted comparisons when evaluating their own economic position in society. The Swedish workers, on the other hand, articulated a greater frequency of relative deprivation and this seems to have been a consequence of the adoption of more broadly-based comparative reference groups, which incorporated both non-manual and manual occupations. The differences in the two groups of respondents were particularly striking in view of the fact that wage differentials, both within the factories and the two countries, were not fundamentally different.

The greater frequency of relative deprivation among the Swedish workers was confirmed by responses to questions which invited comparisons between specific aspects of their own work roles and those of white-collar workers employed in the same factory.[19] Both samples were asked for their opinions about earnings, possibilities for promotion, and conditions of work. Respondents were asked 'What do you think of the money you earn compared with that of white-collar workers. Would you say that it was "much better", "better", "about the same", "worse" or "much worse"?' Among the Swedish workers, 63 per cent claimed that it was 'worse' or 'much worse', while only 4 per cent stated that it was 'better' or 'much better'. A further 30 per cent suggested it was 'about the same' for both manual and white-collar workers. By contrast, 44 per cent of the English sample said their earnings were 'better' or 'much better' and only 23 per cent thought that they were 'worse' or 'much worse'. There were 25 per cent who claimed they were 'about the same'. Clearly the Swedish respondents felt more relatively deprived in terms of their earnings than the English workers.

Asked about possibilities for promotion, both samples were asked to name an occupation which they would be most likely to get if they were given such promotion. For both groups of workers 'foreman', and various supervisory manual occupations such as inspector or chargehand were the most frequently mentioned – by well over 80 per cent of both the Swedish and the English samples. Both groups perceived promotion overwhelmingly in terms of movement within manual jobs, rather than into white-collar occupations. Indeed, both samples had 'realistic' assessments of their life chances; in neither factory was there an effective scheme for recruitment and training which would have enabled manual workers to have become office employees. But the similarity in the responses to this question by the two groups of workers was not sustained when they were asked, 'How likely is a factory worker to get promotion at work. Would you say that it was "very likely", "likely", "unlikely", or "very unlikely"?' Almost twice as many (73 per cent) of the English workers thought it either 'likely' or 'very likely' compared with the Swedish workers (39 per cent). Indeed the Swedish workers were altogether less optimistic about their chances for advancement than were their English equivalents. Among the Swedish sample, 80 per cent claimed their chances for promotion were either 'worse' or 'much worse' compared with those of white-collar workers, and only 3 per cent said they were 'better' or 'much better'. By contrast, the English workers held a more favourable view of their promotion prospects compared with those of white-collar workers with only 33 per cent stating these were either 'worse' or 'much worse', and 29 per cent suggesting they were 'better' or 'much better'. A further 31 per cent of the English sample perceived their chances to be 'about the same', compared with only 12 per cent of the Swedish workers.

The two groups of workers were then asked the open-ended question 'Why is this?', the responses to which were cross-tabulated with their opinions about opportunities for promotion compared with those for white-collar workers. Of the 98 Swedish workers who claimed that their chances were 'worse' or 'much worse', 54 per cent stated this was because promotion was 'automatic' for white-collar workers,[20] but of the 43 English respondents who evaluated their chances in this way, only 16 per cent gave a similar reason. At the same time, 81 per cent of the 37 English workers who claimed that their own opportunities for promotion were 'better' or 'much better', said this was because there were more opportunities available on the shop floor than in the office.[21] These figures indicate that the Swedish workers had a more 'realistic' assessment of their career prospects compared with those of white-collar workers, than the English workers. Indeed the Swedish workers perceived that white-collar employment provided a built-in career structure which was not available to manual workers. The English workers, by contrast, felt that there was much more opportunity in the factory, but they were unaware of the structural differences that existed between manual and non-manual employment.

Both samples were asked 'What about your working conditions compared with those of white-collar workers. Would you say that they were "much better", "better", "about the same", "worse", or "much worse"?' Among the Swedish workers, 89 per cent claimed that their working conditions (meaning physical working conditions) were either 'worse' or 'much worse' than those of white-collar workers, and a further 10 per cent felt that they were 'about the same': only one respondent said they were 'better'. Among the English sample, by contrast, 58 per cent considered their working conditions to be either 'worse' or 'much worse' and 34 per cent thought that they were 'about the same': 7 per cent held they were either 'better' or 'much better'. Unlike their attitudes about earnings and promotion opportunities, the English sample seem to have felt more relatively deprived in terms of working conditions. But the difference in the frequency of this experience for the two samples of workers was still significant; 31 per cent fewer of the English workers considered their working conditions to be either 'worse' or 'much worse' than those of white-collar workers. The difference is particularly noticeable in view of the fact that *actual* differences in the working conditions of manual workers and white-collar workers were less in the Swedish factory than in the English.

The evidence clearly suggests that the Swedish sample demonstrated a greater frequency of relative deprivation than the English. Indeed there was a tendency for this to be reflected in heightened feelings of resentment. Both samples were asked 'How do you feel about all these things – earnings, conditions of work, etc.?' The responses were then coded according to those expressing sentiments of 'approval' and 'disapproval'. Table 10.4 presents, as an example, the data relating to attitudes to earnings analysed in this way.

Among the 77 Swedish workers who claimed that their earnings were either 'worse' or 'much worse' than those of white-collar workers, 26 per cent 'approved' and 72 per cent 'disapproved'. By contrast, of the 30 English workers who thought their earnings were either 'worse' or 'much worse', 43 per cent 'approved', and only a small majority – 53 per cent – 'disapproved'. This suggests that among those workers of both samples who felt they were relatively deprived, the Swedish respondents were more resentful than the English.

But what is more surprising is that 'disapproval' was also expressed by very high proportions of the Swedish sample who felt their earnings were 'much better', 'better' or 'about the same' as white-collar workers. For the first two of these categories the numbers are so small that it is difficult to make further interpretation. However, among the 37 Swedish workers who felt their earnings were 'about the same', as many as 95 per cent 'disapproved' compared with only 25 per cent of the 32 English respondents. Why did such a high proportion of the Swedish sample 'disapprove'? Was it because they felt that their earnings should have been higher or lower than those of white-collar workers? Their responses suggest that they felt

Table 10.4: ·*How do you feel about all these things – Earnings*'

Earnings compared with those of white-collar workers	Swedish workers								English workers							
	'Approval'		'Disapproval'		Don't know		Total		'Approval'		'Disapproval'		Don't know		Total	
	No.	per cent	No.	per cent	No.	per cent	No.	per cent	No.	per cent	No.	per cent	No.	per cent	No.	per cent
Much better	—	—	1	100	—	—	1	100	5	83	1	17	—	—	6	100
Better	—	—	4	100	—	—	4	100	39	77	11	22	1	2	51	100
About the same	2	5	35	95	—	—	37	100	22	69	8	25	2	6	32	100
Worse	20	29	48	70	1	2	69	100	13	46	14	50	1	4	28	100
Much worse	—	—	8	100	—	—	8	100	—	—	2	100	—	—	2	100
Don't know	—	—	—	—	2	100	2	100	—	—	—	—	8	100	8	100
Not recorded	—	—	—	—	—	—	1	100	—	—	—	—	—	—	1	100
Total							122	100							128	100

their earnings should have been higher. For example, 91 per cent of these 35 Swedish workers claimed that white-collar workers had a number of advantages over themselves and felt that this was 'a bad state of affairs'. In view of this, the overall interpretation of Table 10.4 is that a far higher proportion of the Swedish workers than the English felt relatively deprived and resentful about their earnings.

This pattern was reflected in responses to the very general, open-ended question, 'What are the major differences, as you see them, between factory workers and white-collar workers these days?'

Table 10.5: *'What are the major differences, as you see them, between factory workers and white-collar workers these days?'*

	Swedish workers		English workers	
	No.	Per cent	No.	Per cent
Responses suggesting advantages for white-collar workers	109	89	73	57
Responses suggesting advantages for manual workers	–	–	5	4
Claims that there were no differences	11	9	44	34
Claims that they were 'just different'	–	–	5	4
Don't know	1	1	1	9
Not recorded	1	1	–	–
Total	122	100	128	100

As Table 10.5 suggests, a majority of both samples stressed advantages for white-collar workers, but the Swedish workers did so to a far greater degree than the English. Furthermore, the two samples differed considerably in the extent to which they held that there were *no* differences between white-collar workers and manual workers. The responses to this question were also coded according to the reasons workers gave for suggesting that white-collar workers had advantages.

There were important differences between the two groups in the reasons given by those people who thought that the white-collar workers were advantaged. As Table 10.6 shows almost three-quarters of the Swedish sample mentioned economic advantages compared with about one-third of the English workers who, in contrast, tended to mention economic factors with the same frequency as 'status' factors and working conditions. Furthermore, feelings of resentment stimulated by this question were not the same for both samples. Both groups of workers who perceived advantages for white-collar workers were asked, 'Do you think that this is a good

Table 10.6: *Reasons for suggesting the advantages of white-collar workers*[a]

Reason[22]	Swedish workers		English workers	
	No.	Per cent	No.	Per cent
Economic factors	80	73	25	34
Working conditions – noise, lighting, ventilation, etc.	25	23	29	40
'Intrinsic' job factors	18	17	5	7
'Status' factors	20	18	25	34
Other and non-classifiable responses	13	12	18	25

[a] 109 Swedish and 73 English workers said that there were advantages for white-collar workers but some people gave more than one reason, so the answers total to more than 100 per cent.

state of affairs? – "Yes" or "No"?' Only 6 per cent of the Swedish respondents claimed that this was a good state of affairs, while 93 per cent disapproved. On the other hand, 47 per cent of the English workers approved, while only 48 per cent held that it was a bad state of affairs.

Among other things, the study investigated the perceptions which the English and the Swedish workers had of their respective class structures. Both samples were asked 'Some people say that there are no longer social classes in this country today. Others say that there are. What do you think?' The great majority, over 90 per cent, of both Swedish and English workers claimed that there were social classes but differences emerged when they were asked to name 'Which are the major classes in this country today?', and to state, 'Which of these classes would you say that you belong to?'. They were then asked, 'Which class do you think has done best economically over the past few years?' and the responses to this question were coded according to whether the respondent mentioned the class to which he had allocated himself or one of the other classes that he had mentioned.

Among the Swedish workers, 29 per cent claimed that their 'own class' had done best while 71 per cent mentioned 'another class' – those most frequently mentioned including 'The Upper Class', 'Social Group I', 'The Wealthy', 'The Rich', and 'Those with plenty of money'. By contrast as many as 59 per cent of the English sample considered their 'own class' to have done best with 41 per cent mentioning 'another class' which included, 'Middle Class', 'Upper Class', and 'The Rich'.

Both samples were then asked 'How do you feel about this?', and the responses were coded according to 'approval' or 'disapproval'. For both the Swedish and the English workers, 'approval' was expressed by 100 per cent of those who claimed their 'own class' had done best. But there was a striking difference between the two groups of workers when 'another class' was mentioned: only 12 per cent of the Swedish respondents 'approved', compared with no less than 55 per cent of the English workers. The English workers expressed such opinions as 'best of luck to them', 'I would do the same if I were them', 'it doesn't make any difference to me', 'it doesn't bother me', etc.; indeed, statements which indicated that the English workers perceived little or no social link between their own position and that of other groups in society. Accordingly, they experienced little resentment.

Discussion of the results of the enquiry

These results, when taken together, suggest that there was a greater frequency of relative deprivation among the Swedish workers than among the English and that this tended to be associated with heightened feelings of resentment. Clearly the findings show that the experience of relative deprivation differs for similar groups of manual workers in different industrial-capitalist societies. Runciman has argued that in order to explain the experience of relative deprivation among individuals in society, it is necessary to consider the reference groups which they use for the purposes of comparison. He suggests that the awareness and resentment of class inequality is slight in Britain because individuals, particularly manual workers, tend to adopt highly limited reference groups. But this does not occur to the same degree in all industrial societies for this analysis has shown that the Swedish respondents tended to adopt more broadly-based reference groups, which incorporated both manual and non-manual workers. Clearly any adequate explanation for the different responses of the two samples would require a systematic analysis of developments in the social structures and cultural systems of the two countries. Here, consideration will be given to only one factor.

Parkin has suggested that the awareness of inequality in capitalist societies is closely related to the relative influence of different ideologies.[23] He claims that in these societies there are at least three kinds of *meaning-systems*, all of which have as one of their functions, the interpretation of social and economic inequality. These are: (1) the *dominant* value system, which endorses existing structures of inequality and becomes internalised by members of the 'under-class' in either 'aspirational' or 'deferential' terms;[24] (2) the *subordinate* value system, generated by the working-class community and which promotes an *accommodative* response to inequality; this is often reflected in terms of fatalism, resignation, limited levels of aspiration, and an acceptance of existing structures of inequality as legitimate;[25] (3) the *radical* value system, with its source in the mass political party based on the working class, and which promotes an *oppositional* interpretation of class inequality.[26]

Empirical studies that have been conducted in Britain suggest that of these meaning-systems, the *radical* has been the least influential. A number of investigations, for example, have shown that not only the Labour party, but also large sectors of the trade union movement, have given little emphasis to the grass-roots participation of rank-and-file members and to political socialisation.[27] As a result, the *radical* value system is ineffective among large sectors of manual workers in Britain in providing an *oppositional* interpretation of social inequality, with a consequence that inequality has been interpreted according to ideas inherent in either the *dominant* or *subordinate* value systems. Accordingly, the existing structure of inequality has remained fundamentally unquestioned.

In Sweden, on the other hand, could it be that there has been the development of working-class institutions which have been more influential in providing *oppositional* interpretations of social and economic inequality? Differences in the frequency of relative deprivation, the adoption of reference groups, and attitudes of resentment between the two samples of workers could then be regarded as a consequence of the differential degree to which they have been exposed to *radical* values. Of course the reverse is also possible; there could be a more radical labour movement in Sweden simply because workers are more radical. Which, then, is cause and which is effect? This is a difficult relationship to unravel and perhaps it is inappropriate to pose the problem in this way. A better way to conceive of the relationship is in terms of mutual feedbacks; the attitudes of rank-and-file members will impose certain constraints upon the policies of their leaders but at the same time, leaders will shape the attitudes of rank-and-file members. In most circumstances, however, the latter is more likely to occur if only because of the highly bureaucratised structure of working-class institutions, particularly in Sweden.[28] Certainly the evidence lends support to this contention.

In both samples union membership was 100 per cent, but there were striking differences between them in terms of their opinions about the aims of labour unions. Both groups of workers were asked the open-ended question, 'What do you think should be the major aim of trade unions?'

Whereas substantial minorities of the Swedish sample stated either 'socialist' or economic factors, the former were hardly ever mentioned by the English workers, even if those respondents who made the general

Table 10.7: ·*What do you think should be the major aim of trade unions?*'

	Swedish workers		English workers	
Major aim	No.	Per cent	No.	Per cent
Responses suggesting improved social justice, socialism	52	43	2	2
'To represent workers' interests'	3	3	17	13
Economic factors	48	39	72	56
Improved working conditions	12	10	30	24
'To protect the individual'	2	2	4	3
Other	5	4	2	2
Not recorded	–	–	1	1
Total	122	100	128	100

statement, 'to represent workers' interests' are counted. Instead, the English sample tended to stress the need for unions to improve pay and working conditions, factors which suggested that respondents perceived trade unions in instrumental and economic ways rather than in ideological terms.[29] The Swedish workers, by contrast, when they mentioned 'socialist'· factors tended to stress things such as the need to 'increase equality', to 'improve social justice', and 'to remove injustices at work', sentiments which were not evident in the responses of the English sample.

Labour unions in Sweden have adopted as an explicit objective, the need to increase equality. Since the 1950s, the Swedish Trade Union Confederation (Landsorganisationen, LO) has pursued a policy of 'wage solidarity', the objective of which has been to negotiate with employers, wage increases which would, at the same time, reduce differentials between groups of manual workers.[30] Because of factors such as 'wage drift', the shortage of labour in various industries and regions, and local wage bargaining, this policy has had little consequence in narrowing differentials between groups of male manual workers, but it has remained a desirable and a central goal of labour union policy in ·Sweden.[31] In Britain, on the other hand, although the trade union movement has expressed concern over low-wage groups, and the desirability of a national minimum wage, it has never seriously pursued an explicit policy of 'wage solidarity' in the Swedish sense. However, not only have Swedish labour unions attempted to narrow differentials between categories of manual workers, they have also questioned differentials in terms of wages, fringe benefits, conditions of employment and general working conditions as they exist between white-collar workers and manual workers. In Sweden manual and white-collar workers belong to unions which are predominantly affiliated to separate national confederations, so that manual and non-manual differentials are generally more salient in industrial bargaining than they are in Britain.[32] The Swedish Trade Union Confederation can therefore pursue policies of 'equality' between white-collar workers and manual workers in a more explicit manner than is available to the Trade Union Congress (TUC) in Britain, with its affiliation of both white-collar and manual unions.[33]

All this has created, in Sweden, a general awareness of differences in the economic conditions of manual and non-manual workers; a situation which has led to the adoption of broadly-based, cross-class, reference groups among manual workers and a consciousness of relative deprivation.[34] Indeed this pattern has been reinforced by the activities of the Social Democratic party which, over recent years, has questioned the legitimacy of manual/non-manual differentials.

Both samples of workers were asked if they had voted in the last general election; 98 per cent of the Swedish workers claimed they had compared with 88 per cent of the English sample. These respondents were then asked 'If a General Election were to be held in the near future, which party would you vote for?' Among these Swedish workers 81 per cent declared their allegiance to the Social Democratic party and 68 per cent of the English respondents said they would vote for Labour. These respondents were then asked 'Why would you vote in this way?'

Table 10.8: *Why would you vote in this way?*[a]

	Swedish workers		English workers	
Reasons	No.	Per cent	No.	Per cent
General 'working class' identification with Labour/Social Democrat Parties	64	67	50	65
Family traditions	5	5	8	10
Economic factors	42	44	15	20
'Socialist' policies	17	18	4	5
'Welfare' policies	69	72	23	30
Other and non-classifiable responses	26	27	18	23

[a] Asked of those people who said that they had voted in the last general election and who also claimed that they would vote for the Social Democratic or Labour Party in the next. Some people gave more than one answer so that the numbers add to more than 100 per cent.

For both samples there was a 'generalised' working-class identification with the political party. But as Table 10.8 shows, although they were a small minority in both samples, more than three times as many Swedish workers as English, mentioned 'socialist' policies; these responses included such statements as 'they are more likely to increase equality', 'they are more likely to make a more just society', 'we haven't achieved equality yet'. At the same time more than 70 per cent of the Swedish respondents perceived the Social Democrats as the party most likely to improve social benefits and to develop the welfare state; factors mentioned by less than one-third of the English workers.

Over recent years, issues of equality and social justice have been at the centre of political debate in Sweden to the extent that in the 1970 General Election, the Social Democratic party adopted 'Increased Equality' ('Ökad Jämlikhet') as its election manifesto. This was supported by other slogans, many of which were financed by specific labour unions and the Swedish Trade Union Confederation and included, 'We shall remove social injustices at work', and 'Injustices at work will be removed'. The British Labour party, on the other hand, has not stressed issues of inequality when it has been in Government, nor has it made them the centre of its electoral campaign. Therefore, in presenting itself as the champion of social justice, the Social Democratic party has generated a sense of relative deprivation among manual workers which exists to a greater degree than among most members of the working class in England.

Furthermore, Social Democracy in Sweden has lead to the development of an achievement-orientated, 'open', and egalitarian ideology, which has had important implications for the experience of relative deprivation.[35] As Lipset and Trow have suggested: 'An egalitarian, "open class" value system with its less rigid social structures may actually engender more immediate discontent among low socio-economic groups, than does a more rigidly stratified structure. An open class value system leads workers to define inequalities in income and status between themselves and others as illegitimate more frequently than do workers in countries which have more sharply and rigidly defined social structures.'[36] But the evidence suggests that economic inequalities and mobility chances are much the same in Sweden as they are in England; the social structure of the former is no less rigid than the latter.[37] As a result, differences in the frequency of relative deprivation between the two samples of workers must be seen to be more as a consequence of differences in *meaning-systems* than to structural variations between the two countries.

If, then, there is an attempt to explain the experience of relative deprivation among manual workers, it is important to consider, among other things, *meaning-systems* and the ways in which these shape definitions of inequality. But it cannot be assumed that these are similar for all industrial-capitalist societies; indeed, the degrees to which different *meaning-systems* interpret the structure of inequality in various societies is an empirical question. This paper has suggested, if only for extremely limited samples, that differences in the frequency of relative deprivation among English and Swedish workers is a consequence of the differential impact of *radical* values as articulated by working-class institutions.

If this interpretation is correct, then it highlights the dilemma of Social Democratic Governments in capitalist countries; aspirations are heightened and the experience of relative deprivation among rank-and-file supporters, particularly manual workers, increases. But the institutions of capitalism generate various degrees of economic and social inequality. Accordingly, it may be appropriate to consider Social Democracy in capitalist societies as a 'transitional' phenomenon so that, over the long term, two possible developments could be expected. Disillusionment could become so widespread among manual workers that there is a shift in support for more 'right-wing' political parties; indeed, at the time of writing, the likelihood of this occurring in the 1973 Swedish General Election appeared to be a distinct possibility. Alternatively, there could be increased Government intervention in the economy so that ultimately the means of production are publicly owned and a socialist society established. If this were to occur then the whole process could be regarded as one in which in the initial stages Social Democratic and union leaders generate heightened experiences of relative deprivation in order to command and later maintain the support of rank-and-file members, but at a later stage this leads to the adoption of more 'radical' policies. However, irrespective of either of these alternatives, what can be stated with a degree of certainty is that an ideology of egalitarianism and the persistence of structural inequalities generate inevitable tensions in capitalist societies which have long-established traditions of Social Democratic Governments.[38]

NOTES

[1] The data presented in this paper were collected as part of a comparative analysis into aspects of social stratification in England and Sweden. The research, financed by a grant from the Centre for Environmental Studies, London, is investigating manual workers' conceptions of inequality. The

detailed results will be presented in a final report. I am grateful to Mrs Dorothy Wedderburn and to Frank Bechhofer for their comments on an earlier draft of this paper.

2 W. G. Runciman, *Relative Deprivation and Social Justice: a study of attitudes to Social Inequality in Twentieth Century England* (London, 1966).

3 J. Goldthorpe, D. Lockwood, F. Bechhofer and J. Platt, *The Affluent Worker in the Class Structure* (Cambridge, 1969), Ch. 5.

4 A. Inkeles, 'Industrial Man: The Relation of Status to Experience, Perception and Values', *American Journal of Sociology*, Vol. 66 (1960–1).

5 Most sociologists, but particularly Marxists, adopt this approach. For two recent examples see N. Birnbaum, *The Crisis of Industrial Society* (London, 1969); and R. Miliband, *The State in Capitalist Society* (London, 1969).

6 To compare aspects of two social structures without consideration of long-term trends and developments restricts the contribution of any study for the debate about the convergence of industrial societies. See E. Dunning and E. Hopper, 'Industrialisation and the Problem of Convergence: a critical note', *Sociological Review*, N.S. Vol. 14 (1966). The purpose of this paper is not to discuss whether or not England and Sweden are converging in certain respects but to explore the degree to which similar attitudes are shared by workers in different industrial societies. England and Sweden are suitable for this exercise since both are highly industrialised societies with relatively similar occupational structures. See for example, R. Scase, 'Industrial Man: A Reassessment with English and Swedish Data', *British Journal of Sociology*, Vol. 23 (1972): and more fully, 'Inequality in Two Industrial Societies: Class, Status and Power in England and Sweden', in R. Scase (ed.), *Readings in the Swedish Class Structure* (forthcoming).

7 In the absence of national samples and in order to compare workers who were in similar 'structural' positions in the two countries, it was considered more appropriate to study two factories than two communities; with the latter there would have been greater difficulties of comparing like with like.

8 For a brief description of some of these, see the author's 'Inequality in Two Industrial Societies'. For a comparison of differences in *conditions of employment* for separate occupational categories in Britain see Chapter 7 this volume, and D. Wedderburn, 'Inequality at Work', in P. Townsend and N. Bosanquet (eds) *Labour and Inequality* (London, 1972).

9 Whether variation in size contributed to any significant differences in the attitudes of the two samples was not investigated and must therefore remain an open question. For a study and discussion of the relationship between organisational size and workers' attitudes, see G. K. Ingham, *Size of Industrial Organisation and Worker Behaviour* (Cambridge, 1970).

10 At the younger age levels there was often an overlap between the earnings of manual and white-collar workers. See also Chapter 7 this volume. Systematic evidence on the structure of earnings for all occupational groups in the two factories would almost certainly have indicated that there were greater differentials *within* the two factories than those described in this paper. However in the absence of this information it was considered appropriate to focus upon differentials in terms of the *highest* earnings which members of each occupational group could hope to acquire.

11 It was considered that each of these factors would affect perceptions of inequality and the experience of relative deprivation. For a discussion of the relationship between age, stage in the family cycle and work satisfaction, see H. Wilensky, 'Work as a Social Problem', in H. Becker (ed.), *Social Problems: A Modern Approach* (London, 1966).

12 The two industries from which the factories were chosen were remarkably similar in terms of these factors. Both had rather low rates of conflict and

relatively slow technological innovation by contrast with some other industries in the two countries.

[13] There was an attempt to make the schedule as similar as possible for both samples, but in a 'sociological' rather than in a 'grammatical' sense. Instead of grammatically translating the English schedule into Swedish, the investigator 'tested' the schedule with Swedish sociologists and then with 'pilot' respondents in order to use questions which would convey similar 'meanings' to both groups of workers.

[14] If they had been aware of this, there could have been ethnocentric bias in the responses. A Swedish research worker, normally resident in England, conducted the Swedish interviews and most of the English. I am grateful to Anita Ehn-Scase for her kind assistance.

[15] Runciman, *Relative Deprivation*, p. 192.

[16] United Nations, *Incomes in Post-War Europe* (Geneva, 1967). This enquiry also concluded that both pre-tax and post-tax income distributions were much the same in Sweden (1963) as they were in the United Kingdom (1964). For both countries the coefficient of inequality, calculated from Lorenz curves, was 0.40 (Table 6.10).

[17] Indeed, the earnings of Swedish workers employed in the building construction industry, relative to other groups of manual workers, are high compared with the relative earnings of English construction workers. See United Nations, *Incomes in Post-War Europe*, Ch. 5.

[18] Runciman, *Relative Deprivation*, Ch. 10, Table 20.

[19] The term 'white-collar worker' was defined so that it was clear that each respondent understood the kind of occupation with which he was being invited to make comparisons. It was emphasised that the term referred not only to office workers but also to management and other higher officials.

[20] Responses of this kind included statements like, 'White-collar workers get promoted as they get older', 'you just sit there and go up', 'it's automatic for them'.

[21] Some examples of these responses include, 'chances are always cropping up on the factory floor, but you have to wait for dead men's shoes in the office', 'there are always chances', 'jobs are always coming up'.

[22] These reasons included for economic factors – 'better paid', 'higher earnings'; intrinsic job factors – 'their work is more interesting', 'has more responsibility'; status factors – 'looked up upon', 'more prestige', 'better reputations', etc.

[23] F. Parkin, *Class Inequality and Political Order* (London, 1971), Ch. 3.

[24] Parkin defines 'aspirational' as 'a view of the reward structure which emphasises the opportunities for self-advancement and social promotion', and 'deferential' as 'a view of the social order as an organic entity in which each individual has a part to play, however humble. Inequality is seen as inevitable as well as just, some men being inherently fitted for positions of power and prestige.' Parkin, *Class Inequality*, p. 85.

[25] 'In so far as it is possible to characterise a complex set of normative arrangements by a single term, the subordinate value system could be said to be essentially *accommodative*; that is to say its representation of the class structure and inequality emphasises various modes of adaptation, rather than either full endorsement of, or opposition to, the *status quo*.' Parkin, *Class Inequality*, p. 88.

[26] 'The radical value system purports to demonstrate the systematic nature of class inequality, and attempts to reveal a connectedness between man's personal fate and the wider political order.' Parkin, *Class Inequality*, p. 97.

[27] See, for example, J. Goldthorpe, D. Lockwood, F. Bechhofer and J. Platt, *The Affluent Worker: Political Attitudes and Behaviour* (Cambridge, 1968) and B. Hindess, *The Decline of Working Class Politics* (London, 1971).

[28] R. Michels was one of the first to stress that the bureaucratisation of

organisations leads to the development of oligarchical tendencies; R. Michels, *Political Parties* (New York, 1962). For a good summary of the structure of the Swedish trade union movement see T. Johnston, *Collective Bargaining in Sweden* (London, 1962).

One of the major functions of the Workers' Educational Movement (Arbetarnas Bildningsförbund, A.B.F.), the educational wing of the Labour movement, is to convey union and Social Democratic policies to rank-and-file members.

[29] This finding is consistent with the results reported in J. Goldthorpe, D. Lockwood, F. Bechhofer and J. Platt, *The Affluent Worker: Industrial Attitudes and Behaviour* (Cambridge, 1968), Ch. 5.

[30] This objective has often caused conflict within the Swedish labour union movement. One of the factors contributing to a prolonged strike in the iron ore mines in the north of Sweden during the winter of 1969 was the proposal by the Confederation of Trade Unions that lower percentage wage increases should be negotiated for miners than for lower-paid occupations.

[31] For an assessment of 'wage solidarity', see J. Mouly, 'Wages Policy in Sweden', *International Labour Review*, Vol. 95 (1967).

[32] In addition to the Swedish Trade Union Confederation (Landsorganisationen, LO), the principal ones are the Central Organisation of Salaried Employees (Tjänstemännens Centralorganisation, TCO), the Swedish Confederation of Professional Associations (Sveriges Akademikers Centralorganisation, SACO), and the National Federation of Civil Servants (Statsjänstemännens Riksförbund, SR).

[33] J. Fulcher has argued that the structure of collective bargaining in Sweden represents a highly institutionalised representation of class conflict, see his 'Class Conflict in Sweden', *Sociology*, Vol. 7 (1973).

[34] The roles of political and labour union leaders in defining the reference groups of rank-and-file members is discussed by S. Lipset and M. Trow, 'Reference Group Theory and Trade Union Wage Policy', in Mirra Komarovsky (ed.), *Common Frontiers of the Social Sciences* (Glencoe, 1957).

[35] Over the years, Social Democratic Governments have emphasised the need to 'equalise' opportunities for all social groups in society. In view of this, there have been drastic reforms of the school and university systems. Sweden is now the only capitalist country in Europe which has a completely non-streamed comprehensive school system. At the same time, the proportion of university students from working-class homes has increased from 8 per cent in 1947 to 22 per cent in 1968–9.

In the present enquiry, both samples were asked, 'How likely is the son of a factory worker to move from one class to another?' Among the Swedish workers, 48 per cent claimed that it was 'very likely' compared with only 6 per cent of the English sample. Of the Swedish respondents, 96 per cent stressed the need to obtain educational qualifications in order to do this compared with 51 per cent of the English workers.

[36] Lipset and Trow, *Reference Group Theory and Trade Union Wage Policy*, p. 401.

[37] For a review of some of the relevant data see R. Scase, 'Inequality in Two Industrial Societies'.

[38] In addition to generating heightened experiences of relative deprivation, the Swedish labour movement seems to have affected workers' perceptions of social reality in another way. Compared with their English counterparts, they appear to be more likely to perceive of themselves as members of a legitimate and influential working-class movement. In a capitalist society this, in itself, is conducive to heightened feelings of relative deprivation and of resentment if only because 'influence' is not always perceived to produce greater 'social justice'. (See the author's *Industrial Man*.)

11

Social inequality and social integration in modern Britain

JOHN H. GOLDTHORPE

The overall extent and pattern of social inequality in modern Britain are discussed in other chapters in this volume.[1] The concern of this chapter is not to add to this detailed knowledge, nor to produce any new synthesis of the information that exists. It is, rather, with the relatively neglected problem of the implications of inequality for social integration. Prior to broaching this problem, however, three points concerning the general nature of social inequality must be made.

First, social inequality, in societies such as ours, is manifested in a very wide variety of ways – wider than is generally recognised in public discussion of the matter. For example, in addition to great inequalities in the distribution of income and wealth, further marked inequalities are involved in the ways in which economic rewards are *actually gained* – most importantly, in the content of work tasks and roles. There is by now ample evidence to show that wide differences exist between occupations and jobs in the extent to which they offer possibilities of *intrinsic* satisfaction to the individuals engaged in them or, on the other hand, are a source of psychological or social deprivation.[2] To take an obvious contrast, the inequalities in reward between professional employment and factory work are clearly not confined simply to the differences in their income levels.

Again, one aspect of inequality in work which it *has* of late been somewhat fashionable to point to, and to decry, is that of the status differences which operate among different categories of employee in most industrial organisations; for instance, in such matters as methods of payment, 'clocking-in' and lateness rules, toilet, canteen or car-parking arrangements, and so on. But discussion of these questions has usually been carried on without any reference to the far more basic inequality represented by the steep gradient of *authority* within such organisations – which, in fact, status distinctions serve largely to symbolise.[3]

The tendency here illustrated to conceive of inequality in a piecemeal manner, rather than as a multiform and pervasive phenomenon, results

H

from a failure to appreciate in what, fundamentally, social inequality consists. This leads to the second point.

Social inequality in all its manifestations can be thought of as involving differences in social power and advantage: power being defined as the capacity to mobilise resources (human and non-human) in order to bring about a desired state of affairs; and advantage as the possession of, or control over, whatever in society is valued and scarce. Power and advantage are thus closely related. Power can be used to secure advantage, while certain advantages constitute the resources that are used in the exercise of power. Moreover, different forms of power and advantage tend in their very nature to be convertible: economic resources can be used to gain status or to establish authority; status can help to reinforce authority or to create economic opportunities; positions of authority usually confer status and command high economic rewards, and so on.

In this perspective, then, the way in which inequality structures virtually the whole of social life can be readily understood. Differences in social power and advantage, simply because they imply differences across the whole range of life-chances, always tend, other things being equal, to become generalised differences. Furthermore, it is important to add that this effect operates not only from one area of social life to another but also through time. Inequalities of condition at any one point in time create inequalities of opportunity for future achievement. For example, the intergenerational aspects of this phenomenon could be said to constitute the central problem thus far for the sociology of education. The results of research in this field provide impressive evidence of how, notably through the agency of the family, the stability of social strata tends to be maintained – despite the growing importance of education to career chances and the development of policies aimed at reducing non-academic influences on educational attainment.[4]

It has, therefore, to be recognised, thirdly, that structures of social inequality of both condition and opportunity – or, in other words, systems of social stratification – are inherently highly resistant to change. The members of higher strata have the motivation and, in general, the resources to hold on to their position and to transmit it to their children, while the members of lower strata are often caught up in vicious circles of deprivation. This is not, of course, to suggest that change in stratification systems cannot, or does not, occur; but rather that any significant reduction in the degree of inequality will require purposive, well-designed and politically forceful action to this end – that it is unlikely to come about *simply* as the unsought for consequence of technological advance, economic growth, or any such like secular trends.[5] Such developments may well modify certain forms of inequality; but they appear just as likely to accentuate others.

Indeed, far from industrial societies having 'built-in' processes which steadily diminish inequality – as some writers have claimed – what is striking, at least in the British case, is the frequently very limited effect of even the deliberate pursuit of equality through governmental action. For example, as already implied, the egalitarian aspects of educational policy over the last half century or so have resulted in only a very slight lessening in class differentials in educational opportunity – even though over the same period an enormous expansion of educational facilities has occurred.[6] In a similar way, major improvements in medical services and general standards of health have failed over a long period to produce any appreciable reduction in relative class differentials in infant mortality and in many kinds of morbidity.[7] And finally in this respect the stability of inequality in income distribution over the last thirty years may be noted.[8]

In sum, one may say that social inequality, as observed in present-day Britain, takes the general form of a substantially self-maintaining structure of social groupings differentiated multifariously and often extremely in terms of the power and advantage that their members enjoy. What, then, are the consequences of this inequality for the integration of British society; that is to say, for the extent to which the actions of individuals and groups tend regularly to comply with recognised norms, and to be thus consistent with, rather than in conflict with or unrelated to, the expectations and actions of other individuals and groups?[9]

This question, in certain of its aspects, has in fact been examined by a number of recent writers who have adopted a similar initial approach. They have started from the observation that in Britain considerable and abiding inequality does not apparently give rise to deeply divisive conflicts in which the existing social structure, political institutions included, is frequently and fundamentally called into question. They have then gone on to infer from this, not unreasonably, that the resentment of inequality among the less favoured sections of the population is neither particularly widespread nor particularly militant – and especially if comparisons are made with the situation in certain other industrial societies. Thus, the somewhat more specific problem which emerges from this approach is the following: why is it that, given the prevailing degree of social inequality, there is no widely supported and radical opposition to the existing socio-political order, and that at all levels of the stratification hierarchy attitudes of acceptance, if not of approval, are those most commonly found? At this point, analyses tend to divide into two main types which one might conveniently label 'social psychological' and 'culturalist'. The first type is best displayed in the work of Runciman.[10]

Briefly, Runciman's argument is that to account for the discrepancy between the objective degree of inequality in British society and the actual awareness and resentment of this inequality, we must consider the 'reference groups' in terms of which individuals in the lower social strata assess their position. That is to say, we must consider the other groups in society – real or imagined – with which members of less favoured groups habitually *compare* themselves in evaluating their rewards, opportunities and social deserts generally, and in relation to which their expectations and aspirations are formed. If, for instance, the reference groups adopted by a certain membership group are located fairly closely in the stratification hierarchy to the membership group's own position, then the degree of felt inequality is likely to be quite slight, no matter what the overall range of factual inequalities may be. A strong sense of grievance is only to be expected if reference groups are selected in a more 'ambitious' way so that considerable inequality is perceived and is then, on the basis of the comparison made, regarded as illegitimate and unjust. In other words, the degree of *relative* deprivation – deprivation which is subjectively experienced and which may thus influence political behaviour – is primarily determined *by the structure of reference groups* rather than by the structure of inequality itself as the sociologist might describe it.

Runciman's own research, using both historical and survey methods, indicates that among the British working class reference groups are, and generally have been, restricted in scope; and that while some variation in this respect can be traced over time and from one form of inequality to another, no consistent trend is evident towards wider-ranging comparisons. Consequently, the disruptive potential that social inequality might be thought to hold remains in fact suppressed: social integration is furthered through perceptual and conceptual limitations.

Turning secondly to the 'culturalist' type of analysis, it should be said that this has been chiefly elaborated by American social scientists interested in the question of the social bases of stable and effective democracy.[11] In treating Britain as one of the relatively few countries whose polity might be thus described, these investigators have been led to examine – with differing degrees of directness – such issues as the following. Why among lower social strata in Britain is there not far more alienation from a political system which is élitist in itself and under which many other forms of inequality persist? Why is there no longer in Britain, if indeed there ever was, a powerful class-based social movement seeking radical structural changes of an egalitarian kind, and prepared if necessary to challenge existing political institutions in pursuit of its objectives?

In the explanations that are offered for the absence of these possible threats to stable democracy, major emphasis is laid on the nature of British 'political culture'; that is, on the pattern or 'mix' of attitudes which research has shown to exist in British society towards political institutions and political life in general. Like other countries in which democracy flourishes, the argument runs, Britain has, in the course of her historical development, built up a political culture of a distinctive type. It is one characterised primarily by the *balance* that holds, even across lines of class and party, between participant, activist attitudes on the one hand and acquiescent, passive attitudes on the other; between emotional commitment to political principle and cool pragmatism; between consensus on matters of procedure and conflict over particular issues.

Through their socialisation into this culture from childhood onwards, it is held, the majority of citizens come to feel a sense of unfanatical, but generally unquestioning, allegiance to the established political order, and one that is unlikely to be seriously disturbed by any grievances they may have over the distribution of social power and advantage. Such grievances do not lead to alienation from the political system since there is wide acceptance of the 'democratic myth' – the myth that the individual can influence political decisions and outcomes – and the system itself is not therefore seen as exploitive. Moreover, attitudes towards the political élite tend to be ones of trust, if not of deference, and the exercise of governmental authority is generally accepted as legitimate. For example, in one study survey data are presented to show that manual workers who believe that there are inordinately powerful groups in British society (such as 'big business') are just as much prepared to allow Government a wide sphere of authority as are workers who do not share in this belief.[12] In other words, grievances arising out of inequality do not tend to become so highly politicised that established political institutions and processes are themselves challenged. Political awareness is in any case at only a moderate level, and politics is only rarely a central life interest. Consequently, the availability of the ordinary citizen for involvement in 'unstabilising' mass movements is low; the political culture effectively inhibits the radical political action which marked social inequality might otherwise be expected to generate.

Clearly, social psychological and culturalist points of view on the issue in question are not incompatible: they could, rather, be represented as complementary and mutually supportive on the following lines. Because the reference groups of lower strata have remained generally restricted, political issues stemming from social inequality have tended to be relatively 'mild' and capable of being resolved or accommodated by existing political arrangements. This has, therefore, helped a basically 'allegiant' political culture to form. Reciprocally, the development of such a culture has been inimical to the spread of ideological thinking – as, say, on the matter of social justice – which could lead both to a heightened awareness of inequality and deprivation and to greater recognition of their political dimensions.[13] In short, social psychological processes of the kind examined by Runciman could be seen as a necessary condition of the political culture of British democracy, while this culture in turn, once established, favours the persistence of these processes.

Despite the various criticisms with which they have met, the analyses reviewed do, in my opinion, go some important part of the way to explaining why the consequences of inequality in Britain are not socially divisive in an extreme degree. But what has to be kept in mind, and what should be emphasised, is that for the most part these analyses treat the problem of inequality and integration only from one particular angle. As noted earlier the focus of interest is on the possible *political* implications of inequality; and what is in effect illumined is chiefly the question of why among the British working class there is found no significant support for political ideas and movements of a revolutionary cast, nor even the widespread *incivisme* which characterises sections of, say, the French or Italian working class. However, there are other major aspects of the problem which may be distinguished, and ones which have been curiously neglected. In particular, I would advance the view – as the central thesis of this chapter – that the most far-reaching implications of inequality for the integration of British society occur not in the political sphere but rather in that of economic life; and that they are manifested not in a situation of fundamental class struggle but rather in a situation of anomie; that is, in a situation in which to stay close to the original Durkheimian notion, there is a lack of *moral* regulation over the wants and goals that individuals hold. This contention can best be elaborated by reference to two closely related topics of current public concern: industrial relations and incomes policy.

In a recent paper – entitled 'The Reform of Collective Bargaining: from Donovan to Durkheim' – two leading authorities, Fox and Flanders, have in fact argued explicitly and at length that the British system of industrial relations is now in an anomic state.[14] In the post-war period, these authors observe, the wants, expectations and aspirations of industrial workers have expanded notably, and not only in regard to wage levels but also in regard to such matters as security of employment, job rights and control over work organisation. At the same time, generally high levels of employment have given many groups of workers the power to pursue their new goals with some effectiveness. A frequent outcome has then been that such groups have broken through the regulation of work relationships imposed by collective agreements at a national level and have secured agreements of a more favourable kind at company, plant or shop level. Thus, Fox and Flanders argue, industrial relations have become disordered in two main ways: first, as a result of the problems involved in developing new normative systems, capable of accommodating the new issues of industrial conflict which now arise; and second, and more seriously, because the solutions arrived at so far have tended to be *ad hoc* and piecemeal ones of only limited, local application. This tendency has therefore given rise to a proliferation of normative systems based on often unrelated or divergent principles; and such a situation is one rife with anomalies, frustrations and rivalries which constantly generate new tensions and conflicts both between employers and workers and between different sorts of workers: 'Disorder feeds upon disorder'. The consequences of this anomic state are then to be seen not simply in strikes and other dislocations of the productive process, but further 'in such things as chaotic pay differentials and uncontrolled movements of earnings and labour costs'. Thus, it is claimed, threats are posed to the long-term development of the economy (apart from the aggravation of short-term balance of payments problems) and there could, furthermore, be serious political implications: increasing disorder might generate popular demands for State intervention of an authoritarian kind which would mark the end of the present pluralistic and voluntary basis of industrial relations.

The analysis offered by Fox and Flanders is insightful and important. However, I would suggest that it is one that does not go far enough in revealing just how deeply rooted in the structure of British society is the 'disorderly' situation with which it is concerned; and, further, that this limitation results precisely from the fact that Fox and Flanders do not follow Durkeim in relating the problem of anomie to the problem of inequality. This argument can best be illustrated by reference to their recommendations for reform in industrial relations – that is, for the 'reconstruction of normative order'. Briefly, what they stress is the continuing need for an incomes policy, accompanied by the regularising and rationalising of collective bargaining from plant and company levels upwards. In this latter respect, they point to the availability and usefulness of such techniques as productivity bargaining and job evaluation and other means of measuring and rewarding different kinds of work. Through a programme of reform on the lines in question, they see the possibility of achieving a more logical wages structure, greater control over earnings and labour costs, and industrial relations institutions which, through being more adaptable to change themselves, will be better able to manage the conflicts that change inevitably produces.

Fox and Flanders recognise that there is no guarantee that such objectives will in fact be achieved, and they refer to the 'Promethean character' of the task of reform. None the less, I would argue that they still underestimate the difficulties that are involved: in particular, in creating an area of relatively rational and orderly inequality in place of the present 'wages jungle' *when this jungle is simply part of a wider structure of inequality which has no rationale whatsoever* – other, perhaps, than the principle of 'to them that have shall more be given'. For example, at one point in their paper Fox and Flanders remark that 'The debate on incomes policy is often conducted within the trade union movement as if collective bargaining were simply a mechanism for pursuing social justice as between capital and labour, and its function of determining the relative fortunes of different groups of labour is ignored.' This may be fair comment, but it is still highly questionable if an incomes policy of the kind they favour can be effective in establishing a less chaotic and more equitable pattern of earnings *within* the working class in the context of the *overall* degree of economic inequality which statistics on the distribution of income and wealth reveal. An industrial worker seeking a wage increase might be prepared to recognise that his claim was weak in comparison with that of, say, certain of his lower-paid workmates; but he would have no difficulty in finding other groups, possibly outside the working class, in relation to whom his claim could be much better justified – even assuming that his range of reference groups was not extensive. Moreover, it should be emphasised here that while restricted reference groups may inhibit feelings of grievance over inequalities, this is not to say that they actually motivate individuals to *hold back* from attempting to improve their position, especially economically: limited social horizons are not, as Durkheim might have put it, a source of moral restraint.[15]

Now it must be said that Fox and Flanders are well aware – indeed, they emphasise – that the normative regulation resulting from collective bargaining is unlikely ever to rest purely upon consensus; it will also be a product of the balance of power between the parties concerned and of their calculation of what, for the time being, is the most advantageous position they can achieve. What may further be involved, at least in initiating any reform, is some kind of third-party intervention – 'the forceful articulation of common norms by some authoritative source'. However, to follow Durkheim's argument closely here, one has to insist that in so far as the normative order in economic life is *not* based upon consensus, but is rather founded upon coercion or expediency, then the threat of anomie and of chronic malintegration remains – no matter what degree of internal logic or coherence normative systems may be given. For as Durkeim stresses, unless in modern society the regulation of economic life – and, crucially, the regulation of inequality – *does* have some accepted moral basis, then it is unlikely to be effective in any continuing way. To the extent that the normative order is imposed by superior power, fundamental discontent and unrest persist if only in latent form; to the extent that it results from the calculation of advantage under given (non-moral) constraints, it is likely to be called into question as soon as these constraints vary.[16]

Thus, while proposals for reform of the kind that Fox and Flanders put forward might well endow collective bargaining institutions and procedures with a good deal more formal rationality than they at present possess, I find it difficult to believe that such measures could go very far towards ensuring *stable* normative systems, of either a substantive or a procedural kind, at any level of industrial relations. The absence of an accepted moral basis for economic life as a whole in our kind of society must always render precarious the norms which at any time prevail in any specific area – a plant, company, industry, etc. As but one illustration of this point, taken from Durkheim's own discussion of the problem, one may consider the implications of inequalities of opportunity for attitudes towards inequalities of condition. If the former are extreme and without effective legitimation, little consensus can be expected on the latter – even supposing that some hierarchy of social positions and role is generally acknowledged. For, as Durkheim argued, 'it would be of little avail for everyone to recognise the justice of the hierarchy of functions as established by public opinion, if they did not also consider just the way in which individuals are recruited to these functions'.[17] While ever, then, British society is characterised by the present marked degree of inequality in educational and occupational opportunity, it is difficult to see that there is any basis for the achievement of what Fox and Flanders regard as the ultimate objective of industrial relations reform; namely, 'agreed normative codes regulating the production and distribution of wealth in modern industrial society' – or, at all events, agreement will for the majority remain highly qualified, reluctant or uncertain, and thus inherently *unstable*. One need not assume that rank-and-file industrial employees resent the inferior life-chances they have been accorded as keenly as the facts might warrant in order to claim that few will feel *morally* bound by the normative codes which govern their working lives. It is sufficient to ask from what source, given the nature of the British social order, such a sense of moral commitment might stem.[18]

The conclusion must then be that the reconstruction of normative order in British industrial relations which Fox and Flanders pursue is something of an *ignis fatuus*. Within a society in which inequality exists as brute fact – largely without moral legitimation – 'disorderly' industrial relations cannot be understood as a particular pathological development which will yield to particular remedies: rather, to maintain a Durkheimian perspective, this disorder must be seen as 'normal' – as a generalised characteristic of societies of the type in question.[19]

The structural features of British society which stand in the way of the reform of industrial relations are at the same time obstructive, as the foregoing discussion would imply, to the effective administration of an incomes policy. The aim of incomes policy, within a market economy such as our own, is usually stated to be that of controlling the growth of incomes so that inflationary tendencies may be kept in check while still preserving relatively high levels of employment and utilised capacity.[20] However, it is essential to appreciate that an incomes policy is not, and cannot be, just another economic instrument – despite the attempt of certain technocratically minded economists to present it in this guise. Once a Government attempts to regulate incomes, in no matter how piecemeal or partial a fashion, it is forced into the position of arbiter on particular wage levels or wage changes, and issues of social justice thus inevitably arise and have in some way or other to be resolved. Indeed, Government spokesmen in Britain have been generally prepared to acknowledge this situation and even to claim that an incomes policy is, or could be, a means of enhancing social justice; for example, by ensuring a better deal for the lowest-paid workers. But it is basically on account of this normative aspect of incomes policy that its administration runs into serious problems which have not as yet been overcome, and which may, for reasons I shall shortly suggest, be self-aggravating ones.

At the root of the difficulty is again the fact that not only is the existing distribution of income and wealth in British society 'unprincipled' – but further that there appears to be little consensus on the principles which *ought* to apply when it is a question of maintaining or altering any specific income level or relativity. Survey data are of some relevance to this argument,[21] but more significant is the great variety of frequently conflicting considerations which are actually invoked when pay issues are debated. Some criteria, for example, would entail at least the possibility of significant change in the existing pay structure – increased productivity, job evaluation ratings, 'absolutely' low wages or persisting manpower shortages: but other criteria, such as increases in the cost of living, the need to preserve a differential or maintain the social status of a particular group, are essentially conservative in their implications. Moreover, as Professor (now Lady) Wootton has pointed out, claims for more pay based on *any* of these often conflicting criteria can be, and usually are, couched in moral terms, or at any rate the economic arguments are related back to moral premises.[22] Thus, one is again forced to the conclusion that little basis for moral *restraint* is currently to be found in British society – that, in other words, a condition of anomie prevails. Given the diversity of moral positions that are tenable in the existing state of public opinion, virtually any occupational group seeking a pay increase is likely to be able to find some kind of legitimation for pressing its case.[23]

From this standpoint, then, it is to be expected that the amount of 'voluntary' support for an incomes policy will be insufficient to enable it to achieve its ends; and such an expectation seems to be generally in accord with British (and other) experience. Furthermore, even when control over incomes is in some way or other 'imposed', it still appears difficult, at least within the constraints on governmental authority that liberal democracy entails, for such control to be very effective for very long. A 'norm' for pay increases may hold up for a short-run period and even a complete 'freeze' may work under crisis conditions – as in Britain, in 1966–7. But in the longer term control invariably seems to break down, most notably at the level at which coercive methods are least feasible – that is, at the grassroots level of the individual enterprise.[24] A tendency for the actual earnings of many groups of workers to rise above the intended norm, as a result of collective agreements or other less formal arrangements locally made, has to be reckoned as the besetting problem of incomes policy administration – and even, it seems, in 'centrally planned' economies such as that of the USSR.[25]

Thus, as one economist, John Corina, has pointed out, 'the unpalatable facts of wage drift', once recognised, pose a hard dilemma so far at any rate as Britain is concerned. Either an attempt must be made to extend the range and increase the stringency of income control, to the point at which voluntary collective bargaining ceases to exist and at risk of building up a considerable pressure of opposition; or it must be accepted that, under existing conditions, incomes policy initiatives are inherently *unstable* in their effects, and that their progressive breakdown is to be anticipated as a matter of course. Unlike some of his colleagues, Corina is prepared to recognise that 'At bottom, the crucial tangles of incomes policy stem from the intangible concept of "social justice" in income distribution', and are inseparable from issues raised both by the existing structure of inequality and by the lack of accord on what form this structure should possess. As he pertinently asks: '. . . how can incomes policy create consent where social valuations of incomes, within a given incomes distribution, are confused and often obscure?'[26]

Moreover, one point which Corina does not consider is that attempts to implement incomes policy may have quite unforeseen consequences which in fact tend to build up the difficulties involved. It is not simply that a 'freeze' or period of tight control over incomes may be followed by heightened militancy in wage demands, threatening greater inflationary problems than before.[27] There is a further, yet more awkward, possibility: namely, that through increasing information about, and interest in, differences between occupational rewards and conditions, the actual operation of an incomes policy will serve to broaden comparative reference groups among the mass of the population, and at the same time bring issues of equity and fairness into greater subjective salience.[28] Thus, following Runciman's analysis, one would expect, in the case of the working class at least, a growing sense of resentment and grievance over the *status quo* and, in turn, a yet greater unwillingness to accept 'restraint' or to hold back in any way from the direct pursuit of their own maximum advantage. In other words, what are sometimes called the 'educative' functions of incomes policy may well have the effect of undermining the viability of such policy. To the extent that evaluations of income and other economic differences do become less confused and obscure, there is little reason to suppose that what will emerge will be greater consensus from one group or stratum to another: the far more likely outcome, given the prevailing degree of inequality, is that conflicts will become more clearly defined and more widely recognised – that the anomic state of economic life will be made increasingly manifest.

To recapitulate, then, the two central arguments have been the following: first, that social inequality in Britain appears to pose no direct threat to the stability of the political order – because this is, as it were, 'insulated' from the potentially disruptive consequences of inequality by a combination of social-psychological and cultural influences; but second, that the existence of inequality, of an extreme, unyielding and largely unlegitimated kind, does militate seriously against any stable normative regulation in the economic sphere – because it militates against the possibility of effective value consensus on the distribution of economic, and other, resources and rewards.

Of these two arguments, it is the latter that will be the more likely to provoke dissent, and not least perhaps among social scientists with 'applied' interests in the field of industrial and economic policy; for it obviously suggests that much of their endeavour will meet with relatively little success. However, as a way both of rounding off this argument and leading on to my own, concluding observations on policy issues, I would like to draw attention to one further point – somewhat obvious but often neglected – with implications that may be still more unwelcome to those colleagues in question. This is the point that, in spite of frequent attempts, it has not proved possible to give a satisfactory explanation of the persisting degree and form of inequality, in Britain or in any advanced society, by reference primarily to 'external' constraints, and without reference to the purposive exercise of their power and advantage by more privileged groups and strata. In other words, it has not proved possible to explain social inequality otherwise than as a structure with important self-maintaining properties.

For example, attempts to relate social inequality or particular aspects of it – say, in incomes – to differences in the so-called 'natural' attributes of individuals have repeatedly failed; and chiefly because social variation is regularly found to be of a different order of magnitude from natural variation. In advanced societies the dispersion of even earned income has a proportionate range of as wide as 50 or perhaps 100 to 1: no conceivably relevant natural attribute has been shown to vary to such an extent.[29] Again, it is by now evident enough that established structures of inequality yield little to explanation in terms simply of the operation of 'impersonal' market forces – in terms, that is, of the interaction of supply and demand in regard to different types of labour service. Labour economists themselves, as much as educational sociologists, have demonstrated the considerable restrictions that occur on the 'supply' side, as a result of various forms of inequality of opportunity. Consequently, the existence of the essentially 'non-competing groups' which social strata form distorts the labour market into a highly imperfect condition; and the 'imperfections' themselves lie outside the scope of pure economic analysis.[30] Finally, one should note, attempts by sociologists to revamp classical economics in the guise of 'functional' theories of social stratification have scarcely been convincing. Even if one leaves aside the basic problems of how to determine the functional exigencies of a social system or the relative functional importance of positions and roles within it, a logical limitation of such theories must still be stressed: that is, they are adequate only in explaining why *some degree* of social inequality should occur – not why the actual pattern of inequality is as it is.[31]

In short, then, one may assert that attempts to account for observable social inequality in terms simply of constraints, whether ones stemming from genetics, economics or 'societal' imperatives, are at best of very limited value. Through their very inadequacies such attempts point to the degree to which the phenomenon of social stratification must be seen as autonomous: as a phenomenon which has to be explained largely as the outcome of social action and interaction in the form of competition and conflict, the basis for which being always the inequality in power and advantage previously existing.

This being so, there are two implications of note. First, since prevailing patterns of inequality cannot be represented as the direct consequence of ineluctable exigencies, it is hard to see how they can be 'scientifically' legitimated as *necessary* features, either of the human condition in general or of the functioning of a particular type of society. In itself, of course, this fact is unlikely to be of much significance for the attitudes towards social inequality which are actually held among the population at large: it seems probable that inequality is indeed quite widely accepted as deriving either from 'natural' differences or from (what sociologists would call) 'functional imperatives'.[32] But this situation then points to the second important implication. Namely, that when concerned with problems arising out of competition and conflict, such as those found in economic life, applied social scientists must seriously ask themselves whether they do not have an obligation to state, clearly and insistently, that the context of inequality in which these problems typically exist is neither unalterable nor indisputably desirable, and need not, therefore, be taken as a 'given'. In other words, they must consider whether they are not obliged to emphasize what they know about the nature of social inequality, including its self-perpetuating but 'man-made' characteristics, and thus try to redress a situation in which, as Runciman has put it, 'From the moment almost of birth, attitudes to the social structure are conditioned by pressures in which the ideal of social justice plays little if any part.'[33]

If applied social scientists do act in this way, they may well of course make their task of piecemeal social reconstruction even more difficult than I have already suggested; that is, by increasing awareness and resentment of inequality, especially among disadvantaged groups and strata, and thus reducing further the likelihood of their traceability. But if, on the other hand, our social and economic engineers keep silent on the matter of inequality – if they attempt, rather, to build on the fact that the full extent of inequality is often unrealised and its sources misunderstood – then they are, willy-nilly, applying their knowledge and expertise in a partial way. And on this account, whatever their intentions may be, they lay themselves open to the charge of acting as 'the servants of power'.

I am, then, arguing not only that attempts at reconstituting normative order in economic life have small chances of success under existing conditions of inequality, but further that these chances will be still smaller if social scientists acknowledge an obligation to propagate the findings of examinations of this inequality and to relate these findings to the issues in which they seek to intervene. For it can scarcely be denied that such knowledge is likely to be corrosive of those beliefs and attitudes which, it seems, contain grievances arising out of inequality to a level that is 'manageable' at all.

This may be thought a very negative position to adopt, and in certain respects it obviously is. However, there is one conclusion with constructive possibilities to which this analysis does lead on directly; that is, that if the problem of anomie in economic life is to be attacked effectively, then the problem of social inequality must be attacked simultaneously. It can be argued, as a matter of sociology rather than ideology, that in a society that is both industrial and democratic a *relatively* stable normative order in economic life can *only* be created through norms being underpinned by some minimum degree of value consensus – as opposed to merely customary limitations on wants and goals. And such consensus in turn cannot be achieved without the distribution of economic resources and rewards, and indeed the entire structure of power and advantage, becoming in some degree 'principled' – becoming, that is, more capable of being given consistent rational and moral justification. In other words, the advancement of social justice has to be seen not as some lofty and rather impractical ideal, the further pursuit of which must wait upon the attainment of such basic objectives as 'getting the economy right', but rather as an important *precondition* of mitigating current economic difficulties. Such a lesson had to be learnt once in the nineteenth and earlier twentieth centuries, when Governments were forced to recognise, as one historian has remarked, that social welfare policies were not 'mere sweeteners of the hard rigours of a system of individualist compulsions' but represented rather 'social provision against waste of life and resources and against social inefficiency – not concessions'.[34] Governments now apparently need to learn that in a society with a highly complex division of labour, in which the possibilities of malintegration are correspondingly great, social inequality which is extreme and without legitimation will continually frustrate the orderly and efficient conduct of industrial and economic affairs generally: or, as Durkheim more succinctly put it, that 'all external inequality compromises organic solidarity'.[35]

It needs perhaps to be added that nothing in the above argument ignores the sociological truism that *any* distributive system and *any* form of hierarchical social organisation will have at least the potential for generating dissensus and conflict. No claim is made that a state of complete value consensus on economic, or any other, issues would be a possible, let alone a desirable, goal. The contention is, rather, that one can remain clearly this side of Utopianism and still envisage the modification of the existing pattern of inequality in a way that would make it *less* arbitrary, *less* unjust and thus more likely to receive a measure of reasoned acceptance from a wider section of the population; and further, that without such modification, public policy will not find that degree of voluntary, grass-roots support which would appear essential to its effectiveness in the face of current economic problems.

This is not the place to spell out in detail how the normative reconstruction of economic life and the reduction of social inequality might proceed together. However, certain general possibilities are evident enough. For example, several writers have already observed that attempts to regularise industrial relations at enterprise level, so as to facilitate grievance procedures and checks on wage movements, inevitably raise afresh issues of industrial democracy: issues of the right of employees to participate in management and economic decision-making going beyond the scope of collective bargaining. And at least one economist has been prepared to recognise that effective answers to the key 'micro' problems of incomes policy may well entail 'changes in concepts of managerial structure, authority and control'.[36] Again, as regards incomes policy in 'macro' terms, Professor Wootton more than a decade ago argued the need for such a policy to be *expressly related* to egalitarian objectives, in order to counteract the self-reinforcing character of social inequality and to give the structure of earnings a clearer moral basis; otherwise, the support of large sections of the population could neither be asked for nor expected. Professor Wootton in fact points to the genuinely radical conception of an incomes policy addressed not simply to problems of inflation, but, more basically, to those of social integration and the furtherance of democracy. Such a policy, rather than being devised as an essentially economic instrument, would be framed as part of an overall social policy, with economic considerations being admissible only as and when their imperative nature could be actually demonstrated.[37]

In adumbrating such possibilities, there are two things I should make quite clear. First, I do not for a moment under-estimate the difficulties that would be involved in realising them – not least as a result of the direct opposition which could be safely predicted from those whose power and advantage would be diminished. Secondly, I am not attempting here to argue for the desirability of developments of the kind in question in any absolute sense – though such a case might no doubt be made. What I am trying to establish is that these possibilities exist, and that unless and until something on these lines is accomplished, then the present anomic character of economic life will remain. From a number of value positions the goal of greater equality may be given only low priority, or inequality may even be regarded as a good in itself. Moreover, I do not believe that the sociologist *qua* sociologist is able to impugn such positions directly. But what *can* be argued sociologically is that those who are prepared to accept social inequality more or less as it presently exists must *also* be prepared to accept 'disorderly' industrial relations, the 'wages jungle' and general economic 'free for all' more or less as *they* now exist – or, as the one remaining possibility, to support attempts at entirely authoritarian solutions to these problems. This last course of action, however, would be perhaps the most effective way of breaking down the insulation of the British political system from issues and grievances stemming from inequality – the insulation which the national political culture has hitherto provided. In other words, it would carry the very real threat of extending economic into political instability.[38]

Finally, to turn from possibilities to probabilities, one has to accept that for the foreseeable future by far the most likely outcome is the continuance of the present state of affairs; that is, of a situation of persisting, marked inequality and also of chronic industrial unrest and of general economic in-fighting between interest groups under the rules mainly of 'catch as catch can.' Such a forecast is indicated by the fact that the egalitarian restructuring of our society, which could only be achieved as a work of political will, expertise and force, does not now appear to be even on the agenda of any major political party. For those who find this situation an unacceptable one, the main hope, at this stage at least, must lie in attempts at analysis and persuasion; in attempts, that is, to demonstrate, as cogently and as widely as possible, just what the concomitants of existing social inequality are, and how they block the aspirations found in many groups and strata – and not only among the less privileged – for a society in which resources are more rationally and co-operatively used. The highest degree of optimism that egalitarians can permit themselves – the belief that the *need* for great equality will eventually prevail – is aptly expressed in one further passage which is taken from Durkheim, from near the end of *The Division of Labour*:

> The task of the most advanced societies is then, one could say, a work of justice ... Just as the ideal of less developed societies was to create or maintain as intense a common life as possible, in which the individual was absorbed, so our ideal is to invest our social relationships with ever greater equity in order to ensure the free development of all socially useful potentialities. When one thinks, though, that for centuries men have been content with a much less perfect justice, one begins to ask if these aspirations might not perhaps be due to fits of gratuitous impatience; if they do not represent a deviation from the normal state of affairs rather than an anticipation of the normal state of the future; in short, whether the way of curing the disorder they make manifest is through satisfying them or rejecting them. What we have already established ... enables us to answer this question precisely. There are no needs more firmly grounded than these impulsions, for they are a necessary consequence of the changes that have occurred in the structure of societies ... In the same way as earlier peoples needed, above all, a common faith to live by, we ourselves need justice; and we can be sure that this need will become increasingly exigent if, as seems in every way likely, the conditions that govern social evolution remain unchanged.[39]

NOTES

[1] See Chapters 2 and 3 of this volume. I am grateful to Dr A. H. Halsey and Dr Ray Pahl for helpful comments on an earlier version of this paper.

[2] For useful reviews of relevant literature, see Robert Blauner, 'Work Satisfaction and Industrial Trends in Modern Society', in W. Galenson and S. M. Lipset (eds), *Labor and Trade Unionism* (New York, 1960) and John Child, *The Business Enterprise; in Modern Industrial Society* (London, 1969), pp. 64–76.

[3] See, however, Chapter 7 this volume.

[4] See Chapters 5 and 6 this volume as well as the research findings and discussion presented in A. H. Halsey, Jean Floud, and C. Arnold Anderson, *Education, Economy and Society* (Glencoe, 1961), Parts 2, 3, 4; and Olive Banks, *The Sociology of Education* (London, 1968), Chs. 3–5.

[5] It is also, of course, important that changes in the structure of social inequality should be distinguished from the processes of individual, or group, mobility within a given structure. Such mobility can occur without strata losing their identity as collectivities or 'quasi groups'. See Walter Buckley, 'Social Stratification and the Functional Theory of Social Differentiation', *American Sociological Review*, Vol. 23 (1958).

[6] Alan Little and John Westergaard, 'The Trend of Class Differentials in Educational Opportunity in England and Wales', *British Journal of Sociology*, Vol. 15 (1964).

[7] J. N. Morris and J. A. Heady, 'Social and Biological Factors in Infant Mortality: V. Mortality in Relation to the Father's Occupation, 1911–1950', *Lancet*, I (1955), p. 554; and Morris, *Uses of Epidemiology* (2nd ed., Edinburgh, 1964), pp. 52–64.

[8] See Chapters 5 and 6 this volume.

[9] I am thus concerned here specifically with 'social' as opposed to 'system' integration – to apply the important distinction made by David Lockwood. See his paper, 'Social Integration and System Integration', in George K. Zollschan and Walter Hirsch (eds), *Explorations in Social Change* (New York, 1964). It should further be noted that social integration is not taken as implying actors' moral commitment to the norms they observe. As Cohen stresses, '. . . there is a *fundamental difference between the recognition of a normative expectation and a commitment to uphold the norm*'. Percy S. Cohen, *Modern Social Theory* (London, 1968), p. 113. However, what will emerge as a central contention is that a state of social integration will be more *stable*, the greater the degree to which compliance with norms does derive from moral consensus rather than from calculation, coercion, or custom; i.e. the greater the relative importance of 'internal' as opposed to 'external' constraints.

[10] W. G. Runciman, *Relative Deprivation and Social Justice: a study of attitudes to social inequality in twentieth century England* (London, 1966).

[11] The most important studies are Harry Eckstein, 'The British Political System' in Samual H. Beer and Adam B. Ulam (eds), *Patterns of Government* (New York, 1962); Gabriel A. Almond and Sidney Verba, *The Civic Culture* (Princeton, 1963) and Eric A. Nordlinger, *The Working Class Tories: Authority, Deference and Stable Democracy* (London, 1967).

[12] Nordlinger, *The Working Class Tories*, pp. 107–8. The effect in question was the same among Labour and Conservative voters.

[13] In summing up his findings on the relationship between social inequalities and the feeling of relative deprivation, Runciman notes that 'of all its various determinants, one of the least powerful is the abstract ideal of social justice' even though 'the notion of social justice is somewhere implicit in every account of how people feel about social inequality'. *Relative Deprivation and Social Justice*, p. 247. He is further aware of the way in which dominant modes of political socialisation within British society are inimical to a developed awareness of issues of social justice, pp. 202–4. But see Chapters 9 and 10 this volume.

[14] *British Journal of Industrial Relations*, Vol. 7 (1969).

[15] At one point at least Durkheim makes a quite explicit distinction between a 'moral discipline' and one maintained by 'custom' and stresses the greater effectiveness of the former. See *Le Suicide* (new ed., Paris, 1930), p. 278. Moreover the distinction seems to me to be always implicit in, and crucial to, his analyses of the problems of the integration of economically advanced societies, in comparison with those having a less developed division of labour.

The most frequent function of comparative reference groups in industrial negotiations would seem to be to help support claims that an improvement in pay or conditions is necessary in order for a particular group to *maintain* its relative position. See the discussion in S. M. Lipset and Martin Trow, 'Reference Group Theory and Trade Union Wage Policy' in Mirra Komarovsky (ed), *Common Frontiers of the Social Sciences* (Glencoe, 1957). Lipset and Trow in fact advance the view that the extent to which workers feel that wage relationships are morally right will determine the comparative reference groups they adopt – rather than vice versa (pp. 400–1).

[16] See *De la Division du Travail Social* (7th ed., Paris, 1960), pp. 356–7; *Le Suicide*, pp. 278–9; and *Leçons de Sociologie: Physique des Moeurs et du Droit* (Paris, 1950), Ch. 1. Further, as already observed, consensus which reflects moral commitment to norms is in turn seen as more durable, in the context of modern societies, than that which reflects simply the customary observance of norms. Durkheim in fact makes it clear that to increase the integration of such societies and overcome the problems arising from anomie in economic life, it is *not* sufficient simply to have norms or rules articulated: the question of their basis is quite crucial '... ce n'est pas assez qu'il y ait des règles; car parfois, ce sont ces règles mêmes qui sont la cause du mal'.

[17] *Le Suicide*, p. 277. All translations from Durkheim are my own and differ, sometimes significantly, from published versions.

[18] The one possible source would seem to be in the close and highly personalised relations between workers, and between workers and the employer, which may prevail in very small-scale establishments. See G. K. Ingham, *Size of Industrial Organisation and Worker Behaviour* (Cambridge, 1970). Durkheim himself noted how small enterprises might in this way escape the consequences of an anomic division of labour. *De la Division du Travail Social*, pp. 344–6. The major objective of the 'human relations in industry' movement might in fact be described as that of recreating the characteristic quality of interpersonal relations in small establishments in the context of large scale, bureaucratised concerns. It has yet to demonstrate any widespread and lasting success.

[19] See *Les Regles de la Methode Sociologique* (Paris, 1895), Ch. 3. Fox and Flanders argue that at the present day industrial relations are more disorderly than at any time since Britain became an industrial society. This claim is, I think, debatable; but in any case their explanation of why disorder was not greater in earlier periods is essentially in terms of 'custom' or of imbalances of power, i.e. 'coercion'; and order thus based cannot be regarded as the converse of anomie. What Durkheim contrasted with the

anomie of economic life in modern societies was the idea of a 'moral economy' such as was pursued, and in some measure realised, in pre-industrial Europe. See the remarks in E. P. Thompson, *The Making of the English Working Class* (London, 1963) Ch. 14. It should, however, be added that Durkheim fully realised the need to create quite *new* institutions and processes for the moral regulation of economic life within advanced industrial societies. See the much misunderstood Introduction to the second edition of *De la Division du Travail Social*, 1902.

[20] See National Board for Prices and Incomes, *Third General Report, August, 1967 to July 1968*, Cmnd. 3715 (HMSO, London, 1968), pp. 6–7.

[21] For example, results from an Opinion Research Centre Study (February 1967) showed that when members of a quota sample of electors were asked to choose the one most important objective of an incomes policy out of three suggested, significant differences emerged on class lines, and especially between 'AB' and 'DE' respondents. Seventy-one per cent of the former selected 'that people with special skills are fully rewarded' while 52 per cent of the latter selected 'that lowest paid workers get a reasonable wage' and a further 10 per cent 'that incomes become more equal'. For a report on the survey, see R. P. Kelvin, 'What sort of Incomes Policy', *New Society*, 6 April 1967.

[22] *The Social Foundations of Wage Policy* (2nd ed., London, 1962), Chs. 4 and 5.

[23] Nor can it be thought likely that many individuals will support control over incomes on a purely calculative basis – i.e. on the basis of an understanding, or supposed understanding, of the interrelationships between money incomes, costs and prices, and thus of the nature of inflation. Survey research has demonstrated the not very surprising fact that the bulk of the population has little grasp of macro-economics. See Hilde Behrend, 'Prices Images, Inflation and National Incomes Policy', *Scottish Journal of Political Economy*, Vol. 13 (1966). and Behrend *et al.*, *A National Survey of Attitudes to Inflation and Incomes Policy*, Edutext Publications, Occasional Papers in Social and Economic Administration, No. 7 (London, 1966). In any case, no amount of macro-economic understanding could ensure general consensus on the actual application of an incomes policy, the crucial problems of which concern what shall happen to *particular groups* rather than to the aggregate of incomes.

[24] See the valuable review of the working of incomes policies provided by John Corina, 'Can an Incomes Policy be Administered?' in B. C. Roberts (ed.), *Industrial Relations: Contemporary Issues* (London, 1968).

[25] See A. Nove, 'Wages in the Soviet Union: a comment on recently published statistics', *British Journal of Industrial Relations*, Vol. 4 (1966).

[26] Corina, 'Can an Incomes Policy be Administered?' pp. 284–8, 290–1. It may be noted that an earlier review of incomes policies in western societies arrived in effect at the conclusion that an essential condition of controlling wage drift was some measure of moral restraint: '. . . a willingness on the part of individual trade unions, groups of workers, and employers to sacrifice some autonomy in matters of wage fixing under circumstances which may be particularly favourable or conducive to their exercise of it'. H. A. Turner and H. Zoeteweij, *Prices, Wages and Incomes Policies* (ILO, Geneva, 1966), p. 142.

[27] *Prices, Wages and Incomes Policies*, pp. 135–6.

[28] See Lipset and Trow, 'Reference Group Theory and Trade Union Wage Policy', pp. 397–400; also the comments by Bob Rowthorn, 'Unions and the Economy', in Robin Blackburn and Alexander Cockburn (eds), *The Incompatibles: Trade Union Militancy and the Consensus* (London, 1967), pp. 221–2. See also Chapter 10 this volume.

[29] See Wootton, *The Social Foundation of Wage Policy*, pp. 51–4; and Harold

Lydall, *The Structure of Earnings* (Oxford, 1968), pp. 68–88. It should of course be said that *all* human attributes that might be treated as 'abilities' or 'capacities' are determined by *both* genetic *and* environmental influences. See J. M. Thoday, 'Geneticism and Environmentalism' in J. E. Meade and A. S. Parkes (eds), *Biological Aspects of Social Problems* (Edinburgh, 1965).

[30] See Guy Routh, *Occupation and Pay in Great Britain, 1906–60* (Cambridge, 1965); A. H. Halsey (ed.), *Ability and Educational Opportunity* (O.E.C.D., Paris, 1961); and J. W. B. Douglas *et al.*, *All Our Future* (London, 1968).

[31] For a relevant collection of papers, see Reinhard Bendix and S. M. Lipset (eds), *Class, Status and Power* (2nd ed., New York, 1966), Part I, 'The Continuing Debate on Equality'. Also Buckley, 'Social Stratification and the Functional Theory of Social Differentiation'.

[32] See the data referred to by John H. Goldthorpe, David Lockwood, Frank Bechhofer and Jennifer Platt, in *The Affluent Worker in the Class Structure* (Cambridge, 1969), pp. 154–6; also, Goldthorpe, 'L'image des classes chez les travailleurs manuels aisés', *Revue Française de Sociologie*, Vol. II (1970), pp. 311–38.

[33] Runciman, *Relative Deprivation and Social Justice*, p. 294.

[34] H. L. Beales, 'The Making of Social Policy', Hobhouse Memorial Lecture, 1945, p. 9.

[35] Durkheim, *De la Division du Travail Social*, p. 373. By 'inégalité exterieure' Durkheim refers to all inequality resulting from sources other than differences in individual potentialities. See also *Leçons de Sociologie*, Ch. XVIII.

[36] Corina, 'Can an Incomes Policy be Administered?', p. 286.

[37] Wootton, *The Social Foundations of Wages Policy*, Ch. VI especially. Particularly pertinent here, for example, would be the requirement that arguments on the functions of economic inequalities as work incentives should be precisely stated and empirically tested, rather than being merely asserted in the form of vague generalities.

[38] See Turner and Zoetweij, *Prices, Wages and Incomes Policy*, p. 147.

[39] Durkheim, *De la Division du Travail Social*, pp. 381–2.

NAME INDEX

SUBJECT INDEX